English Tour Guide for
YUNNAN, GUIZHOU, SICHUAN AND CHONGQING

云贵川渝
英语导游讲解词

英汉对照

（第2版）

杨天庆 ◎ 编著

北京·旅游教育出版社

图书在版编目（CIP）数据

云贵川渝英语导游讲解词：英汉对照 / 杨天庆编著. 2版. -- 北京：旅游教育出版社, 2025. 1. --（"魅力中国"导游外语丛书）. -- ISBN 978-7-5637-4833-4

Ⅰ.K928.97

中国国家版本馆CIP数据核字第2025G4F457号

"魅力中国"导游外语丛书
云贵川渝英语导游讲解词
（英汉对照）
（第2版）

杨天庆　编著

策　　划	李红丽　陈卫伟
责任编辑	陈卫伟
出版单位	旅游教育出版社
地　　址	北京市朝阳区定福庄南里1号
邮　　编	100024
发行电话	（010）65778403　65728372　65767462（传真）
本社网址	www.tepcb.com
E - mail	tepfx@163.com
排版单位	北京旅教文化传播有限公司
印刷单位	北京泰锐印刷有限责任公司
经销单位	新华书店
开　　本	880毫米×1230毫米　1/32
印　　张	12
字　　数	268千字
版　　次	2025年1月第2版
印　　次	2025年1月第1次印刷
定　　价	75.00元

（图书如有装订差错请与发行部联系）

再版前言

云南、贵州、四川、重庆四省市（以下简称"云贵川渝"）位于中国西南部，以其丰富多彩的旅游资源吸引了无数的海外游客，旅游业发展喜人，成为当地的重要产业。同时，云贵川渝地缘相近，人文相亲，互动频繁。在其旅游业蓬勃发展的过程中，随着入境游人数的不断增加，各地对高素质英语导游人才的需求也越来越大。为此，国家文旅部每年都要组织导游资格考试，其中包括各省市的现场英语考试，目的就是发现人才，壮大各地的英语导游队伍。

在现场英语考试中，景点讲解一般要求在5~10分钟内完成，占总分值的30%，景点讲解的优劣直接关系着考试的通过率。讲解过程要体现景点的概况、旅游价值、旅游特色及主要景点介绍等方面。然而，因考生多是大专院校学生和已通过中文笔试的导游，他们在翻译、编译、改译中文导游词的过程中可能会感到力不从心，难以在讲解时详略得当、重点突出，有一份较好的英语导游讲解词范本对他们来说会很有帮助。

目前市面上的英语导游书籍，景点讲解词篇幅往往较长，不适用于现场英语导游考试。针对以上情况，结合考生实际需求，笔者编写了这本《云贵川渝英语导游讲解词》（英汉对照），旨在满足云南、贵州、四川、重庆四地英文导游考生的需求，让考生在考前有所准备，增加考试信心，帮助其顺利通过现场英语考试。

本书第2版依据全国导游资格考试大纲，精选了云贵川渝四省市共计71个景区，对其进行模拟现场讲解，其中包括云南省19个（新增"普者黑景区"）、贵州省29个、四川省15个（新增"眉山三苏祠博物馆"）、重庆市8个，均为当地重要的自然或人文景观。本书不仅涵盖了云贵川渝四省市最新导游考试大纲要求的外语类考生备考景点讲解词，同时还补充了多个其他景点的讲解词，供有余力的考生或在职导游人员学习充电。

每篇讲解词的编排皆参照景点讲解英文口试的评分细则，做到有的放矢。编排模块如下：景点的导向性知识（景点所在的位置、游览景点的注意事项、景点的参观游览路线）；景点的说明性知识（景点的历史沿革，景点的风光或文化特色，有关景点的名人、名家、名言、名句及传说故事）；景点讲解的重点。

此外，本书英文讲解词分段给出了对应的中文文本。一方面可以帮助考生更好地理解英文讲解词，另一方面，中文文本也不失为中文类考生景点讲解的参考资料。

在本书编写过程中，承蒙美国 Ysidro Vega III 先生的大力支持。他对本书的英文语句修改提出了中肯的意见，使英语文本更自然流畅，特对其表示感谢。

杨天庆
于四川成都

Contents
目　录

辅助资料

Yunnan Province
云南省

01. Stone Forest Park

　　石　　林 ··· 003

02. Old Town of Lijiang

　　丽江古城 ··· 008

03. Meili Snow Mountain in Deqin County

　　德钦县梅里雪山 ··· 014

04. Xishuangbanna Tropical Botanical Garden

　　西双版纳热带植物园 ···································· 018

05. Cultural Landscape of Honghe Hani Rice Terraces

　　红河哈尼梯田文化景观 ································· 025

06. Three Pagodas in Dali

　　大理崇圣寺三塔 ··· 031

07. Potatso National Park

　　普达措国家公园 ··· 036

08. Dai Nationality Park in Xishuangbanna

　　西双版纳傣族园 ··· 041

09. The Village of Yunnan Nationalities

　　云南民族村 ·················· 046

10. Dali Ancient Town

　　大理古城 ·················· 051

11. Yulong Snow Mountain

　　玉龙雪山 ·················· 056

12. World Horti-Expo Garden in Kunming

　　昆明世博园 ·················· 061

13. Gardan Songzanlin Monastery

　　噶丹·松赞林寺 ·················· 066

14. Heshun Old Town in Tengchong County

　　腾冲和顺 ·················· 072

15. Fuxian Lake in Chengjiang County

　　澄江抚仙湖 ·················· 077

16. Colorful Sand Forest in Luliang County

　　陆良彩色沙林 ·················· 082

17. Temple of Confucius in Jianshui County

　　建水文庙 ·················· 087

18. Dinosaur Valley in Lufeng County

　　禄丰恐龙谷 ·················· 092

19. Puzhehei Scenic Area

　　普者黑景区 ·················· 097

Guizhou Province
贵州省

01. Qingyan Ancient Town

　　青岩古镇 ·················· 105

Contents 目录

02. Yangming Cultural Park in Xiuwen County

   修文阳明文化园···110

03. Tianhetan Scenic Area

   天河潭景区···114

04. Scenery of Huangguoshu Waterfalls

   黄果树大瀑布景区··118

05. Longgong Caves in Anshun

   龙宫风景名胜区···123

06. Fanjing Mountain Nature Reserve

   梵净山自然保护区··128

07. Zhusha Old Town

   朱砂古镇···133

08. Zhangjiang Scenery in Libo County

   荔波樟江景区···137

09. Chishui Danxia Tourist Area

   赤水丹霞···142

10. Zunyi Conference Site

   遵义会议会址···147

11. Hailongtun Castle

   海龙屯··153

12. The Center of the Tea Sea in Fenggang County

   凤冈茶海之心···157

13. The Tea Sea in West China

   西部茶海···161

14. Shuanghe Karst Cave in Suiyang County

   绥阳双河洞··166

15. Zhijin Cave in Bijie

   毕节织金洞··170

16. Baili Azalea Scenery
    百里杜鹃景区 ·················· 174
17. Thousand-household Miao Village in Xijiang
    西江千户苗寨景区 ·················· 179
18. Zhenyuan Ancient Town
    镇远古镇 ·················· 184
19. Wanfeng Forest Scenery in Xingyi
    兴义万峰林景区 ·················· 190
20. Yeyuhai Scenic Site
    野玉海 ·················· 195
21. The Third Line Construction Museum in Liupanshui
    六盘水市三线建设博物馆 ·················· 199
22. Ancient Ginkgo Scenic Spot in Tuole Village
    妥乐古银杏 ·················· 204
23. Qianling Mountain Park
    黔灵山公园 ·················· 208
24. Jiaxiu Pavilion
    甲秀楼 ·················· 213
25. Sidonggou Scenic Area
    四洞沟风景区 ·················· 217
26. Tianlong Old Town
    天龙屯堡 ·················· 223
27. Culture of Miao Ethnic Minority
    苗族文化 ·················· 227
28. Culture of Dong Ethnic Minority
    侗族文化 ·················· 232
29. Culture of Bouyei Ethnic Minority
    布依族文化 ·················· 237

Sichuan Province
四川省

01. Sanxingdui Museum
    三星堆博物馆·················· 245
02. Jiuzhaigou National Park
    九寨沟景区·················· 251
03. Chengdu Research Base of Giant Panda Breeding
    成都大熊猫繁育研究基地景区·········· 257
04. Mt. Emei
    峨眉山景区·················· 261
05. Dujiangyan Irrigation System
    都江堰景区·················· 267
06. Daocheng-Yading Nature Reserve
    稻城亚丁··················· 272
07. Mount Guangwu Scenic Area
    光雾山风景区················· 277
08. Bifengxia Scenic Area
    雅安碧峰峡·················· 283
09. Leshan Giant Buddha
    乐山大佛景区················· 288
10. Mt. Qingcheng
    青城山景区·················· 294
11. Wuhou Temple
    武侯祠景区·················· 300
12. Du Fu's Thatched Cottage
    杜甫草堂景区················· 306

13. Shunan Bamboo Sea

蜀南竹海 ·············· 312

14. Wangjiang Tower Park

望江楼 ·············· 317

15. Meishan San Su Shrine Museum

眉山三苏祠博物馆 ·············· 322

Chongqing Municipality
重庆市

01. Yangtze Three Gorges

长江三峡 ·············· 331

02. Dazu Rock Carvings

大足石刻 ·············· 336

03. Urban Landscape in Chongqing

山水都市 ·············· 342

04. Three Natural Bridges in Wulong County

武隆天生三桥 ·············· 346

05. The Capital of Hot Springs

温泉之都 ·············· 351

06. Hechuan Diaoyu Town

合川钓鱼城 ·············· 355

07. White Crane Ridge in Fuling County

涪陵白鹤梁 ·············· 360

08. Fengjie Tiankeng Difeng

奉节天坑地缝 ·············· 365

Yunnan Province
云南省

云南省《导游服务能力》考试大纲

01. Stone Forest Park
    石　林 /003
02. Old Town of Lijiang
    丽江古城 /008
03. Meili Snow Mountain in Deqin County
    德钦梅里雪山 /014
04. Xishuangbanna Tropical Botanical Garden
    西双版纳热带植物园 /018
05. Cultural Landscape of Honghe Hani Rice Terraces
    红河哈尼梯田文化景观 /025
06. Three Pagodas in Dali
    大理崇圣寺三塔 /031
07. Potatso National Park
    普达措国家公园 /036
08. Dai Nationality Park in Xishuangbanna
    西双版纳傣族园 /041
09. Yunnan Nationalities Village
    云南民族村 /046
10. Dali Ancient City
    大理古城 /051
11. Jade Dragon Snow Mountain
    玉龙雪山 /056
12. World Horti-Expo Garden in Kunming
    昆明世博园 /061
13. Gadan Songzanlin Lamasery
    噶丹·松赞林寺 /066
14. Heshun Ancient Town in Tengchong
    腾冲和顺古镇 /072
15. Fuxian Lake in Chengjiang County
    澄江抚仙湖 /077
16. Colorful Sand Forest in Luliang County
    陆良彩色沙林 /082
17. Temple of Confucius in Jianshui County
    建水文庙 /087
18. Dinosaur Valley in Lufeng County
    禄丰恐龙谷 /092
19. Puzhehei Scenic Area
    普者黑景区 /097

(注：根据2024年全国导游资格考试大纲，云南省外语类考生景点讲解范围包括01、02、04、14、19共计5个景点，其余为补充内容。)

01

Stone Forest Park
石 林

The Stone Forest Park is located about 78 kilometers southeast of Kunming in Yunnan Province. Its tourist attractions cover an area of 350 square kilometers, which are mainly divided into several scenic sections: the Greater & Lesser Stone Forests, Naigu Stone Forest, Changhu Lake, Qifeng Cave, Yuehu Lake, Zhiyun Cave, and Dadie Waterfall. The Stone Forest is a karst geological park, with stone forest landform as the main landscape. In the late Palaeozoic Era, this area was a shallow sea with a large amount of limestone and dolomite deposited. Later, as the earth's crust moved, the sea turned into land, the flat ground became hills, and limestone and dolomite pushed their way out of the receding sea. During this period, the underground and surface water constantly eroded stones within and around rock cracks. As a result, the area eventually developed into a vast composite-type and multiple-shaped forest of stone landscape. The earliest stone-forest was formed about 250 million years ago in the late period of the early Permian Era.

石林公园位于云南省昆明东南约 78 公里处，景区占地面积 350 平方公里，主要分为大小石林、乃古石林、长湖、奇峰洞、月湖、芝云洞和大叠水瀑布。石林是一个以石林地貌景观为主的岩溶地质公园。在晚古生代时期，这里为浅海，沉积了大量的石灰岩和白云岩。后因地壳变动，海洋变陆地，平地变高山，石灰岩和白云岩从退去的浅海里显露出来。在此期间，地下水和地表水不断侵蚀岩石裂缝内部和周围的石头，最终形成了广阔的组合类型多样的石林地貌景观。最早的石林形成于2.5亿前的早二叠纪晚期。

The formation of the Stone Forest is a true geological miracle and is considered as an extraordinary natural phenomenon. In the stone forest scenic areas, sharp cone-shaped rocks and stone pinnacles rise abruptly from the ground in numerous layers. Like a vast black forest, the greystone formations stretch all around as far as the eye can see. Some stones are almost as high as a six-story building, some are treated as superhuge rockeries, some remain secluded, while many others are interconnected in a crisscross pattern, occupying an area ranging from a few *mu* (1 *mu*≈0.067 hectare) to acres.

石林的形成是一部真正的地质传奇，是非常奇特的自然现象。在石林风景区，尖锥形岩石、石峰拔地而起，层层叠叠，灰色的岩层向四周伸展，一望无际，像一片辽阔的黑色森林。有的岩石近六层楼高，有的像超大型的假山，也有的独立成景，还有许多岩石纵横交错，连成一片，占地几亩（1亩≈0.067公顷）到上百亩不等。

In the Stone Forest, the main tourist area is Lizijing (plum cluster) Stone Forest. According to legend, there was a man who saw plum trees at nightfall. The trees grew on cliffs and had large and red plums. The next day, he went there for plums, but there was no sign of the trees, hence the name of the "Lizijing" Stone Forest. This area covers a space of about 12 square kilometers, where its sightseeing territory is mainly composed of the Stone Forest Lake, the Greater & Lesser Stone Forests and the Lizijing Yard. In the Stone Forest, this is the largest zone, where the scenery is the most concentrated and impressive. As visitors enter this place, the geographical wonders come into view, which makes them get lost in admiration of the scenic beauty. They will see nothing but pinnacles, stone cliffs in different postures. These stones appear extremely unique and look like wonderful pictures, attracting many visitors to stop and feast their eyes on the view. Such stones seem like beautiful verses chanted by countless writers and poets throughout the ages. If you look more closely, you will find that some large stones have titles, such as a baby elephant on the top of a stone peak, cows crouching calmly in the woods, or a sword falling into a pond; some other look like the Tang Monk or Monkey King. One stone is titled as a "Bell Stone". It is said to be a treasure bestowed upon the Stone Forest by the Deity of Music. If you knock it, the stone will give out different sounds. According to legend, the Stone Forest is the birthplace of Ashima, a beautiful Sani girl. By the pool, there is a pinnacle, like a slim Sani girl carrying a bamboo basket on the back. Local people affectionately call it "Ashima".

在石林，主要游览区为李子箐石林。相传，有人在傍晚看见了李子树，树长在石崖上，结着又红又大的李子。第二天，他去那里摘李子，却没有李子树的踪迹，"李子箐"石林由此得名。景区面积约12平方公里，游览区主要由石林湖、大石林、小石林和李子园组成，是石林景区内最大，也是景点最集中、最美的区域。走进这个区域，地质奇观映入眼帘，风景之美让游客赞不绝口。山峰、石壁奇特无比，姿态各异，看起来像一幅幅绝妙图画，吸引众多游客驻足凝神，欣赏景色。这样的岩石似是一首首美丽的诗句，让历代无数的作家和诗人为之吟唱。如果仔细观看，会发现有些较大的岩石都有称谓，如像石峰顶上的小象；状若牛，在林间静卧；像一把剑柄，投入池中。还有的岩石像唐僧、像孙悟空。有一块岩石称为"石钟"，据传说是乐神赐给石林的宝贝。如果敲击它，"石钟"能发出不同的声音。据传说，石林是美丽的撒尼少女阿诗玛的出生地。在水池旁，有一座石峰，宛如一位身材苗条，背着竹篓的撒尼少女。当地人民亲切地称之为"阿诗玛"。

The Stone Forest

The Stone Forest is a huge treasure of natural rock-scape art. Hailed as the "first miracle in the world", it enjoys equal popularity with the Palace Museum(the Forbidden City) in Beijing, the Terra-cotta Warriors in Xi'an and Guilin Karst. As early as in the Ming Dynasty, the Stone Forest had become an attraction. In 2007, the Stone Forest was inscribed on the World Heritage List. In addition, it has been crowned with other titles such as National 5A-level Tourist Attraction, China's Key National Scenic Attraction, the National Geological Park and the World Geological Park.

石林是一座天然岩石景观艺术的瑰宝，被誉为"天下第一奇观"，与北京故宫、西安兵马俑、桂林山水齐名。早在明朝，石林就成为游览胜地。2007年，石林被列入《世界遗产名录》。此外，石林还获得了其他的称号："国家AAAAA级旅游景区"、中国国家重点风景名胜区、中国国家地质公园、世界地质公园。

Well, so much for the introduction to the Stone Forest. Today, we are scheduled to go for the tour of the Greater Stone Forest, the Lesser Stone Forest and the Naigu Stone Forest. The tour takes three hours. Please stick with me all the time because the Stone Forest is so big, and it is easy to get lost. A final word of advice. Please wear sturdy hiking shoes or sneakers to ensure that the shoes are suitable for walking on steep stone slopes.

好了,石林讲解到此结束。今天,我们计划去参观大小石林和乃古石林片区。游览时间为三小时。石林太大了,容易迷路,请一直跟着我。最后,还有一个建议:请穿上结实的登山鞋或运动鞋,确保所穿的鞋适合在陡峭的石坡上行走。

02
Old Town of Lijiang
丽江古城

Lijiang lies in a beautiful valley north of Dali, bordering Tibet. Located in Lijiang City, Old Town of Lijiang is one of the four best preserved ancient towns in China. The other three towns include Langzhong in Sichuan, Pingyao in Shanxi and Shexian in Anhui.

丽江坐落在大理北边美丽的谷地,与西藏接壤。丽江古城位于丽江市内,是中国保存最为完好的四大古城之一,其他三座古城分别为四川阆中、山西平遥和安徽歙县。

For the tour of the old town, you will have much free time to walk around. You can climb up the Lion Hill and sit on the slope for a panoramic view of the old town. Or you can go and observe the crisscrossing streams and canals in the old town, where main streets are close to streams and alleys by canals. Or you can stroll along streets or walk into a courtyard to watch the architecture of the old town. Also, you can go to the market or cross bridges to have a view of the old town's layout and folk customs. Please note that you are expected to return to the hotel for dinner at 6:00 p. m. Also, please wear a sun-hat and use sun-creams to protect your skin when you take part in outdoor activities.

这次古城游览,你们会有许多空闲时间四处走动。或登上狮子山,坐

Yunnan Province
云南省

在斜坡上观古城全貌；或去看看古城纵横交错的溪水河道，主街傍河、小巷临渠；或走街入院，欣赏古城建筑；或入市过桥，一览古城布局，民风民俗。请注意：下午6点返回酒店用餐。进行户外活动时，请戴上太阳帽，涂抹防霜，以保护皮肤。

A Bird View of Old Town of Lijiang

The Old Town of Lijiang, located in the Yunnan-Guizhou Plateau, is at an elevation of about 2,400 meters and occupies an area of 3.8 square kilometers. The town was built in the period between the late Song and early Yuan dynasties. In ancient times, it remained known far and wide as a bazaar or a place of strategic importance. People of the Naxi ethnic nationality occupy the vast majority of the total local population. Thirty percent of the local residents are still engaged in traditional handicraft production and commercial activities related to the manufacture of copper and silver, as well as in sectors such as fur and leather, and textiles and brewage.

丽江古城地处云贵高原，海拔2400余米，全城面积达3.8平方公里。古城始建于宋末元初，在古代就是远近闻名的集市和重镇。纳西族占总人口绝大多数，30%的居民仍在从事与铜银器制作、皮毛皮革、纺织、酿造业相关的传统手工业和商业活动。

Old Town of Lijiang has blended the essence of architectural styles from the Naxi, Bai, Tibetan, and Han nationalities. The town has no walls. At present, it still preserves a large number of local residential houses built in the Ming and Qing dynasties. These are all made of wood, with tile roofs. Many buildings are in the shape of three-section compound, each with a screen wall facing the entrance gate. These residential compounds are enclosed by walls and appear square. Porches remain spacious. Flowers and birds are carved on doors and windows. Plants and flowers grow in compound yards. These tile-roof buildings highlight the structural patterns and pursue carving or painting decoration, thus architectural experts at home and abroad regard such architectures as the "Museum of Folk Residential Dwellings". As for streets and alleys, they are restricted to neat and orderly formation. Instead, they sprawl without external constraints. Main streets are close to streams, and alleys by canals. More than 300 ancient stone bridges are connected with rivers, forming an agreeable contrast with rivers, trees, and age-old lanes and houses. Along the canals are some inns and cafes, a good place to sit outside and sip a cup of tea or café as the water gurgles by. Besides, there are a number of interesting spots in the old town, such as the North Entrance Gate, the Mu Family Mansion, the Wenchang Pavilion, the Lijiang Three-Eye Wells and the Old Market Square.

丽江古城融合了纳西族、白族、藏族和汉族建筑风格的精华。古城没有城墙，目前仍保留着大片明清时期的民宅，均是瓦顶土木结构，许多建筑是三坊一照壁。所居院落四周为墙，呈方形，门廊宽敞，门窗雕有花鸟图案，院内还种植草木花卉。这些瓦屋楼建筑突出结构布局，又追求雕绘装饰，由此被中外建筑专家誉为"民居博物馆"。而大街小巷呢，不拘于工整有序，而是自由延伸，主街傍水，小巷临渠，300多座古石桥相连，与河水、绿树、古巷、古屋相映成趣。沿着渠道有一些客栈、咖啡馆，人坐在外面，喝口茶或啜饮咖啡，渠水从旁边汩汩流过，十分惬意。此外，古城内还有众多景点，如：北门入口、木府、文昌楼、丽江三眼井、四方街，等等。

Well, compared with other attractions in the town, the Old Market Square is particularly impressive. The square is the center of the old town. Why is it called Sifangjie or the market square? One of the stories tells the origin of its name. It is said that the shape of the square is similar to the regular four-sided official seal owned by a prefecture magistrate, hence a Tusi named the square after the seal shape. The old town was once a strategically important place on the Ancient Tea Horse Road. It remains as the town's open-air trade center and the distribution center of logistics, where four main streets stretch from the square to the surrounding area. Many side streets and alleys sprawl from each main street, and all of them are connected and boundary on all sides. When tourists enter the market square, they will find interesting sights. In the early morning, as the square comes to life and mist begins to dissipate, some locals walk out of their houses to buy their breakfast. Around 10 a.m., the square begins to bustle up. Shops, inns and tea houses start their business. The square is crowded with people. Vendors from different ethnic groups dressed in traditional costumes trade in goods, selling snacks, mountain products or souvenirs. The locals come and go, and the elderly sit sunning themselves on old bridges. Some of tourists stroll around the square for good photograph, some of them sit in front of tea houses or on the second floor of the inns or cafés, a good place to look out onto the old market square, allowing them to enjoy the sights and sounds of the market, while sipping tea, cold beer or hot coffee. At nightfall, shops are closed, and business people depart from the square. The elderly are back home, and children begin playing by the bridges. Soon lamps are on in the windows of the inns and pubs, shining for hours. At around two o'clock, the market square was completely empty, except for the sound of the streams and the gurgling of the canals.

当然，在这些景点中，四方街尤其令人难以忘怀。四方街是古城的中心。为什么叫四方街呢？其中一种说法道出地名的由来。据说，广场方形的形状与知府拥有的四方大印很相似，故土司以大印形状命名四方街。丽江古城是茶马古道上的重镇，是一露天贸易中心，也是物流集散地。四条主道从四方街向四周辐射，许多小街小巷又从每条主道分出，街巷相连，四通八达。当游客来到四方街，他们会发现有趣的景象。清晨，四方街苏醒过来，薄雾慢慢散去，当地的一些居民走出家门，购买早点。大约上午10点，四方街变得热闹起来。商店、旅馆、茶馆开始营业；四方街上挤满了人，来自不同民族的小商贩们身着传统服装，在此交易商品，销售零食、山货及纪念品。当地居民来来往往，年长的坐在古桥上晒太阳；有的游客在四方街闲逛，寻找摄影的好目标；有的坐在茶馆前或在客栈、咖啡馆二楼上，目视四方街，一边啜饮茶水、冷啤酒或热咖啡，一边欣赏四方街的景象，聆听街上的声响。夜幕降临，商店打烊了，商人离开了四方街，老人回家了，孩童却开始在桥四周玩耍，客栈和酒吧窗户里的灯亮了，灯光一直持续数小时。凌晨两点左右，四方街空无一人，只有小溪和水渠汩汩的流水声。

The Old Market Square and the Old Town of Lijiang have a long history and unique cultural connotations. In 1986, Old Town of Lijiang was listed as a famous historical and cultural city in China by the state Council. On December 4, 1997, it was formally listed as a World Cultural Heritage Site by UNESCO. In 2002, it was crowned as one of "China's 10 Most Desirable Small Cities".

四方街、丽江古城历史悠久，具有独特的文化内涵。1986年，丽江古城被国务院列为中国历史文化名城，1997年12月4日被联合国教科文组织正式列为世界文化遗产，2002年荣登"中国最令人向往的10个小城市"行列。

Well, so far for the brief introduction to the Old Town of Lijiang. Now let's walk into the town for sightseeing! The easiest way to enter the old town is to go in the direction of the cinema, turn east into a small square and then head south. The old town is like a pleasant labyrinth with twists and turns. Although it is small, it is easy to get lost in here, which, of course, is part of the fun.

好了，丽江古城的简介到此结束，现在让我们走进古城观光吧！进入古城最简单的办法，就是先向电影院方向走去，再朝东转，走小广场，然后朝南行。古城如同迂回曲折的快乐迷宫。虽然不大，但在这里容易迷失方向，当然，这也是乐趣之一。

Meili Snow Mountain in Deqin County
德钦梅里雪山

Meili Snow Mountain is also known as "Kawakarpo Snow Mountain". In the Deqin Tibetan language, meili is pronounced "mainri", which means "medicine mountain" due to the fact that the mountain is rich in a variety of rare and precious medicinal herbs. At present, this mountain is a national 4A-level scenic site, with a total area of 960 square kilometers.

梅里雪山也称"卡瓦格博雪山"。"梅里"一词在德钦藏语里读"mainri",意思是"药山",因盛产各种名贵药材而得名。梅里雪山景区是国家AAAA级旅游景区,总面积960平方公里。

Meili Snow Mountain is a vast snow-capped mountain group, where the north section is Meili Snow Mountain, the middle section is Taizi Snow Mountain, and the south section is Biluo Snow Mountain. Its main peak, 6,740 meters above the sea level, is considered to be the first peak in Yunnan Province.

梅里雪山是一座庞大雪山群体,北段为梅里雪山,中段为太子雪山,南段为碧罗雪山,主峰海拔6740米,是云南的最高峰。

Most of visitors, who come to Meili Snow Mountain from different places, will choose to stay in the place where Feilai Lamasery is located.

The lamasery is not only a temple, but also the first observation platform of the mountain. On the platform, visitors can overlook the spectacular canyon, where the Lancang River flows rapidly. In the front of the platform is majestic Kawakarpo, the main peak of Meili Snow Mountain. At sunrise, the sun shines on the peak, as if the snow-capped mountain sparkles with golden light. At night, the starry sky can be seen from the platform, too; countless stars add splendor to the mountain, making visitors feel like they were in another world.

来到梅里雪山的游客，大多数都会选择来飞来寺。飞来寺不仅是一座寺庙，还是梅里雪山第一观景台。从观景台上，可以俯瞰壮观的峡谷，那里的澜沧江水流湍急。观景台正面是雄伟的梅里主峰卡瓦格博；日出时，阳光洒在主峰上，仿佛雪山闪耀着金色的光芒。夜晚，从观景台上还可以看到满天星斗的夜空，无数的星星为梅里雪山增添了光彩，游客感到仿佛置身于另一个世界。

Traditionally, in late autumn and early winter, pilgrims from Tibet, Sichuan, Qinghai or Gansu, usually come to worship the Thirteen Peaks. The main peak, Kawakarpo, commonly known as "the God of Snow Mountains", is a pilgrimage site of Tibetan Buddhism. Kawakarpo and its surrounding peaks, collectively known as the Thirteen Peaks, are densely vegetated and species rich, with spruce forests extending to grass marshland of the plateau. Of these peaks, the most famous peaks are Meantsmu and Jiwa Ren'an. Legend has it that the Meantsmu Peak (Goddess Peak) was the concubine of the Mountain God Kawakarpo. This peak is 6,054 meters above the sea level, and its summit covers an area of 30 square kilometers, where snow does not melt all year round. Jiwa Ren'an consists of five flat, pointed snow peaks that look like the cap worn by Buddhas. Therefore, in Tibetan language, Jiwa Ren'an means "the Crown of Five Buddhas". This peak is located on the north side of Meantsmu Peak, and its summit covers an area of about 10 square kilometers, where snow does not melt all year round.

深秋和初冬，藏川青甘香客通常会来朝拜"十三峰"。主峰卡瓦格博，俗称"雪山之神"，是藏传佛教的朝圣地。卡瓦格博及周围诸峰，统称"十三峰"。那里植被茂密，物种丰富，云杉森林延伸到高原草甸。在这些山峰中，较有名的是缅茨姆峰、吉娃仁安峰。传说中，缅茨姆峰（神女峰）是卡瓦格博山神的妃子。这座山峰海拔6054米，峰顶范围30平方公里，终年积雪不化。吉娃仁安由五座扁平而尖削的雪峰组成，很像菩萨戴的五佛冠帽。因此，在藏语中，吉娃仁安意思是"五佛之冠"。此峰位于缅茨姆峰北侧，峰顶范围约10平方公里，终年积雪不化。

At the foot of Kawakarpo Peak lies Mingyong Glacier, one of several glaciers on Meili Snow Mountain, stretching from the summit to Mingyong Village at the foot of the mountain. Seen from a distance, the glacier looks like a silvery dragon descending from the sky toward the Lancang River. Visitors can hikeuphill along the mountain trail, pass through Taizi Temple and then ascend the glacier observation platform, where visitors can have a close view of the winding glacier and magnificent Kawakarpo peak. The distance is about 8 kilometers from the main entrance of the scenic site at the foot of the mountain to Taizi Temple, and about 2.5 kilometers further up from the temple to the platform. For easy hiking, visitors can rent a horse at the entrance and ride it up to the deck.

主峰卡瓦格博脚下是明永冰川，是梅里雪山上几条冰川之一。它从峰顶一直延伸到山脚下的明永村。从远处看，冰川犹如一条银龙从天而降，直到澜沧江边。游客可以沿着山路上山，穿过太子庙，登上冰川观景台，在那里可以近距离看到蜿蜒曲折的冰川和壮美的卡瓦格博峰。从山脚的景区大门到太子庙大约8公里，从太子庙再往上约2.5公里。如果想要轻松游览，可以在景区门口雇一匹马代步。

Yubeng Waterfall is located on the south side of Kawakarpo Peak. The best time to see Yubeng Waterfall is in the period between autumn and winter. At that time, not much water flows down from the top, but as the wind blows, the water disperses itself and even forms in shapes. When the sun shines, there appears a rainbow, which locals consider to be a good omen. Visitors can follow the Tibetan tradition of walking three times clockwise along the base of the waterfall for good fortune. On the way to the waterfall, there are many *mani* stone heaps piled up by Tibetan visitors who come to worship the sacred mountain. At the foot of Meantsmu Peak, there is a Tibetan community named Yubeng Village. It takes about 4-5 hours to get from the village to the waterfall back and forth.

雨崩瀑布位于卡瓦博格峰南侧，观赏雨崩瀑布最佳时间是秋冬之际。那时的瀑布水量不大，但风吹之时，瀑水就会自动散开，甚至呈现各种形状。阳光照耀时，彩虹出现，当地人称之吉兆。游客可以按照藏族传统，在瀑布底下顺时针绕瀑布走三圈祈福。在通往瀑布的路上，有众多的玛尼堆，是藏族游客朝拜神山时堆砌而成的。在神女峰脚下，有一座藏族村寨叫雨崩村，从村庄到瀑布来回需要4~5个小时。

Well, so much for my brief introduction to Meili Snow Mountain. Here are some points for your attention. Meili Snow Mountain is a sacred mountain in Tibetan areas. When hiking, please follow a local tour guide and be sure to respect the local religion and customs. Those who plan to go to Yubeng Waterfall should prepare waterproof and warm clothes, as well as antislip and waterproof hiking shoes.

好了，讲解到此结束。以下几点需要大家注意：梅里雪山是藏区的神山。徒步旅行时，请跟随当地导游，并要尊重当地的宗教和习俗。徒步去雨崩瀑布需要防水保暖的衣服和防滑防水的登山鞋。

04
Xishuangbanna Tropical Botanical Garden
西双版纳热带植物园

Xishuangbanna Tropical Botanical Garden is locally known as Menglun Botanical Garden, and its full name is the Xishuangbanna Tropical Botanical Garden of the Chinese Academy of Sciences. The garden is located in Menglun Town, Mengla County under Xishuangbanna Dai Autonomous Prefecture of Yunnan Province. Specifically, it lies on the Huludao, at the intersection of Luosuo River and Menglun District. It covers an area of about 11.25 square kilometers and preserves about 2.5 square kilometers of virgin tropical rainforests. As a local saying goes, "Without a trip to the Huludao, that means you have never been to Xishuangbanna."

西双版纳热带植物园，当地人称勐仑植物园，全称为中国科学院西双版纳热带植物园。该园林位于中国云南省西双版纳傣族自治州勐腊县勐仑镇，在罗梭江与勐仑地区交会处的"葫芦岛"上。植物园占地面积约为11.25平方公里，并保存着一片面积约2.5平方公里的原始热带雨林。当地流传着一句话："不到葫芦岛，等于没到过西双版纳"。

Xishuangbanna Tropical Botanical Garden was founded in 1958. In the early stage of the garden development, the botanical garden mainly develops and utilizes plant resources according to the needs of economic construction and builds experimental fields for various economic plants. In the late 1980s, according to the trend of botanical gardens at home and abroad, as well as its own scientific research development, the botanical garden adjusted its scientific research tasks to "development, utilization and protection of plant resources". Gradually after the completion of a few projects, the experimental sites were transformed into special botanical gardens or zones for specific plants. In the 1990s, some more special botanical gardens or zones were established in the original experimental fields. In 2000, the botanical garden introduced and cultivated about 4,000 tropical plants from 58 countries and regions. It established 13 special botanical gardens or zones, such as the Palm Garden, the Hundred-Bamboo Garden, the Banyan Tree Garden, the Kapur Garden, the Garden of Hundred Tropical Fruits, the Garden of Various Aromas, the Garden of Exotic Flowers and Rare plants, the Garden of Celebrities and Famous Trees, the Botanical Garden of Ethnic Nationalities, the Shade-Tolerate Botanical Garden, the Garden of Ornamental Trees and Shrubs, the Zone of Aquatic Plants, as well as the Reserve of Endangered Plants Relocated from South Yunnan.

西双版纳热带植物园，始建于1958年。在建园初期，植物园根据经济建设的需要，主要进行植物资源的开发和利用，建设各种经济植物的试验地。在20世纪80年代后期，根据国内外植物园及其科研发展的趋势，植物园调整科研任务为"植物资源的开发、利用和保护"，把少数课题结束后的试验地逐渐改建为某类植物专类园（区）。20世纪90年代，又在原有的试验地上建立一些植物专类园（区）。在2000年，植物园从58个国家和地区引种栽培了4000种左右的热带植物，建立了13个植物专类园（区），如：棕榈园、百竹园、榕树园、龙脑香园、热带百果园、百香园、奇花异卉园、名人名树园、民族植物园、荫生植物园、树木园、水生植物区、滇南濒危植物迁地保护区。

A View of the Palm Garden

At present, the botanical garden is divided into the Western Section, the Eastern Section and the Greenstone Forest. The Western Section is composed of several small botanical gardens. It includes the Garden of Celebrities and Famous Trees, the Hundred-Bamboo Garden, the Wild Orchid Garden, the Garden of Exotic Flowers and Rare plants, the Zone of Aquatic Plants and the Garden of Tropical Wild Flowers and Plants from South Yunnan. The Eastern Section is a strip of tropical rainforests, which are suitable for hiking. There are seven tropical botanical gardens or zones, including the Ginger Garden, the Garden of Rhizoma Arisaematis, the Orchid Garden, the Zone of Ferns, the Zone of Wild Flowers, etc. In addition, the Eastern Section preserves more than 2,000 species of seed plants, including more than 100 species of rare and endangered plants. The scenic area of the Greenstone Forest is located in the eastern Huludao, and more than 90% of the area is covered by forests. In this area, pictographic stones are of various shapes, the rainforest is luxuriantly green, and trees and stones mixed together. All this makes for a rare miracle of which "Up above is the forest, and below is the stone forest".

现在，植物园分为西区、东区和绿石林。西区由多个小的植物园组成，有名人名树园、百竹园、野生兰园、奇花异木园、水生植物区、滇南热带野生花卉园等等。东区是一片狭长的热带雨林，适合徒步旅行，有姜园、天南星园、兰园、蕨类植物区、野花区等7个热带植物专类园/区，保存有种子植物 2000 余种，其中稀有和濒危植物 100 余种。绿石林景区位于葫芦岛东部，森林覆盖率在 90% 以上，区内象形奇石千姿百态，雨林郁郁葱葱，树石交织一起，构成了世间少有的"上有森林，下有石林"的奇观。

Of course, the most popular tourist attraction in the Western Section is the Garden of Exotic Flowers and Rare Plants. The section covers an area of 12 *mu* (0.8 hectares) where various exotic tropical flowers and trees are mainly collected and presented to the public as gardening landscapes. It is divided into the Zone of Fruit-Viewing Plants, the Zone of Grass and Flower Plants, the Zone of Flower and Leaf Plants, the Zone of Sensitive Plants, the Zone of Stem-Plant Admiration and other sites, with a collection of 254 species of exotic flowers and rare trees. In the Western Section, there are plenty of plants worth seeing, such as the Saraca dives Pierre, a species of old stem flower plants; plants with ornamental fruits—Synsepalum dulcificum (miracle fruit), Burmese grapes, cocoa, Gomphocarpus fruticosus (a species of milkweed) and Solanum mammosum (nipple-fruit); stem-bulging plants with ornamental stems—Mascarena lagenicaulis (champagne palm), Beaucarnea recurvata (elephant's foot, ponytail palm), Moringa thouarsii (bottle tree), Jatropha podagrica (Buddha belly plant, bottle-plant shrub) and so on. There are also some other plants worth seeing as below: the Stephania epigaea with bulging tuberous roots and stem tubers; the Aristolochia grandiflora (pelican flower), the world's largest flowers; the Tair-conca chishrieri (tiger-whiskerplant) and Clerodendranthus spicatus (cat-whisker plant) with floral-module beards; the Passiflora coccinea (scarlet passion flower) and Hunnemannia fumariifolia (tulip poppy or Mexican tulip poppy) in a peculiar and bright-colored shape; the grass flower plants such as the Callispidia guttata (shrimp plant or false hop) and sun flowers; floral-leaf plants such as the Acalypha wilkesiana (copperleaf and Jacob's coat) and Agave angustifolia (Caribbean agave); sensitive plants such as the Desmodium gyrans (tick-trefoil, tick clover, hitch hikers or beggar lice), the Mimosa arborca (tree with balls of yellow flowers and leaves that are sensitive to touch and light) and the Apple-fruited Granadilla (passion flower genus); the Ochroma lagopus (balsa tree), a very lightweight material; and the Dendrocnide stimulant (stinging nettle or nettle tree), a plant under state protection. The core of the Eastern Section is the virgin tropical rainforests, which display the typical features of the tropical rainforests and greatly show the wonders of nature, such as the upright and strong "Large Buttress Roots", the merciless "Strangler Figs", the majestic "Single Tree Forest", the colorful "Garden in the Air" and the unique "Old Stem Flower". In addition, it has something spectacular, such as the giant vines that fly in various shapes through the forests; the flowers that can change colors; the miracle fruits that make sour fruits sweet; the Desmodium gyrans that quiver to the rhythm of music; the Apple-fruited Granadilla that blossoms on time; and the upas-tree (poison arrow wood) that has a highly poisonous pulp.

当然，西区最受游人喜爱的是奇花异卉园。该园占地面积12亩（0.8公顷），主要收集热带各种奇花异木，并以园林园艺的方式向公众进行展示。该园分为观果植物区、草花植物区、花叶植物区、感应植物区、赏茎植物区等，收集奇花异木254种（品种）。在西区，有许多值得看的植物，如：老茎生花植物——无忧花；观果植物——神秘果、木奶果、可可、气球果、乳茄；茎秆膨大的观茎植物——酒瓶椰、酒瓶兰、象腿树、佛肚树等。还有别的可看的植物：山乌龟植物块根和块茎；被誉为世界花之最的巨花马兜铃；有花构件似胡须的老虎须和猫须草；花形奇特艳丽的红花西番莲、金杯花；虾衣花和太阳花等草花植物；红桑及白缘龙舌兰等花叶植物；跳舞草、含羞树及时钟花等感应植物；最轻的木材——轻木；国家保护植物火树麻。东区的核心部分是原始热带雨林，集中展示了热带雨林的典型特征，尽显大自然造化之神奇，如：顶天立地的"大板根"、残忍的"绞杀植物"、气势磅礴的"独木成林"、五彩缤纷的"空中花园"、奇特的"老茎生花"。此外，还有令人叹为观止的林间飞舞的巨藤、会变颜色的花、能让酸水果变甜的神秘果、随音乐节律颤动的跳舞草、按时开花的时钟花，以及树浆剧毒的"见血封喉"等奇观。

In July 2011, Xishuangbanna Tropical Botanical Garden was rated as a National 5A-level Tourist Attraction. Besides, it has been crowned with several other titles, such as the National Knowledge Innovation Base, the National Environmental Protection and Popular Science Base, the Base of Science Popularization and Education Base, the Scientific Education Base for China's Youth, the National Civilization Unit, One of China's Top Ten Bases of Science, Technology and Tourism, as well as the High-Quality Popular Science Base in Yunnan Province.

2011年7月，西双版纳热带植物园被评为国家AAAAA级旅游景区。此外，西双版纳热带植物园还获得了其他的称谓："国家知识创新基地""国家环保科普基地""全国科学普及教育基地""全国青少年科技教育基地""全国文明单位""中国十大科技旅游基地""云南省精品科普基地"。

Well, so much for the introduction to Xishuangbanna Tropical Botanical Garden. This morning, we will go sightseeing in the Western Section, and it will take about three hours. At noon, we will have lunch in the Tengben

Garden. In the afternoon, we will go to the Eastern Section for sightseeing. It will take about one hour.

好了,西双版纳热带植物园的简介到此为止。今天上午游览西区,游览时间约3小时。中午在藤本园内用餐。下午游览东区,游览时间约1小时。

05
Cultural Landscape of Honghe Hani Rice Terraces
红河哈尼梯田文化景观

Cultural landscape of Honghe Hani Rice Terraces is located in Honghe Hani and Yi Autonomous Prefecture of Yunnan Province. The rice terraced fields cover four counties, namely Yuanyang, Honghe, Jinping and Luchun, with a total area of about one million *mu* (67,000 hectares) of which Ailao Mountain in Yuanyang County is the core zone of the terraced fields. The Hani Rice Terraces on Ailao Mountain are considered to be a representative work of Yunnan's rice terraced fields and are reputed as the most beautiful mountain sculpture in China. In November 2007, the State Forestry Administration approved Hani Rice Terraced Wetland Park in Honghe as a national wetland park. In 2010, Honghe Hani Rice Terraced Field System became a "Globally Important Agricultural Cultural Heritage". In 2013, Honghe Hani Rice Terraces were listed as a World Cultural Landscape Heritage Site.

红河哈尼梯田文化景观位于云南省红河哈尼族彝族自治州。梯田遍及元阳、红河、金平和绿春四县，总面积约100万亩（6.7万公顷），其中元阳县哀牢山为哈尼梯田的核心区。哀牢山哈尼梯田为云南梯田的代表作，被誉为"中国最美的山岭雕刻"。2007年11月，国家林业局批准红河哈尼梯田湿地公园为国家湿地公园。2010年，红河哈尼稻作梯田系统成为全球重要农业文化遗产。2013年，红河哈尼梯田被列为世界文化景观遗产。

Honghe Hani Rice Terraces are the miracle of farming civilization created mainly by Hani people, as well as other ethnic groups. According to ancient documents, it has a history of more than 1,300 years. As the water in mountainous area flow all year round, the Hani people have diverted water into ditches to allow it to flow into their rice fields, ensuring that rice is grown and harvested in the terraced field. Over the years, Hani people have cultivated rice terraces based on the mountainous terrain. Specifically, large rice fields have been cultivated on large, gentle slopes, while small rice fields have been cultivated on small, steep slopes.

红河哈尼梯田是以哈尼族为主的各族人民创造的农耕文明奇观。据古代文献记载，已有1300多年的历史了。由于山区的水四季长流，哈尼族人将流水引入沟渠，让水流入稻田，确保梯田里的稻谷生长和丰收。多年来，哈尼族根据山势地形垦殖梯田。具体来说，坡缓地大，则开垦出大田；坡陡地小，则开垦小田。

In Yuanyang County, Hani rice terrace ecosystem has the following characteristics. Above each village there must be a dense forest that provides abundant water. Below the village are hundreds and thousands of rice terraced fields that provide food for the local Hani people. In the middle is the village composed of mushroom-shaped houses, forming a place where people live in peace. This structure is highly praised by cultural ecologists, because rivers, forests, villages and rice terraced fields are highly coordinated and virtuously cycled between man and nature.

在元阳，哈尼族梯田生态系统具有以下特点：每个村寨上方，一定有茂密的森林提供丰富的水源。村寨下方是千百级梯田，为当地的哈尼族提供食物。中间是蘑菇形房屋组成的村寨，形成人们平安生活的居所。这一结构受到了文化生态学家的高度赞扬，因为河流、森林、村庄、梯田体现了人与自然的高度协调和良性循环。

Also, in Yuanyang County, Hani Rice Terraces are composed of four scenic sites by the name of Qingkou, Bada, Duoyishu and Laohuzui. The following is the brief introduction to some of them.

元阳梯田一共有四个景区：箐口、坝达、多依树、老虎嘴。以下是部分景区的介绍。

Qingkou Rice Terraces are named after Qingkou Village. The local rice terraces, just like the endless sea, cover an area of nearly ten thousand *mu* (667 hectares) on the steep slopes. There, most of the villages are built on the hillside, and the hills behind the villages are covered with dense forests. On either side of each village flow streams, which are diverted into the village, or down into the rice terraced fields. The miracle of Qingkou Rice Terraces lies in the beauty of the overlapping of terraces, the magic of the intersection of the terraced lines, as well as the elegance of the fusion of these lines with the terraced surfaces.

箐口梯田因箐口村而得名。当地的梯田在陡坡上占地近万亩，宛如一望无际的大海。在那里，村寨多建在半山腰，寨后山上有茂密的森林。每个寨子两边有溪水流淌，水或引入寨里，或引进梯田。箐口梯田的神奇之处在于梯田面与面交叠之美、线与线交汇之神奇、线与面交融之优雅。

Bada Scenic Site is located 43 kilometers south of the county seat. Its main attractions include Quanfuzhuang, Bada, Malizhai and Shangmadian Rice terraces. The rice terraces in the Bada Scenic Site are vast, extending from the Malizhai River at 1,100 meters above the sea level to the top of the mountains at an altitude of 2,000 meters. At four o'clock in the afternoon, as the sun is setting, the vast rice terraces gradually turn pink and red in colors, and then become pink and white. In other words, the best time to visit Bada Scenic Site is late afternoon, when the sun sets and the sky turns red. Some photographers say that this site is the best place to take photos of sunsets and an ideal spot to view the rice terraces, sea of clouds and villages.

坝达景区位于县城南部43公里处，主要景点有全福庄梯田、坝达梯田、麻栗寨梯田和上马点梯田。坝达景区梯田面积广阔，从海拔1100米的麻栗寨河起，一直延伸至海拔2000米的高山之巅。每当下午四时，随着夕阳西下，茫茫梯田逐渐变成粉红色、红色，然后又变成粉红色和白色。也就是说，观赏坝达景区的最佳时间，是每天夕阳西下、满天红霞的傍晚之时。有摄影家称之是夕阳晚照最佳的地方，也是观赏梯田、云海、村寨的理想场所。

Duoyishu Rice Terraces are located in Duoyishu Village, with an altitude of 1,900 meters. In the scenic site, the rice terraces are connected to each other, covering a total area of tens of thousands of *mu* (667 hectares). The scene of the sunrise at Duoyishu is considered to be the most beautiful. In addition, its morning mist also presents a dynamic landscape painting. Among many photos taken in Yuanyang County, the most beautiful ones come from Duoyishu Scenic Site, where the terraces look like colorful prints. Especially at sunrise, the water in the rice terraces constantly changes colors, setting off against the misty village, which seems to be partly hidden and partly visible.

多依树梯田位于多依树村境内，海拔1900米。景区梯田相连，面积上万亩。多依树的日出景色最美。此外，晨雾也呈现出动态风景画情景。在元阳拍摄的很多照片里，最美的照片来自多依树景区，那里的梯田像多彩的版画。尤其是日出时分，梯田水不断变换颜色，衬托着烟雨迷雾下的村寨若隐若现。

Laohuzui Scenic Site, also known as Mengpin Scenic Site, is located 50 kilometers south of Yuanyang County. Laohuzui Rice Terraces, like a huge "abstract painting", has been hailed as "the most magnificent pastoral scenery in the world". Its main attractions include Mengpin, Amengkong and Baoshanzhai rice terraces. Standing on the top of Laohuzui Scenic Site, you can find 3,000 *mu* (200 hectares) of Mengpin Rice Terraces in different shapes. In the sunshine, these rice terraces look like lakes or blue waves rising from the sea. Looking west from the same top, you can see more than 2,000-*mu* (133 hectares) Amengkong Rice Terraces, extending from the deep valley to the three ridges, thus making the ridges covered with layers of rice terraces. Then looking far into the east, you can see more than 2,000 *mu* (133 hectares) of Baoshanzhai Rice Terraces, which cover seven semicircular ridges, like a crescent-shaped ladder leading to the sky.

老虎嘴景区，又名勐品景区，位于县城南部50公里处。老虎嘴梯田，好似巨幅"抽象画"，被誉为"世界上最壮美的田园风光"。该景区主要景点有勐品梯田、阿猛控梯田、保山寨梯田等。站在高高的老虎嘴景区上，可以看到3000亩（200公顷）形状各异的勐品梯田；阳光照射下，这些梯田像湖泊，或似蓝色海浪从海上升起。往西遥望，可以看到2000多亩（133公顷）阿猛控梯田，从深谷一直延伸到三座山脊，使山脊披挂着层层梯田。再往东远眺，可以看到2000多亩（133公顷）保山寨梯田，覆盖着七座半圆形山脊，像是通向苍穹的弯月天梯。

Of course, speaking of the Hani Rice Terraces, the mushroom-shaped houses inhabited by Hani people have to be mentioned. Traditionally, Hani people tend to build their villages along sunlit hillsides. This typical Hani house is shaped like a mushroom and consists of earthen walls, bamboo frames and a thatched roof. Legend has it that in ancient times, Hani people used to live in caves. Later, they moved to a place called Reluo, where they saw large mushrooms everywhere. These mushrooms could not only resist wind and rain, but also allowed ants and other insects to build their nests underneath, so Hani people began to build houses in imitation of mushrooms. These houses are unique in that they are warm in winter and cool in summer. In Hani Rice Terrace Scenic Site, mushroom-shaped houses have a strong local flavor, and visitors can also learn more about the folk customs in the local villages composed of mushroom-shaped houses.

当然,说到哈尼梯田,就不得不提及哈尼族人所居住的蘑菇房。按照传统习惯,哈尼族人常常在向阳的山腰修建村寨。独特的哈尼族蘑菇房状如蘑菇,由土墙、竹框架和茅草屋顶构成。传说远古时候,哈尼人住的是山洞。后来他们迁到一处叫"惹罗"的地方。在那里,随处可见的是大蘑菇。这些蘑菇不仅可以抵御风雨,还能让蚂蚁和其他小昆虫在下面做窝栖息。于是,哈尼人就模仿蘑菇的样子盖起了房屋。蘑菇房独特之处就是冬暖夏凉。在哈尼族梯田景区,蘑菇房具有浓郁的地方风味,而游客还可以在蘑菇房组成的村寨了解更多哈尼族的民俗。

Well, so much for my brief introduction to Honghe Hani Rice Terraces. As for the suggestions for photo-taking, I'd like to tell you that Tuguozhai Rice Terraces are located five kilometers away from the old county seat of Yuanyang. The best time to take photos is in the morning. In addition, eleven kilometers away from Tuguozhai Rice Terraces are Mengpin Rice Terraces, where the best time to take photos is in the afternoon or at dusk. All these scenic sites look very beautiful, and you can easily drive to the entrance to each scenic site.

好了,红河哈尼梯田讲解到此结束。关于拍照的建议,土锅寨梯田在距离元阳老县城五公里处,拍照最佳时间是早晨;另外,距离土锅寨11公里处是勐品梯田,那里拍照的最佳时间是下午或黄昏。景区很漂亮,可以轻松自驾到达每个景区入口处。

Three Pagodas in Dali
大理崇圣寺三塔

Three Pagodas in Dali, one kilometer north of Dali City, are backed by Mt. Cangshan and face the Erhai Lake. Seen from a distance, the three pagodas look splendid, standing like the three legs of a tripod. The tallest pagoda is called Qianxun Pagoda, and the other two small ones are collectively known as the Southern and Northern Small Pagodas. Today, we will pick up a route to a park called the Three Pagoda Reflection Park, then we go and see the Ruins of Chongsheng Temple, Qianxun Pagoda and the other two small pagodas. The whole tour takes 60 minutes. Please come with me to tour Dali Three Pagodas. I will further interpret some of inscriptions, plaques, poetic couplets and paintings. I wish my interpretation will be of great help to your tour of this place of historic interest and scenic beauty.

大理三塔，位于大理城北约1公里处，背靠苍山，面朝洱海。从远处看，三塔雄伟壮观，呈鼎立之态，大塔叫千寻塔，小塔统称南、北小塔。今天，我们的旅游线路是，先到三塔倒影公园；游玩公园后，去观摩崇圣寺遗址、千寻塔和南、北小塔。游览时间为60分钟。请跟我一起游览大理三塔，我将继续讲解一些题词、匾额、对联、绘画，希望我的讲解对你们的参观游览有较大的帮助。

The Three Pagodas in Dali is the brand of the Dali tourism and the symbol of the Dali ancient culture. It is also among the oldest and most majestic architectures in southern China. The construction of these pagodas started during the reign of Quan Fengyou, the seventh king of the Nanzhao Kingdom (824 A.D.–859 A.D.). Qianxun Pagoda, the tallest pagoda, was first constructed. Later, the Southern and Northern Small Pagodas were built. According to ancient records, the construction of the three pagodas totally lasted eight years, used 7.7 million craftsmen and cost about 40,000 *jin* of gold. After the construction of the three pagodas, Chongsheng Temple was built up. The temple was huge in scale, but was destroyed during the Xianfeng's reign (1851–1861) of the Qing Dynasty. However, the three pagodas, located west of the temple, still stood as tough as rocks. In 1925, when an earthquake occurred, the top of the pagodas was shaken off, and the pagodas thus became increasingly dilapidated. After the founding of the People's Republic of China, the government attached great importance to the protection of the three pagodas. As early as March 1961, the Three Pagodas in Dali were admitted into the first group of the national key cultural relic sites under the state protection. In 1978, the three pagodas were repaired on a large scale by relevant departments. In July 2011, the Cultural and Tourist

Three Pagodas in Dali

Zone of the Dali Three Pagodas was listed as a National 5A-level Tourist Attraction.

大理三塔是大理旅游的标志,是大理古文化的象征,也是中国南方最古老、最雄伟的建筑之一。三塔始建于南诏王劝丰祐时期(公元824—公元859),先建了大塔"千寻塔",稍后又建了南、北小塔。据古籍记载,修三塔共"役工匠七百七十万,耗四万余金,历时八年建成"。三塔建成后,又建了崇圣寺。该寺庙规模宏大,但毁于清咸丰年间(1851—1861);然而,位于寺庙西的三塔却巍然屹立。1925年,大理发生了地震,塔顶震落,残破益重。中华人民共和国成立后,政府高度重视对三塔的保护。早在1961年3月,大理三塔就被列入首批全国重点文物保护单位;1978年,相关部门对三塔进行了大规模的修复;2011年7月,大理三塔文化旅游区荣膺国家AAAAA级旅游景区。

Of course, the most impressive are the three pagodas. They stand like the three legs of a tripod. The distance between the Qianxun Pagoda and the Southern Small Pagoda is 70 meters, roughly equivalent to the distance from the Qianxun Pagoda to the Northern Small Pagoda. The Qianxun Pagoda is one of the highest extant towers in China. It is similar in shape to the Small Wild Goose Pagoda in Xi'an, belonging to the Tang-style architecture. Typically, it is a brick pagoda with multiple eaves. It is square shape and hollow inside, with 16 tiers. It is 69.13 meters in height, while its width is 9.9 meters at the bottom. The pagoda is coated with white lime substance. Each tier has niches on its four sides. There are two opposite niches for Buddhist images, and the other two niches are windows for lighting and ventilation. The inner wall of the pagoda is equipped with a wooden spiral staircase from the bottom to the top of the pagoda. Tourists can climb up the pagoda and view the Dali ancient town through the windows of the niches. The marble stone on the pagoda base is inlaid with four large characters "Yong Zhen

Shan Chuan" which literally mean to "dominate the mountains and rivers forever". The base of the pagoda is square and consists of three storeys. The side lengths of the bottom and top layers are 33.5 meters and 21 meters respectively. There are stone railings around the bottom layer, with stone lions carved on the top of the square-shaped columns at the four corners. As for the two small southern and northern pagodas, they were built in the period of the Dali Kingdom dating back to the time of the Five Dynasties (907 A.D. – 960 A.D.). Typically, these two pagodas are very similar in shape and structure, belonging to the Song-style architecture. They are multi-eave brick pagodas. Each pagoda has 10 tiers and is 42.4 meters in height. The interior is hollow and the exterior is decorated like a loft. In addition, the small pagodas appear octagonal. Each tier has an extended-eaves gallery, with the extended eaves upturned at the end of the eaves. The top of the small pagodas looks very spectacular, for it is gilded and preciously ornamented. These small pagodas, coated with white lime substance, look like high-rise jade columns. At that time, Buddhism prevailed in Dali area, so the three pagodas were built to further popularize Buddhism. In addition, there was another important reason for the construction of the pagodas. In the ancient times, the Dali kingdom abounded in rivers and lakes, which frequently caused floods. In accordance with an ancient book named *The Compilation of Epigraphy*, "It has been said through the ages that the dragon was spiritually in awe of pagodas and feared the roc; in ancient times, Dali area was once dragons' watery land, so the pagodas were built in hope to control dragons." In April 2005, a large-scale reconstruction of Chongsheng Temple was completed, thus ending the history of the three pagodas in Dali, where for the past 100 years "there have been only pagodas, but not one temple".

当然，最令人注目的是这三座塔。它们呈三足鼎立，千寻塔与南小塔的距离为70米，与北小塔的距离也大致相同。千寻塔是中国现存座塔最高者之一,在造型上与西安小雁塔相似,属于唐代建筑风格,其特点是多檐砖塔,呈方形,内部中空,共16层,高度69.13米,底宽9.9米。塔以白灰涂面,每层四面有壁龛,相对两壁龛供佛像,另两壁龛为采光通风的窗口。塔身内壁设有从底到顶部的木制螺旋楼梯,游客可以登上塔楼,在壁龛的窗洞后面观赏大理古城。塔底的大理石上镶嵌着四个大字"永镇山川"。塔的基座呈方形,共三层,底层和顶层边长分别为33.5米和21米。底层四周有石栏杆,栏杆的四角柱头雕有石狮。而南、北二小塔,均建于五代(公元907—公元960)大理国时期。两塔的形状和结构都很相似,属典型的宋代建筑风格,为多檐砖塔,每塔10层,高42.4米,内部中空,外观装饰像阁楼建筑。此外,小塔为八角形,每层设平座(出檐廊),出檐角上翘;小塔顶镏金华丽装饰,非常壮观;塔通体抹石灰,好似玉柱擎天。当时,大理地区佛教盛行,故修建三塔的目的是为进一步传播佛教。另外,还有一个重要原因,古代大理为"泽国多水患"。古籍《金石萃编》中记载:"世传龙性敬神塔而畏鹏,大理旧为龙泽,故为此镇之。"2005年4月,崇圣寺大规模恢复重建竣工,从而结束了大理三塔近百年来"有塔无寺"的历史。

Well, so much for my brief introduction to the Three Pagodas in Dali. Let's start our tour of the three pagodas to see the pagodas and other historical relics.

好了,大理三塔简介到此结束,让我们开始游览三塔景区,看三塔,了解其他历史文物吧。

Potatso National Park
普达措国家公园

Potatso National Park is located in the heartland of the world natural heritage area, where the "three rivers flow in parallel rows" in Northwest Yunnan Province. It is the first national park in the Chinese mainland and a national 5A-level tourist attraction. The park is about 22 kilometers away from Shangri-La and is composed of the Wetland Bita Lake Nature Reserve, the Hongshan Section and the Niru Section, with a total area about 1,313 square kilometers. The word "potatso" comes from the transliteration of Sanskrit. "Pota" means "a boat", while "tso" is a Tibetan word, which refers to the "sea" or "lake". Accordingly, potatso is referred to as the boat-lake that floats off all living beings into their Nirvana.

普达措国家公园，位于滇西北"三江并流"世界自然遗产中心地带，是中国大陆第一个国家公园，国家AAAAA级旅游景区。公园距香格里拉22公里，由湿地碧塔海自然保护区、红山片区、尼汝片区等构成，总面积约1313平方千米。"普达措"一词源于梵文音译，"普达"为舟船，"措"是藏语，意为"海""湖"。"普达措"意为普度众生到达理想彼岸的舟湖。

The Potatso National Park is high in elevation. The highest point is at the top of the northern Militang and about 4,159 meters above the sea level. The lowest point is in the Golden Gully east of the Bitahai, at 3,200 meters above the sea level. In the park, the mountain lakes are like bright mirrors, the pastures are extensively covered with verdant grass, the wetlands are full of blooming flowers, and forest trees are in different forms. In addition, there are many fault cliffs, small forest gullies and deep canyons. All these have extremely high geographic scientific value and tourist appreciation value.

普达措国家公园海拔较高，最高点在弥里塘北部山顶，海拔为4159米；最低点在碧塔海东部金子沟，海拔为3200米。公园内高山湖泊宛若明镜，牧场草色青翠，湿地百花盛开，原始森林里林木千姿百态。此外，还有多处断层崖、林间小涧、深沟峡谷等，具有极高的地理科学价值与旅游观赏价值。

The cultural landscape of the park is dominated by the traditional Tibetan culture. There are many folk workshops in Xiagei. Village near the park, such as earthen pottery workshops, tangka workshops, wood-ware workshops, horn carving workshops, Tibetan-incense production workshops, the museum of folk houses, as well as Tibetan silver manufacture workshops. Those places are filled with all kinds of exquisite Tibetan handicrafts, demonstrating the wisdom and art of the Tibetan people. Beside the scenic spot area, there are a number of Mani stone piles and barrel-shaped prayer wheels by streams, carrying the Tibetan people's faith and sustenance.

公园的人文景观以藏族传统文化为主。公园边的霞给村里有土陶坊、唐卡坊、木器坊、牛角雕刻坊、藏香坊、民居博物馆、藏银坊等民间作坊，那里摆满了精美的各式各样藏族手工艺品，彰显着藏民族的智慧和艺术。景区周边有若干玛尼石堆和溪边的转经桶，承载着藏族人民的信仰和寄托。

The park's main attractions include "two lakes", "one village" and "one subalpine pasture". The Shudu Lake is in the north of the park, while the

Bita Lake is in the south. Between the two lakes are the Militang Subalpine Pasture and the Luorong Village of Ethnic Ecological Culture and Tourism. There is an "8-shaped" sightseeing lane running through the scenic areas. Along the way, there are 16 observation platforms and 19 stops.

公园主要景点为"两湖""一村""一坝"。属都湖在公园北部，南面是碧塔海，两湖之间是弥里塘亚高山牧场和洛茸民族生态文化旅游村。公园内有"8"字形观光车道贯通旅游景区，沿途有16个观景台和19个停靠站。

Among many scenic spots, Bita Lake and Shudu Lake are known as pearls on the plateau. The Shudu Lake is a poetic place. In spring and summer, the azalea bushes around the lake are reflected on the lake, various wild flowers bloom on the ground, and flocks of yaks and sheep roam the green pastures along the shore of the lake. In autumn and winter, the birch forests take on distinctive colors, with red alternating with yellow, white, golden yellow or emerald green. In the middle of the dark blue lake, the white clouds are set against the faint morning mist, forming a quiet and poetic picture. In the lake, there is plenty of "Shudu Schizothorax", a genus of golden yellow carp with cracks on its belly, whose flesh tastes tender and tasty. The lake is also home to a large number of wild birds, such as mallard ducks and yellow ducks. In Diqing, the pasture by the lake is a famous ranch, where the grassland is vast, vegetation is lush, and yaks and sheep flock around the lake.

在众多的景点中，碧塔海和属都湖被称为高原明珠。属都湖是一个充满了诗意的地方。春夏之时，属都湖畔四周的杜鹃花丛倒映在湖面上，各种野花在地面上开放，湖岸边，成群的牛羊悠然徜徉于绿色牧场。秋冬季节，一片片白桦林呈现出独特的颜色，红色与黄色、白色、金黄色或翠绿的交相辉映；在碧蓝的湖心，白色的云朵映衬着淡淡晨雾，构成一幅平静而富有诗意的画面。湖中盛产"属都裂腹鱼"，鱼身金黄，腹部有一条裂纹，其肉细嫩鲜美。湖内还栖息着野鸭、黄鸭等大量野禽。湖畔是迪庆有名的牧场。这里的草场广阔，水草丰茂，成群的牛羊漫步于湖畔。

Bita Lake is located 25 kilometers east of Zhongdian County, surrounded by towering mountains, steep hills, lush forests and rolling snowy peaks. The blue water of the lake comes from streams on the snow-capped mountains, and the shadows of the snow-capped mountains and trees are reflected on the lake. In the lake there are islands, where spruce, alpine pines, alpine oak and birch grow, dense azalea plants grow around the lake. According to legend, Bita Lake is said to be incarnated from a piece of mirror of a fairy lady who broke her mirror when combing in the heaven. This piece was the most beautiful one, inlaid with emeralds. In May rhododendrons are in full bloom. The petals of rhododendrons by the lake fall into the water and attract fish to eat. After swallowing petals, the fish will get drunken, floating on the water. Thus, the drunken fish and azaleas form a unique picture on the lake. It is said that old bears in the forest would take advantage of the moonlight to catch the drunken fish. Feng Mu, a famous writer, once described such a scene. Since then, the view of the rhododendrons and drunken fish in the Bita Lake is known far and wide.

碧塔海位于中甸县城东25公里处，四周环抱高山峻岭、林木苍翠、雪峰连绵。碧蓝的湖水来自雪山上的溪流，雪山树影倒映湖中。湖中有岛，生长着云杉、高山松、高山栎、白桦，湖四周生长着浓密的杜鹃花林。相传天女梳妆时，她的镜子不小心掉落，破碎后立刻形成了许多高原湖泊。其中一块破镜碎片变成了碧塔海，那块碎片最漂亮，镶嵌着绿宝石。每逢五月杜鹃花盛开时，碧塔海湖畔的杜鹃花瓣纷纷飘落于水，引来游鱼。鱼儿吞食花瓣后，醉倒而漂浮在水面，由此醉鱼和杜鹃就形成了湖面上的奇特景观。据说林中的老熊也会趁月色来捞食昏醉之鱼。著名作家冯牧曾描写了这种景象，从此碧塔海"杜鹃醉鱼"的景观就扬名于世。

The Potatso National Park is very large. We will tour the Shudu Lake, the Militang Subalpine Pasture and the Bita Lake. Each scenic spot is far away from each other, so we plan to walk around the Shudu Lake, tour the pasture by sightseeing van and take a boat on the Bita Lake. The tour of the park will take at least 3-5 hours. The Potatso National Park is located at a high altitude, and the plateau climate is unpredictable. So I'd like to give you some advice: don't do strenuous exercises, take along with the relevant drugs, and bring warm clothes and rain gears.

普达措国家公园很大，我们将游览属都湖、弥里塘亚高山牧场和碧塔海。每个景点相隔甚远，所以我们选择在属都湖徒步，在弥里塘亚高山牧场坐车游览，在碧塔海坐船。游玩普达措公园至少需要3~5小时。普达措国家公园海拔较高，高原气候变幻莫测，建议不要剧烈运动，并带上相关药物，携带保暖衣物和雨具。

Dai Nationality Park in Xishuangbanna
西双版纳傣族园

Dai Nationality Park lies on the Ganlanba in the southern suburb of Jinghong City. It is listed as a national 4A-level tourist attraction and a famous tourist resort in Xishuangbanna. The park is composed of five well-preserved Dai villages, where local villagers have been mainly engaged in agricultural production for generations. As we visit the park, we will experience the life and customs of the Dai people and watch the typical stilt-style architecture and traditional handicrafts. We will also watch the Dai folk song and dance performances. Our tour route goes like this: we pose for photos at the entrance, walk through the Welcome-Guest Plaza, visit Manga Village, and then view the Tower-Wrapping-Tree and the Princess Well. However, we have also opportunities to go to the Song and Dance Theater, the Water Splashing Square, the Peacock Garden and Manchunman Ancient Buddhist Temple. I'd like to remind you that when you visit the temple, be sure to dress appropriately and take off your shoes before entering the temple. In addition, don't take any photos indoors without permission.

傣族园位于景洪市南郊橄榄坝，是国家AAAA级旅游景区，是西双版纳的旅游胜地。它由五个保存完好的傣族村寨组成，当地村民世代以从事农业生产为生计。我们此次游览傣族园，将体验傣家生活习俗，观赏典型的干栏式建筑和传统的手工艺制作。我们还要观看傣族民间歌舞表演。我们的旅游线路是：景区大门照相留影，穿过迎宾广场，参观曼嘎村，再去看看塔包树和公主井。此外，我们还有机会去歌舞剧院、泼水广场、孔雀园、曼松满古佛寺。注意：进寺庙时，要衣着得体，脱鞋；未经允许不得在室内照相。

A View of Dai Village

It is often said that Xishuangbanna is like a beautiful green peacock. Its beautiful tail feathers grow in Ganlanba, and the Dai Nationality Park is the most beautiful feather on the peacock's tail. The scenic zone of the park totally covers an area of 336 hectares, with its main scenic sections composed of five villages, such as Manjiang Village, Manchunman Village, Manzha Village, Manga Village and Manting Village. Thus, the park has become a tourist attraction featured by folk characteristics. It focuses on displaying the Dai religion, history, culture, customs, architecture, costume and diets in Xishuangbanna. The following are the routine activities provided by the Dai Nationality Park. The first is the Greeting-guest Performance at the entrance. Every day when tourists pass through the entrance, many young Dai girls dance the welcome dancing, sing greeting songs and sprinkle water with the blessing. The tour of the Dai Villages is another activity for tourists to enjoy the sights of the subtropical Dai-style courtyards, the different types of tropical fruits and the Dai stilt-style architecture. There is something special about visiting Manchunman Ancient Buddhist Temple, where tourists can participate in Buddhist activities, such as chanting scriptures, burning incense and drawing lots. In addition, in the Dai Folk Music Demonstration Area, tourists can watch performances, such as cucurbit flute solo, Zanha dance, Bawu flute solo and love songs of bamboo houses. In the Dai Handicraft Demonstration Area, tourists can observe the manufacture of brocade, the production of Dai jewelry, the squeezing of sugar, the making of pottery and others. Also, tourists are arranged to visit Dai houses to know about the dwelling conditions of the Dai people and the features of their bamboo buildings. In the Dai Ganbai fair, tourists will enjoy tasting the Dai-flavor barbecue food and various fresh fruits. According to the Dai language, Ganbai originally refers to a grand festival or gathering. The water splashing activity is held every day. It is a large-scale event involving 100-200 participants. Remember, the wetter you are, the more luck you get. The whole tour in the park takes about three hours.

人们常说，西双版纳是一只美丽的绿孔雀，美丽的尾羽在橄榄坝，而傣族园就是孔雀尾羽上最美丽的羽翎。傣族园景区总面积为336公顷，主景区由曼将、曼春满、曼乍、曼嘎、曼听五个村寨组成；傣族园由此成为具有民俗特色的旅游景区，集中展示了西双版纳傣族宗教、历史、文化、习俗、建筑、服饰及饮食。以下是傣族园提供的活动项目。首先是寨门迎宾：每天当游客进入寨门时，众多傣家小卜哨为游客跳迎宾舞，唱祝词，洒水祝福。另一项活动是参观傣族村寨，游客可以观赏亚热带傣家庭院、各种热带水果，以及傣家干栏式建筑。曼春满古佛寺别具特色，游客可以在古佛寺参加念经、烧香、抽签等佛教活动。此外，在傣族民间音乐演示区还可观看表演节目,如:葫芦丝演奏、赞哈表演、巴乌笛子独奏、竹楼恋歌。在傣族手工艺展示区,游客可以观摩织锦生产、傣首饰制作、榨糖、陶器的制作等。此外,游客还会被安排参观傣家民居,了解傣族居住环境和竹楼建筑的特点;在赶摆场上,游客可以尽兴品尝傣家风味烧烤和各种新鲜水果;按傣语的原意,"赶摆"最初指的是盛大节日或集会活动。泼水节活动每天举行,是由100~200人参与的大型活动;记住,身上越湿,好运越多。整个傣族园游览时间为3小时。

Of course, the most impressive is the Dai bamboo houses, which form an important part of the scenery in the park. These Dai houses are the stilt-style buildings, well distributed in the five Dai villages. Most of them are square and have two stories. The lower storey is built on stilts, with no walls. It is used for raising livestock and stacking utility items. House-owners and their family live on the upper story. In old times, this area was once a primeval forest infested with wild animals, so living upstairs would prevent wild beasts and moisture. On the upper storey are bedrooms and a central room. A fireplace or a fire pit is set in the central room for tea making, cooking and family gatherings. Outside the central room, there is a balcony and porch. The porch is where the host has meals, rests and receives guests during the day, while the balcony is where the host does washing, air-dry clothes and crops, and stores water tanks. On the either side of the central room are two to three bedrooms for the couple and their children. Usually, outsiders are not allowed to get into bedrooms because the Dai people believe that people have a soul, and the soul of the family is kept in the bedrooms. If an outsider opens the bedroom door, the soul inside may be disturbed. Well, bamboo houses are warm in winter and cool in summer. Some of houses have been converted into wooden structures, but their appearance has not changed, so those buildings are also known as bamboo houses. In addition, the Dais extensively grow fruit trees and flowers in their courtyards. Most of these plants bloom in spring, and the fruits mature in summer or autumn, such as grapefruits, mangos, jackfruits, lychees, plums, etc. Around the village are patches of age-old cassia siamea. When visitors stroll in the villages, or around the village, or amid the eye-catching vegetation, a pleasant feeling always arises.

当然，最引人瞩目的是构成园内景区重要部分的傣家竹楼。这些傣家竹楼为干栏式建筑，分布在五个傣族村寨。竹楼多呈方形，分上下两层。底层架空，多不用墙壁，供饲养牲畜和堆放杂物。上层住的是房屋的主人和他们的家人。从前，这里是一片原始森林，常有野兽出没。住在楼上可以防野兽侵犯，还可以防潮。楼上有堂屋和卧室，堂屋设火塘，是烧茶、做饭、家人团聚的地方；堂屋外有晒台和前廊，前廊是白天主人吃饭、休息和接待客人的地方；晒台是主人盥洗、晒衣、晾晒农作物和存放水罐的地方。堂屋侧旁有两到三间卧室，供主人夫妇和孩子使用。通常，卧室是不允许外人进去的，因为傣族人相信人有灵魂，而一家人的灵魂就关在卧室里。如果外人打开卧室的门，就会惊动灵魂。竹楼冬暖夏凉。虽然有些房屋改成木结构，但其形状并无改变，还称为竹楼。此外，傣家人在庭院里广种果树和花草；植物大多都是春季开花，在夏秋季果实成熟，有柚子、杧果、菠萝蜜、荔枝、李子等等。村寨四周，有成片的古铁刀林地。游客漫步于村寨里，或村寨周边，或置身于引人注目的植被之中，一种愉悦的感觉会油然而生。

Well, my brief introduction to the Dai Nationality Park is over. Now please follow your local tour guide for the sightseeing in the park, where you will watch the Dai bamboo houses, view the courtyard scenery and experience the daily customs of the Dai people.

好了，傣族园的讲解到此结束，请随傣族园的导游在傣族园游览吧，参观傣家竹楼，观赏庭院风光，体验傣家生活习俗！

09
Yunnan Nationalities Village
云南民族村

Yunnan Nationalities Village is located in the southwestern suburb of Kunming, close to Dianchi Lake, about seven kilometers away from the urban area. Covering an area of 89 hectares, the village consists of a number of typical ethnic sub-villages. On February 18, 1992, the village was open to the public. Its ultimate goal was to build 25 sub-villages of ethnic nationalities within the space of the village. At present, Yunnan Nationalities Village have built sub-villages of the Dai, Yi, Naxi, Wa, Jinuo, Bulang, Lahu, Bai, and Tibetan. In addition, the "Home of the Mosuo People" is also housed here. In the village, there are other venues for activities, such as the Ethnic Nationalities Dance Hall and the National-Unity Square.

云南民族村位于云南省昆明市西南郊，靠近滇池，距市区约7公里。该村占地面积89公顷，由一系列典范式的民族村寨组成。1992年2月18日，民族村开园，拟在村寨范围内修建25个少数民族村寨。目前，民族村已建成傣、彝、纳西、佤、基诺、布朗、拉祜、白、藏村寨。此外，"摩梭之家"也在这里落成。在村寨里，还有其他活动场所，如：民族舞厅、民族团结广场。

Yunnan Province
云南省

Yunnan Nationalities Village is a national 4A-level tourist attraction and an important part of the Kunming Dianchi National Tourist Vacation Zone. In the scenic area, water and land crisscross and the sub-village scenic spots are well spaced. There, pathways are shaded with greenness, pavilions and winding corridors are dotted, and arch bridges and stone steps are well connected. The village is filled with flowering branches, which glisten in colors through seasons. In addition, in the village, there are several such special programs worth watching carefully as the laser fountain, the water-screen movie, the folk songs and dancing, as well as the elephant performance. Also, tourists can taste local snacks and buy handicrafts. Village tour guides, who are dressed in the costumes of ethnic nationalities, provide tour guide services for tourists, interpreting the architecture, costumes and customs of local ethnic groups. The village also holds the festival activities of ethnic nationalities, such as the Bai's Third Month Fair, the Dai's Water-Splashing Festival, the Yi's Torch Festival, or the Lisu's Knife-Ladder Climbing Festival. These festivals not only enable tourists to enjoy the charm of the festivals, but also allow them to wander leisurely about in the ocean of the people of all nationalities.

云南民族村是国家AAAA级旅游景区，是昆明滇池国家旅游度假区的重要组成部分。景区内，水陆交错，各村寨景点错落有致。其间，林荫道绿意盎然，亭台楼阁星罗棋布、拱桥石阶相衔相接，民族村内树枝浓密，花儿盛开，四季缤纷。在村寨里，还有几个值得仔细观看的特别节目：激光喷泉、水幕电影、民族歌舞、大象表演。此外，游客还可以品尝风味小吃，购买工艺品。导游身着民族服饰，为游客提供导游服务，讲解当地各少数民族的建筑、服饰及习俗。村民们还举行民族节日活动，如：白族的"三月街"、傣族的"泼水节"、彝族的"火把节"、傈僳族的"刀杆节"。这些节日活动不仅让游客尽情领略节日的风采，而且还能够徜徉于各民族的海洋里。

Of course, the architecture of each sub-village is an important part of the village scenery, displaying the best model of the buildings of the ethnic nationalities in Yunnan. As tourists walk into the villages, what they can see is the village buildings with different styles and features. We will visit such villages as the Bai Village, the Yi Village, the Miao Village, the Dai Village and the Tibetan Village. As for the Bai village, it is mainly composed of traditional residences of the Bai People. Its buildings have strong decorative effects, with overhanging eaves and bracket sets, as well as carved beams and painted rafters. These residences are arranged in rows and look spacious and tidy, with a layout of "three-residential-walls-and-one-screen-wall courtyard", or "four-residential-walls-and-five-patios courtyards". In addition, the Bai village has a tie-dye workshop, a wood carving workplace, a garden tea houses, a drama stage, the Benzhu Temple, as well as the "Three Pagodas in Dali". The Yi village occupies an area of about 50 *mu* (3 hectares), where the Wall of the Three-Tiger-Relief and the Modeling of the Tiger Hill embody the feature of the tiger culture of the Yi ethnic minority. In the center of the Solar Calendar Square stands a totem pole carved with the images of the sun, the tiger, the fire and the Eight Trigrams. There are ten black and white balls shaped like the moon around the pole and beyond the balls are encircled with the 12 stone sculptures in the shape of Chinese animal zodiac. The "soil-rammed houses" are built on the hillside, such an architectural complex truly embodies the outlook of the Yi People's living in harmony with nature. The Miao's village is built on the mountainous area. The stilted houses are usually three-storey wooden buildings, which are believed to reflect the heritage of the architectural styles from the ancient inhabitants. The Dai village is hidden under thick trees and surrounded by water on three sides. Inside the Dai village are blocks of "stilt-style" bamboo houses, spectacular white towers, delicately wind and rain bridges, as well as wind and rain pavilions, wells and a bell pavilion. The Tibetan village is made up of dwellings of different sizes, with sloped roofs. Also, the village has carving-tower-style dwellings, with flat roofs. These unique Tibetan architectures smoothly coordinate and complement with the solemn Tibetan Buddhist temple, the spectacular white towers and the sculptures of auspicious "white yaks."

当然，民族村各村寨建筑是民族村景区的重要组成部分，展示了云南少数民族建筑的最佳模式。游客走进民族村，映入眼帘的便是不同风格特点的村寨建筑。在这次的游览中，我们将去参观以下的村寨：白族村、彝族村、苗寨、傣族村和藏族村。白族村主要建有白族传统民居；其建筑呈现很强的装饰效果，飞檐斗拱，雕梁画栋；院落鳞次栉比，宽敞整齐，布局有"三坊一照壁"或"四合五天井"。此外，白族村还有扎染坊、木雕屋、花园茶社、戏台、本主庙，以及"大理三塔"。彝族村占地50余亩（3公顷），三虎浮雕墙与虎山造型表现了彝族虎文化的特色；太阳历广场中央矗立着图腾柱，上面刻有太阳、虎、火、八卦图像；有10颗形似月亮的黑白球环绕四周，球外还围绕着12座形似中国生肖的石雕。"土掌房"依山而建，其建筑群真实体现了彝家与自然和谐相处的生活观。苗寨建造在山地上，吊脚楼通常为三层木楼，人们认为这传承了来自远古居民建筑风格。傣族村绿树掩映，三面环水；村内有一幢幢"干栏式"竹楼、壮观的白塔、精致的风雨桥、风雨亭、水井和钟亭。藏族村由大小不一的民居组成，屋顶呈斜坡状。此外，村里还有碉楼式的平顶民居。这些独特的藏族建筑，与庄严的藏传佛教寺庙、壮观的白塔、吉祥的"白牦牛"雕塑相互照应，相得益彰。

Well, so much for my brief introduction to the Village of Yunnan Nationalities. Today, our tour route goes like this: We walk through the north gate into the village. Then we go to the sub-villages I mentioned above. During our stay in the village, we have the opportunity to watch the elephant show, as well as the folk song and dance performance. It takes about 2.5 hours. As you tour the village, please follow the village tour guide and respect the religion and customs of each sub-village.

好了，云南民族村的简介到此结束。今天，我们行走的线路是：由北门进入民族村，然后去我所提及的村寨。在村寨逗留期间，还可以观赏大象表演和民族歌舞。游览时间约两个半小时。注意：在游览时，请跟随村寨导游，尊重各村寨宗教和习俗。

⑩ Dali Ancient Town
大理古城

Dali Ancient Town is also known as Yeyucheng or Zicheng. It is located 415 kilometers west of Kunming and lies on the western edge of Erhai Lake at an altitude of 1,900 meters, with imposing Cangshan Mountain Range behind it. The Kingdom of Nanzhao (738 A.D.–902 A.D.) and the Kingdom of Dali (937 A.D.–1253) established their capital right here. In those days, Dali remained as the political, economic and cultural center of Yunnan. Dali also acts as an important crossroad in the Western Yunnan, where the Ancient Tea Horse Road meets with the Ancient Shu Yuandu Path, and the ethnic cultures of the Han, Tibetan, Yi, Bai, Naxi and Dai are also interwoven. Along these trade routes, Dali became a place where the cultures of Central Plains, Southeast Asia, South Asia and West Asia were blended. It was the civilization of the Ancient Tea Horse Road and the Ancient Shu Yuandu Path that made Dali become an "ancient capital city standing at the crossroad of Asian cultures".

大理古城又名叶榆城、紫城，位于昆明以西415公里处，在洱海西端，海拔1900米，居于雄伟的苍山山脉之下。南诏国（公元738—公元902）、大理国（公元937—1253）在此建都，是当时云南的政治、经济、文化的中心。大理还地处滇西要冲，"茶马古道"和"蜀身毒道"于此交会，汉、藏、彝、白、纳西、傣等民族文化也在此交织。在商贸通道上，大理成为中原、东南亚、南亚、西亚文化的交融之地。正是"茶马古道"和"蜀身毒道"的文明,使大理成了"站在亚洲文化十字路口的古都"。

The existing Dali Ancient Town covers an area of three square kilometers, with a width of more than 1,000 meters from east to west and a length of more than 2,000 meters from north to south. The ancient town has been renovated on the basis of the town of Yangxiemie in the early Ming Dynasty. The town is square in shape, complete with original four gates. The towers stand on the top of the gates. They are surrounded by refurbished walls, with the wall facade made of brick. What's more, there are three streams, which flow from south to north, serving as natural barriers. Five main streets traverse the town from south to north and eight streets run through from west to east, making the whole town like a checkerboard. On the top of the gate tower, you can get a good view of the East Gate, the South Gate, the West Gate, the North Gate and part of the wall. At present, the town still retains some well-preserved slate streets and traditional stone buildings, where streams encircle the streets, every family grows flowers, and trees and flowers look luxuriant and well-arranged.

现存的大理古城占地面积3平方公里,东西宽1000余米,南北长2000余米。古城是以明朝初年在阳苴咩城的基础上恢复的,城呈方形,开四门;城楼屹立于城门上,城墙环绕,外墙为砖砌的。更有三条溪水,从南到北流淌,成了天然屏障。城内由南到北横贯五条大街,自西向东纵穿八条街巷,整个城市呈棋盘式布局。登上城楼,可以看到东门、南门、西门、北门和部分城墙。古城现在还保留着一些保存完好的石板街道和传统的建筑,流水环绕街道,户户养花,花木繁茂而错落有致。

There are many places of historic interest in the town, such as the Jianggong Temple, the Dali Martial Temple, the Catholic Church, the

Tomb and Former Residence of Generalissimo Du Wenxiu, Honglongjing Waterscape Street, the Foreigner's Street and others.

城内景点众多，如：蒋公祠、大理武庙、天主教堂、杜文秀帅府遗迹、红龙井水景街、洋人街等。

In recent years, the Honglongjing Waterscape Street has been especially popular with tourists and has become a hot spot in Dali Ancient Town. This is a beautiful side street, where there used to be a well, known as Honglongjing (Red Dragon Well). Later, the locals used the term "Honglongjing" to refer to this 400-meter-long street. In 2003, the Dali Municipal Government established a new waterscape cultural and leisure area, integrating accommodation, shopping and entertainment. A stream flows down from Cangshan Mountain, passes through the western part of the town and rushes straight down along the Honglongjing Waterscape Street. The stream touches the four disc-shaped stone troughs, where the water is clear, flowing gently, splashing and gurgling. Along the sides of the stream, the sidewalks ascend step by step. What you can see is green willow makes a pleasant shade and flowers are in full blossom. Some children chase one another, jumping on stones in the water. Some children are in the stream, paddling, screaming or laughing. In the center of Waterscape Street is a small pavilion, known as the original site of Honglongjing. In the center of the pavilion is the sculpture that depicts "the Legendary Jade Cabbage". On the walls around the sculpture are carved with the legends of the "Honglongjing and Jade Cabbage", the "Twelve Chinese Zodiac Signs" and the "Construction Process of the Honglongjing Waterscape Street". Along the way, you can see so many small bars and restaurants, with many tables and chairs placed beside the water. If anyone is tired from walking, he/she can sit in a chair by the water and enjoy the sights and sounds of the street, while drinking tea, cold beer or hot coffee. At nightfall, the street lamps light up one after another, flickering in the water. The music sounds melodious, moving gently through the air. All this makes people feel as if they were in a world of idyllic beauty.

近年来,红龙井水景街备受游客青睐,已成为大理古城热点景区。这是一条美丽的小街,那儿曾经有过一口水井,名红龙井。后来,当地人就用"红龙井"一词来指代这条400米长的街道。2003年,大理市政府全新打造了一个集食宿、购物、休闲娱乐为一体的水景文化休闲区。溪水从苍山流淌下来,穿过西城,沿红龙井水景街直泻而来。溪水抚过四个盘形石水槽,水清澈,轻轻流淌,溅起水花,汩汩作响。沿着溪水两旁的人行道拾级而上,绿柳成荫,鲜花盛开。有的孩童相互追逐,在水里的石头上跳来跳去。有的孩童在溪水里戏水、尖叫、欢笑。在水景街的核心区有一个小亭子,是红龙井的原址。亭子中心是传说中的"玉白菜"雕塑。雕塑四周墙壁上刻有"红龙井与玉白菜"的传说、"十二生肖图"、"红龙井水景街的建造过程"。一路上,可以看到许多小酒吧、小餐馆,水边摆放着许多桌椅。如果有谁走累了,可以坐在水边椅上,一边啜饮茶水、冷啤酒或热咖啡,一边欣赏街道景象和声响。夜晚来临,街灯依次亮起,灯光在水中摇曳;古乐悠扬,在空中缓缓流转,让人仿佛置身于世外桃源。

In March 1982, the State Council listed Dali as a famous historical and cultural city. In December of the same year, Dali was announced by the State Council as the first batch of the National Key Tourist Attractions.

1982年3月,国务院将大理列为历史文化名城。同年12月,大理又被国务院公布为首批国家级重点风景名胜区。

Well, my brief introduction to Dali Ancient Town is over. Our tour route goes like this: We start from the Shuanghe Tourist Service Center. We pass through the Nancheng Gate and Fuxing Road before we arrive at the

Dali Town Museum. After that, we visit the Wuhua Tower and walk along Honglongjing Waterscape Street and the Foreigner's Street. Finally, we return to the Shuanghe Tourist Service Center via the Yu'er Road and the Erhai Gate. It takes about 80 minutes. In Dali, the temperature varies widely during the day. It is hot when the sun comes out, and cool when there is no sun in the early morning or at night. It is advisable to bring warm clothes. In addition, the ultraviolet ray is strong, so a sun hat or a pair of sunglasses is necessary.

好了，大理古城讲解到此结束。今天，我们参观游览路线如下：从双鹤游客服务中心出发，经南城门、复兴路，到大理市博物馆；之后，我们观五华楼，漫步红龙井街、洋人街，最后经过玉洱路、洱海门，再返回双鹤游客服务中心。游览时间约80分钟。大理一天之内温差很大。太阳出来时候热，早晚没有太阳的时候就会凉一些，最好备上防寒服装。此外，紫外线强烈，遮阳帽或太阳镜是必备的。

11

Yulong Snow Mountain

玉龙雪山

Yulong Snow Mountain lies in Baisha Town, 15 kilometers north of Yulong County, Yunnan Province. The snow mountain is a sacred mountain in the eyes of Naxi people and other ethnic groups in Lijiang. In Naxi language, Yulong Snow Mountain is called "O Lu", which means "Tianshan". In addition, the mountain is called the "Black and White Snow Mountain" because its limestone and basalt are in a sharp contrast between black and white on the mountain.

玉龙雪山位于云南省玉龙县以北15公里处的白沙乡境内。雪山是纳西族及丽江各民族心目中一座神圣的山。在纳西语中，玉龙雪山被称为"欧鲁"，意为"天山"。又由于山上石灰岩和玄武岩黑白分明，故又称为"黑白雪山"。

Yulong Snow Mountain has 13 snow-capped peaks that remain in an unbroken line, like a flying "gigantic dragon". The mountain stretches 35 kilometers from north to south, about 13 kilometers from east to west. In addition, it faces Haba Snow Mountain, while the Jinsha River surges forward between the two mountains.

玉龙雪山有十三座雪峰，连绵不绝，宛若一条飞舞的"巨龙"。其山呈南北走向，东西宽约13公里，南北长约35公里。此外，玉龙雪山与哈

Yunnan Province
云南省

巴雪山对峙，金沙江在两山间奔腾向前。

Yulong Snow Mountain is a very high subtropical mountain in Yunnan. From the valley at the foot of the mountain to the peaks, it presents from subtropics, temperate zone to frigid zone, forming a complete vertical landscape. Yulong Snow Mountain looks magnificent. With the changes of seasons and weather, the snow mountain is sometimes shrouded in clouds and mist and it appears at one moment and disappears next. Sometimes, the peaks are enveloped in clouds, making the mountain mysterious. Sometimes, clouds and mist drift away, only floating around the mountainside. Sometimes, the sky is blue for thousands of miles, while the peaks are glistening with silvery light.

玉龙雪山是云南亚热带的极高山地。从山脚下的山谷到山顶，雪山呈现亚热带、温带、寒带，形成了完整的垂直带景观。玉龙雪山蔚为壮观。随着时令和阴晴变化，雪山时而云雾缠裹，时隐时现；时而山顶云封，看上去深奥莫测；时而云雾飘散，只飘浮在半山腰；时而碧空万里，群峰闪烁着银光。

The snow mountain is rich in natural tourism resources, which can be roughly divided into glacier landscape, alpine grassy marshland, primitive forests and waterscape on the snow mountain. The main attractions include the Ice Tower Forest, the High-Rise Jade Columns, the Spruce Ground, the Snow Mountain Cableway, Heishui River, Baishui River, the Baoshan Stone Castle and others. Here, the "Baishui No. 1" Glacier and Ganhaizi Meadowland particularly impressive. According to *the Glacier Catalogue* published in 1994, Yulong Snow Mountain has 19 modern glaciers. Specifically, there are 15 glaciers on the east slope and four glaciers on the west slope, with a total area of 11.6 square kilometers. Every year, millions of people visit the glaciers. The huge body of ice is called the Third Pole that holds the world's third largest ice group after Antarctica and Greenland. Among them, the "Baishui No. 1" Glacier is the largest one, which is located on the east slope of the main peak of the mountain and occupies an area of 1.5 square kilometers. It is 2.7 kilometers long, and its equilibrium line is about 4,800 meters above the sea level. If you stand at the foot of the mountain and look up, you will find that the glacier looks amazing, just like a waterfall hanging from the sky. The "Baishui No. 1" Glacier is also known as the Ice Tower Forest depicted as the "green snow and unique peaks" in the writing by Mr. Li Lincan, the late former deputy director of Taipei Palace Museum. The forest looks like knives and halberds piercing the sky. In the sunlight, it seems as if huge chunks of jade blocks embedded in jagged rocks. When you reach the glacier, you can hear the sound of rushing water in the river from the melting glacier. Ahead is a steep, fan-shaped slope that frequently produces huge noises. That is the sound of ice slides or avalanches, like rolling bulls. For thousands of years, the fan-shaped slope has remained the same all along, replenishing the glacier with fresh snow. As for the Ganhaizi Meadowland, it is a vast grassy marshland on the east of Yulong Snow Mountain. It is about 4 kilometers long, 1.5 kilometers wide and about 2,900 meters above the sea level. As you arrive at the Ganhaizi Meadowland, it gives you a sense of vastness. Such a large meadow provides a good place for you to clearly see the snow mountain, the fan-shaped slopes and the mountain peaks. From the Ganhaizi Meadowland to the snow line, you can also see orchids, wild peonies, snow lotus and other flowers. The tall trees include Yunnan pines, cedars, firs, thorn-chestnut trees, hemp-chestnut trees, etc. Of course, the large meadowland is also a natural ranch. Every spring, when flowers bloom and grasses sprout, herders from the Tibetan, Yi and Naxi ride horses to the meadowland, where they herd yaks, cattle, or flocks of sheep. In addition, there are many recreational facilities, such as the sand boarding, grass sliding, motorcycle racing and horse racing. The reserve in the Ganhaizi Meadowland is a national-level forest park, where the good ecosystem remains as a natural habitat for wild animals.

雪山自然旅游资源丰富,大致可分为冰川景观、高山草甸、原始森林、雪山水景等。主要景点有冰塔林、玉柱擎天、云杉坪、雪山索道、黑水河、白水河及宝山石头城等。"白水一号"冰川和甘海子尤其令人难以忘怀。据1994年出版的《冰川编目》记载,玉龙雪山分布有19条现代冰川,即:东坡15条,西坡4条,总面积11.6平方千米。每年,数以百万计的人参观冰川。这个巨大的冰体被称为第三极,拥有世界上第三大的冰群,仅次于南极洲和格陵兰岛。其中,"白水一号"冰川为规模最大的冰川,位于玉龙雪山主峰东坡,面积1.5平方千米,长2.7千米,平衡线海拔约4800米。站在山脚向上望去,你会发现瀑布悬挂天际,令人震撼。"白水一号"冰川也被称为冰塔林,在已故的原台北故宫博物院副院长李霖灿先生笔下为"绿雪奇峰"。冰塔林像一把把刀戟直刺苍穹。在阳光照射下,冰川仿佛又是一块块巨大的翡翠碧玉,镶嵌在怪石嶙峋之间。靠近冰川,你可以听到冰川融化的河水的奔流水声;前方是扇子陡,经常发出阵阵巨响。那是冰崩、雪崩、岩块崩落的响声,就像"滚雪牛"似的。千万年来,扇子陡始终如一,为冰川补给新雪。又如:甘海子是玉龙雪山东面的一个开阔草甸,全长4公里左右,宽1.5公里,海拔约2900米。来到甘海子,会给人一种开阔空旷的感觉。这样一个大草甸是个好场地,在那里可以清楚地观赏玉龙雪山、扇子陡和雪山山峰。从甘海子草甸到雪线,还可以看到兰花、野生牡丹、雪莲等花卉;高大乔木有云南松、雪松、冷杉、刺栗、麻栗,等等。当然,大草甸也是一个天然大牧场。每年春天,鲜花盛开,百草萌发,藏族、彝族、纳西族牧民们就骑着马来到草甸,在那里放牧牦牛、黄牛或成群的羊。此外,这里还有滑沙、滑草、赛车、赛马等众多的游乐设施。甘海子草甸保护区是国家级森林公园,其良好的生态系统也是野生动物的自然栖息地。

In 1984, Yulong Snow Mountain became a provincial nature reserve. In 2001, the mountain was rated as a national 4A-level tourist attraction. In 2007, it became one of the first batch of the 5A-level tourist attractions in China.

1984年,玉龙雪山成为省级自然保护区。2001年,玉龙雪山被评为国家AAAA级旅游景区,2007年成为全国首批AAAAA级旅游景区。

Well, my brief introduction to Yulong Snow Mountain is over. Following is our tour route. In the morning, after we arrive at the main scenic area, we first take the Grand Cableway and stay in the Glacier Park for two or three hours. In the afternoon, we visit the Lanyue Valley and Baishui River. The sightseeing takes one or two hours. Finally, I'd like to advise you to bring warm clothes and sunglasses because the temperature varies widely, and the wind is strong in the Glacier Park. In addition, you'd better wear hiking boots or sneakers for easy walking on steep rocky steps.

好了,玉龙雪山讲解到此结束。今天,我们参观游览路线计划如下:早上到主景区,先上大索道,在冰川公园逗留需要2~3小时。下午游览蓝月谷、白水河,观光需要1~2小时。最后,我建议带着保暖衣服和墨镜,因为冰川公园温差大,风大。此外,穿上登山靴或运动鞋,便于在陡峭的石路上行走。

Yunnan Province
云南省

⑫
World Horti-Expo Garden in Kunming
昆明世博园

The World Horti-Expo Garden, called the Expo Garden for short and used to be the site of the 1999 Kunming World Horticultural Exposition, is located in the Golden Temple Scenic Area and about four kilometers away from Kunming urban district. At the end of the 20th century, the Chinese government successfully held the World A1 Horticultural Exposition in Kunming, the world's largest international pageant that lasted from May 1 to October 31 in 1999. The Expo Garden covers about 218 hectares, which are a large space with many attractions. The Expo Garden can be generalized as follows: three large exhibition zones—the International Exhibition Zone, the Domestic Exhibition Zone and the Exhibition Zone for Enterprises; four large squares—the Guest Plaza, the New Century Square, the Huaxia Square and the Plaza of Arts; five large exhibition halls—China Hall, the Man and Nature Hall, the Grand Green Hall, the Science and Technology Hall, and the International Hall; and seven large theme gardens—the Bamboo Garden, the Tea Garden, the Bonsai Plant Garden, the Medicinal Herb Garden, the Tree and Wood Garden, the Fruits and Vegetable Garden and the Garden of Famous Flowers and Strange Stones.

世界园艺博览园,简称"世博园",是1999年昆明世界园艺博览会会址,位于金殿风景名胜区,距昆明市区约4公里。20世纪末,中国政府在昆明成功举办了世界 A1 园艺博览会。这是世界上规模最大的国际盛会，该博览会从 1999 年 5 月 1 日持续到 10 月 31 日。世博园占地面积约 218 公顷，面积大，景点也多。纵观世博园，可以概括如下：三大展区：国际、国内、企业展区；四大广场：迎宾广场、新世纪广场、华夏广场、艺术广场；五大展馆：中国馆、人与自然馆、大温室、科技馆、国际馆；七大专题园：竹园、茶园、盆景园、药草园、树木园、蔬菜瓜果园、外花艺石园。

Since the end of the Expo, Kunming has maintained the Expo site intact, turning it into a theme park, where it integrates the courtyard architecture with technological achievements, fully reflecting the theme of the times of the "Harmonious Development of the Man and Nature". The park remains as a world-class grand landscape and a particularly good gardening showplace with the "Yunnan regional features and Chinese styles". Also, the park has become an Expo-site cultural heritage that possesses its global and national characteristics, unparalleledly high quality and uniqueness, as well as sustainable and productive value.

博览会结束后，昆明完整保留了世博会会址，并将其转化为主题公园，融庭院建筑、科技成就于一园，充分体现了"人与自然、和谐发展"的时代主题；世博园是一座具有"云南特色、中国气派"世界一流的园林园艺精品大观园，成为具有世界性、民族性、高品位性、唯一性、价值可持续性的会址文化遗产。

As is well known, China Hall is one of the five large exhibition halls. Its total construction area is up to 19,927 square meters and floor space 33,000 square meters. Its architecture, constructed with white walls and green tiles, skillfully blends the features of the Han-dynasty imperial gardens with the charm of the traditional southern style residences. White represents peace and harmony, while green symbolizes life. Its central inner gardening area is divided into the gardens in the regions south of the Yangtze River, the northern-style courtyards, as well as the local Dali walled land with flowers, vegetables and other plants; such an area not only showcases the best Chinese landscape gardening, but also serves as a tourist attraction and offers an ideal place for short rests. China Hall is the Expo's largest indoor exhibition hall. On the first floor along the inner corridor lie six sub-exhibition-halls, where 34 booths display typical achievements of China's provinces and regions, including Hong Kong, Macao and Taiwan, in the fields of gardening, horticulture, biology and environment. China Hall constitutes the Expo's main venue of exhibition, together with the Man and Nature Hall and the New Century Square. It directly faces the central square and is situated on the northern side of the square; a viewing platform is provided to facilitate visitors who attended the Expo opening and closing ceremonies or watched activities held in the Expo period. The viewing platform covers an area of 3,600 square meters. On the platform stands a pair of ornamental columns donated by Beijing Municipal People's Government. In addition, a pair of stone lions, located in front of the hall entrance, is the gift from the People's Government of Hebei Province. The Zero Sub-Hall mainly displays precious gifts presented to the Expo by all provinces and cities, such as ceramic vases from Henan Province and the pyrographic picture of the "Huangguoshu Waterfalls" from Guizhou Province. There is a purple-clay mural painting named the "Man and Nature". It is 27 meters long and three meters high, and so far, is considered as the largest purple-clay mural painting made in China. The painting consists of five parts: the Hundred Days, the Laboring Activities, the Happy Togetherness, the Bumper Harvests and the Auspicious Dates, all these vividly depicting the scenes of the unity and harmony, and the thriving and prosperity of all the nationalities in the country.

众所周知，中国馆是五大展馆之一，总建筑面积达 19 927 平方米，建筑面积 3.3 万平方米。建筑为绿瓦白墙，将汉代宫苑建筑特色和南方传统居民建筑巧妙地融合在一起。白色代表和平与和谐，绿色代表生命。中央内庭分为江南庭园、北方庭园和大理庭园，既集中表现了中国园林园艺风采，又是观光、休息的理想场所。中国馆是世博会最大的室内展馆，一楼沿内走廊设有 6 个展厅、34 个展位，充分展示了我国包括香港、澳门和台湾的省区园林、园艺及生物、环保等方面的代表性成果。中国馆与人与自然馆、新世纪广场构成世博会主场馆区，它正对着中心广场，处于广场北面，设有供开幕、闭幕和博览会期间活动使用的观礼台。观礼台面积 3600 平方米，台上矗立着一对北京市人民政府赠送的华表。此外，一对石狮位于正门前，是河北省人民政府赠送的礼物。零号展厅主要展示了各省市向世博会赠送的珍贵礼物，如：河南的陶瓷花瓶、贵州的烙画"黄果树瀑布"。有一幅"人与自然"的紫砂壁画，长 27 米、高 3 米，是目前我国最大的紫砂壁画，画面由"百日""劳作""欢聚""收获""吉日"五个部分组成，生动地描绘了全国各族人民团结和睦、兴旺发达的景象。

China Hall

Well, so much for my brief introduction to the World Horti-Expo Garden in Kunming. Today we will visit the five large exhibition halls, the seven large theme gardens and the three outdoor exhibition zones. The tour of garden can take six to eight hours, for its route covers the distance of more than 10 kilometers. Our tour ends at around 5:00 p. m. Note that if you want to see more of the attractions in the garden, please take the battery park-vans or the free-of-charge mini-train.

好了，昆明世博园讲解到此结束。今天，我们将去参观五大展馆、七大专题园、三大室外展区。世博园游览路程共10多公里，需要6~8小时，大约下午5点结束行程。请注意：如果想看更多的景点，可乘坐园内的电瓶车或免费的小火车。

Gadan Songzanlin Lamasery
噶丹·松赞林寺

Gadan Songzanlin Lamasery is located at the foot of the Foping Hill, four kilometers from Shangri-La, covering an area of more than 500 *mu* (33 hectares). It is the largest Tibetan Buddhist lamasery in Yunnan Province. Because its exterior layout is exactly like the Potala Palace, the lamasery is also known as "Little Potala Palace". Today, our tour route goes like this: we first enter the main entrance of the lamasery and then walk through the passageway in front of Zhacang Lamasery Hall, where we watch murals. On the way, we set out on a flight of 147 steps that eventually lead us into Zhacang Lamasery Hall, where I will explain the architectural style of the building, the connotation of the murals, as well as the meaning of the altar of the Buddhas. Finally, we climb onto a platform perched on the high point of the lamasery, where you can have a bird's eye view of the entire Shangri-La. The tour takes about 60 minutes.

噶丹·松赞林寺，位于佛屏山麓，距香格里拉4公里，占地500余亩（33公顷），是云南省规模最大的藏传佛教寺院。因其外观布局酷似布达拉宫，所以寺庙也被称为"小布达拉宫"。我们今天参观游览路线是：首先进入噶丹·松赞林寺的正门口，然后通过扎仓大殿正门前的走廊，同时观看壁画；接着，上147级台阶，进入扎仓大殿，在那里我将讲解大殿的建筑风格、壁画，以及佛台的含义；最后，我们将登上寺庙高处的平台，鸟瞰整个香格里拉。参观时间约60分钟。

Yunnan Province
云南省

Gadan Songzanlin Lamasery began its construction in 1679 and was completed in 1681. It is said that the Fifth Dalai Lama sought divine advice before deciding on the location of the lamasery. Prophesy said, "Woods remain vast and quiet, and there emerge transparent springs; from Heaven descend golden ducks, who frolic among woods and in springs." In addition, the Fifth Dalai Lama named the lamasery. Gadan denotes the inheritance of Gadan Lamasery, the first temple built by Tsongkhapa, the founder of the Yellow Sect Lamaism; Songzan refers to the playground of the three heavenly gods—Sakra, Mengli and Sheratan. After its completion, the lamasery became the supreme institution of the local political-and-religious-integration system. Besides, the lamasery served as an extraordinary Bodhimanda (Buddhist rite) in the Tibetan areas located in Yunnan, Tibet, and Sichuan. In the second year of Yongzheng reign of the Qing Dynasty (1724), Emperor Yongzheng bestowed on the lamasery with a Chinese name called "Gui Hua Si". In the summer of 1936, the Second Front Red Army, led by He Long, passed through the Shangri-La area as the army was on the Long March. He Long, Xiao Ke and others made a special trip to the lamasery. There, they visited living Buddhas and lamas and presented a brocade scroll entitled "Prosperity of Ethnic Nationalities". The lamasery raised grains for the Red Army and sent monks as the guides for the Red Army. They greatly supported the Red Army toward the north for the fight against the Japanese aggression. After the founding of New China, Eminent Monk Song Mou, a living Buddha who took charge of the lamasery in those days, was elected as the first governor of Diqing Tibetan Autonomous Prefecture.

噶丹·松赞林寺始建于1679年，竣工于1681年。据说，寺址是五世达赖喇嘛占卜求神所定，神示曰："林木深幽现清泉，天降金鹜嬉其间。"寺名为五世达赖喇嘛所赐。"噶丹"表示传承黄教祖师宗喀巴首次建立的噶丹寺;"松赞"即指天界三神帝释、猛利和娄宿的游戏场所。松赞林寺建成后,便成为本地区政教合一制度的最高机构,也成为滇、藏、川藏区的殊胜道场。清雍正二年(1724年),雍正皇帝赐汉名"归化寺"。1936年夏,贺龙率领红二方面军长征经过香格里拉。贺龙、萧克等来到归化寺,拜访活佛、喇嘛,并赠"兴盛番族"锦幛一幅。归化寺为红军筹粮,还派出僧侣为红军当向导,支持红军北上抗日。中华人民共和国成立后,松赞林寺寺主高僧松谋活佛当选为迪庆州首任州长。

The architectural style of Gadan Songzanlin Lamasery is consistent with that of other Tibetan Buddhist architectures. Zhacang Lamasery Hall, the main building in the lamasery, is located above all the other buildings and surrounded by eight major Kangcan(sangha) houses, monks' residences and other buildings. These buildings, high or low, are well-spaced and stretch uphill layer upon layer, making Zhacang Lamasery Hall tall and majestic. The hall, constructed during the reign of Emperor Kangxi in the Qing Dynasty, is a multi-storey and Tibetan-style carved architecture. In Tibetan language, Zhacang means "Buddhist Academy", a place where monks study Buddhist scriptures or doctrines. Specifically, the first storey mainly serves as the place where the Dharma assembly and Buddhist activities are held, Buddhist scriptures are chanted and Buddhist sermons are delivered. On the northern side of the second and third storeys enshrine the statues dedicated to the Five Grand Buddhas. In the central area of the two storeys stands a group of access-to-sky pillars encircled by winding corridors. Also, these storeys house the Golden Chapel of the Ten Thousand Buddhas. The fourth and fifth storeys are mainly used for monks' daily living rooms, chanting rooms, and living Buddhas' cultivation chambers. In addition, on the fourth storey there is the Dharmapala Hall, which is about two floors in height. The sixth and seventh storeys are the lamasery administration area, with offices and management rooms for the living Buddhas, Khenpos and eight major Kangcans. There is a scripture library on the seventh storey. The main building on the top storey is the Vihara Hall, which houses the statues dedicated to the Fifth Dalai Lama and the Seventh Dalai Lama. A tall drum tower stands on the south side of the hall. When the drum is struck in the early morning, by midday and at dusk, the sound of the drum travels ten miles around.

噶丹·松赞林寺建筑与藏传佛教建筑样式相同。扎仓大殿是寺庙的主要建筑，位于其他建筑物之上，四周簇拥着八大康参、僧舍等建筑。这些高矮错落的建筑，层层递进，使扎仓大殿显得高大雄伟。大殿建于清康熙年间，为多层藏式碉楼建筑。"扎仓"藏语意指"僧院"，是僧众学习经典或教义的地方。具体来讲，第一层主要为寺院法会、佛事活动、诵经讲经之处。在第二、三层北部供奉五大佛像，在两楼层的中心区域，矗立着通天柱群，并环绕于蜿蜒回廊；此外，这两楼层还有万佛金堂。四、五层主要为僧侣日常起居室、念经房、活佛静室；四层还有护法殿，约两层楼高。六、七层为寺院管理办公场所，设有活佛、堪布、八大康参的办公室和管理用房；七层还有藏经阁。顶层正楼设精舍佛堂，供奉五世达赖、七世达赖佛像。高大的鼓楼矗立在大厅南面，清晨、正午、黄昏击鼓之时，声闻十里。

If Gadan Songzanlin Lamasery is the museum of the Tibetan culture in Yunnan, then the essence of the museum is in Zhacang Lamasery Hall. Right above the main entrance hangs a plague inscribed by Shuoguo Prince Yinli, a younger brother of Emperor Yongzheng of the Qing Dynasty. The inscription reads, "The Clouds of Benevolence, Far and Wide". On the sides of the main entrance are Buddhist murals, which have profound metaphorical meanings. These murals include the "Driving the Elephant onto the Buddhist Path", the "Six Great Divisions in the Wheel of Karma", "Kalachakra Tantra (Ten

Aspects of Unconstraint)" and the "Holy Monks". The walls of the hall are covered with murals of Buddhas, Bodhisattvas, Dharma protectors with different postures expressions. The east wall is painted with Bodhisattvas, including Atisha, the Goddess of Mercy with Thousand Hands and Eyes, the Medicine Tathagata Buddha and the Twenty-One Taras. The murals on the south wall are the Dharma protectors, such as Ushnishavijaya, Mahakala, Mahakala with Six-Arms, the Lord of Hell, Pelden Lhamo (the Auspicious Fairy) and Qujia Dharmapala (the rhinoceros-shell-armored custodian). The west wall is painted with the images of Arhats and Buddhas, such as the Sixteen Venerable Arhats, the Eighteen Arhats, the Magic Change of Sakyamuni, Yamantaka (Buddha's Great Powerful and Benevolent Warrior Attendant), as well as the incarnations of Tsongkhapa in different forms. In the rear chamber of the hall, there are the statues of Tsongkhapa, Maitreya and the Seventh Dalai Lama, each more than three *zhang* in height (each *zhang* being about 3.13 meters in length). In addition, the top floor houses pattra-leaf scriptures, Thangka paintings and ritual-service objects handed down from ancient times. Here, people find that the architecture is magnificent, while the essence of Tibetan religion and culture is vividly revealed, showing the depth of the Dharma and the rich connotation of Buddhist scriptures.

如果说噶丹·松赞林寺是云南藏族文化的博物馆，那么博物馆的精华就在扎仓大殿。正门上方有一匾额，上面刻有清雍正皇帝弟弟硕果亲王胤礼题字"慈云广覆"，正门两侧为佛教壁画，具有深刻的寓意，包括"驱象入道""六道轮回""十相自在图""圣僧图"。大殿画满了佛、菩萨、护法神的壁画，其姿势和表情各不相同。东墙壁画为菩萨，有阿底峡、千手千眼观音、药师佛八如来、二十一度母等。南墙壁画为护法者，有尊胜佛母、大黑天、六臂大黑天、地狱主、吉祥天女、犀甲护法等。西墙壁画是罗汉与佛像，有十六尊者，十八罗汉图，释迦牟尼神变图，大威德金刚，宗喀巴化身等。在后殿，有塑像宗喀巴、弥勒佛、七世达赖，每座塑像三丈（1丈＝3.13米）多高。顶层藏有贝叶经卷、唐卡、传世法器等。在这里，人们发现建筑金碧辉煌，藏族宗教文化精华荟萃，显现了佛法的深度，诠释着佛经的丰富内涵。

Well, so much for my brief introduction to Gadan Songzanlin Lamasery. Now let us walk into the main entrance for the tour of the lamasery and Zhacang Lamasery Hall.

好了，噶丹·松赞林寺的介绍到此为止。现在让我们走进正门，游览寺庙和扎仓大殿吧！

Heshun Ancient Town in Tengchong
腾冲和顺古镇

Heshun Ancient Town is located four kilometers southwest of Tengchong, about 723 kilometers away from Kunming. The town stretches for two or three kilometers. On this small flatland stand age-old temples, shrines and ancient buildings of the Ming and Qing dynasties. As you walk into the town, the smooth stone roads, the simple and quiet old houses, the clear streams and the silent night, all make you feel peaceful and calm.

和顺古镇位于腾冲市西南4公里处,距昆明约723公里。全镇绵延2~3公里,在这片面积不大的平地上矗立着古刹、祠堂、明清古建筑。走进和顺,光滑的石板路、古朴沉静的老房子、清澈的溪流、安静的夜晚,让人感觉生活的宁静与安详。

In ancient times, there was a South Overland Route, which passed through Sichuan, Yunnan, Burma, and India. Tengchong, located along the route, was once the only place where "jade, precious stones and jewelry were transported". Heshun Ancient Town was located on the side of the route, and many residents in the town were thus engaged in the business of jade, precious stones and jewelry. In ancient times, Heshun Ancient Town was also a part of the Ancient Tea Horse Road, where horse-caravans constantly came to and departed from the town, which greatly promoted the prosperity of Heshun and formed a unique caravan culture.

古代有一条滇、川、缅、印南方陆路，腾冲就位于沿线上，曾是"玉石珠宝之路"必经之地。和顺古镇坐落在这条大道一侧，镇上的许多居民经营珠宝玉石。和顺古镇在古代也是茶马古道的一部分，马帮在那里络绎不绝，推动了和顺的繁荣，形成了独特的马帮文化。

Heshun remains as a place propitious for giving birth to great men. In the past 600 years, Heshun has nurtured a large number of historical celebrities, such as Philosopher Ai Siqi and Educator Cun Shusheng. Nowadays, Heshun has still well preserved the Memorial Hall of Ai Siqi's Former Residence, as well as numerous precious historical photos. Meanwhile, Heshun is one of the largest hometowns of overseas Chinese in Yunnan. Its overseas Chinese live in more than a dozen countries, including Burma, Thailand, Indonesia, Singapore, Japan, Canada and the United States.

和顺人杰地灵。在过去的600年里，和顺养育了一大批历史名人，如：哲学家艾思奇、教育家寸树声。时至今日，和顺仍然完好地保存着艾思奇故居纪念馆，以及许多珍贵的历史照片。与此同时，和顺是云南省最大的侨乡之一，其海外华人分布在缅甸、泰国、印度尼西亚、新加坡、日本、加拿大、美国等10多个国家。

However, what is the most attractive about Heshun is the near-perfect natural ecology and idyllic rural life in the town. Heshun is situated at the foot of hills and beside the river. The pleasant shade of trees makes the town beautiful and quiet. Daying River meanders around the town, forming a sharp contrast with the remote towering volcanic hills. In spring, the earth revives with life, flowers blossom, and the town is coated with green. In the fields outside the town, yellow rape flowers are found everywhere, and the air is filled with the delicate odour of the plants. In summer, lotus flowers bloom in the ponds around the Yuzhou Pavilion, in front of Liu Family's Ancestral Hall and in the Xianhe Wetland. Children swim in the river, frolicking along with egrets or wild ducks. In autumn, osmanthus flowers bloom in the Yunnan-Burma War of Resistance against Japanese Aggression Museum, Heshun Household Restaurant and the Waterfront Restaurant, and the golden rice sway in the wind. By the side of the Laundry Pavilion, there are more people than ever before. Perhaps because of the autumn harvest, their gathering is filled with joy and laughter. In winter, when the sun is warmer, flocks of wild ducks are playing in lakes. Early in the morning, the Dragon Pool is shrouded in thick mist, like a fairyland or a legendary paradise. There is a couplet written for Heshun Ancient Town. It says, "The path meanders all the way along brooks, flowers and overlying waters; a few houses remain in thick trees and buildings hidden in greenness." Li Genyuan, the former acting Prime Minister of the Republic of China, wrote a poem to eulogize Heshun Ancient Town. It says, "Hills afar appear vast; rivers nearby flow in pleasant tunes; at the foot of slopes seat thousands of households; such scenery is exceedingly better than little Suzhou or Hangzhou."

然而，和顺最吸引人的是古镇近乎完美的自然生态和田园般的乡村生活。和顺依山傍水，绿树成荫让古镇秀丽宁静，大盈江蜿蜒环绕，与远方矗立的火山相互辉映。春天，大地复苏，百花盛开，小镇披上绿装；在小镇外的田间里，油菜花遍地金黄，镇里弥漫着植物的清香。夏天，雨洲亭、刘氏宗祠、陷河河塘荷花盛开，孩童们在河里游泳，与鹭鸶、野鸭一起嬉戏。秋天，滇缅抗战馆、和顺人家、水上餐厅里桂花绽放，田间金灿灿的稻谷随风摇曳。洗衣亭边，出现比往时更多的身影；也许是秋收的缘故，他们的聚集充满着喜悦和欢笑。冬天，阳光温暖，成群的野鸭在湖里嬉戏；清晨，龙潭笼罩在浓浓的雾气中，宛如仙境或传说中的世外桃源。

有一副写和顺古镇的对联:"一路沿溪花覆水,数家深树碧藏楼"。民国代总理李根源有诗赞和顺:"远山茫苍苍,近水河悠扬,万家坡坨下,绝胜小苏杭。"

Liu Family's Ancestral Hall

Due to all those facts, Heshun Ancient Town was listed as one of China's Top Ten Famous Charming Towns in 2005. In 2006, it was admitted on to the list of China's Most Beautiful Ten Towns. Besides, Heshun has been crowned with several other titles, such as the First Charming Town in China, the Famous Town of Chinese History and Culture, the Beautiful Town of National Environment, and the Demonstration Base of National Cultural Industry.

2005 年,和顺古镇获得"中国十大魅力名镇"的称号,2006 年被评为中国最美的十个小镇之一。此外,和顺古镇还获得"中国第一魅力名镇""中国历史文化名镇""国家环境优美乡镇""国家文化产业示范基地"等多项殊荣。

Well, my brief introduction to Heshun Ancient Town is over. Now please follow the local tour guide for the tour of the town. As you are in the old town, the tour guide will continue to tell you more about the local history and culture. Around the town, there are many tourist attractions, so our tour route is as follows: Ai Siqi's Former Residence, the Dragon Pool, Yuanlong Temple, the Double Age-Old Fir Trees, Heshun Library, Wenchang Palace, as well as the Yunnan-Burma War of Resistance against Japanese Aggression Museum. Of course, we will also visit local residential houses, called "Wan Lou Zi", so named because the walls of those dwellings are built along the winding alleys. Also, I'd like to remind you that the temperature difference in the morning and evening in Tengchong is relatively large, so you'd better bring a warm coat with you wherever you are in the town.

好啦，和顺古镇的简介到此结束，现在请大家随当地导游参观古镇吧。在游览古镇时，导游会继续讲述有关当地历史与文化。古镇有众多旅游景点，我们参观线路是：和顺古镇艾思奇故居——龙潭——元龙阁——双杉——和顺图书馆——文昌宫——滇缅抗战博物馆。当然，我们还要去参观被称为"弯楼子"的民居。另外，要提醒大家，腾冲每天早晚温差较大，在古镇游览时最好带件保暖外套。

Yunnan Province
云南省

15
Fuxian Lake in Chengjiang County
澄江抚仙湖

Fuxian Lake is located in Yuxi area of Yunnan Province, bordering Chengjiang, Jiangchuan and Huaning counties. It is the third largest lake in Yunnan. It's about 60 kilometers away from Kunming at an elevation of 1,721 meters, covering an area of 212 square kilometers.

抚仙湖位于云南省玉溪地区，与澄江、江川、华宁三县接壤，是云南省的第三大湖泊，距昆明约60公里，海拔1721米，总面积212平方公里。

Fuxian Lake

According to legend, the Emperor of Heaven (the Jade Emperor) once sent two immortals to inspect the world. One immortal was called Shi, and the other was Xiao. When they arrived at Yunnan, they saw this clear blue lake. Its natural beauty and surroundings fascinated them and made them forget to return to Heaven. Later, they turned into two huge rocks side by side, standing by the lake forever.

相传，玉皇大帝派了石、肖二仙来到人间巡查。他们来到云南，看见清澈湛蓝的湖水。自然的美景和周围的环境迷倒了两位仙人，使之忘记了返回天上。后来，他们变成了两块并肩的巨石，永远矗立在湖边。

Around the lake there are many tourist attractions. To the west is Jianshan Hill, which appears tall and steep like jade-bamboo shoots. On the east side, there are several hot springs, known as hot water ponds locally. The water temperature is around 40°C, and the hot springs are ideal resort for bathing and health recuperation. In the northeast there is Huilong Hill that looks like an elephant's trunk, hence it is called the Elephant Trunk Ridge. At the southern end of the lake, there is a one-kilometer-long river that connects Fuxian Lake and Xingyun Lake of neighboring Jiangchuan. Remarkably, fish from the two lakes swim to the junction of Xingyun Lake and Fuxian Lake, but they never cross the boundary stone overlooking the water, so this stone is known as Jieyu Stone. About 100 meters west of the Jieyu Stone there is a beautifully carved bridge known as the Bridge of the Sea Gate, which was built in the fourth year of Tianshun's reign of the Ming Dynasty (1460). In the southwest of the center of the lake, there used to be two tiny islets, one called the Large Solitary Hill, and the other the Small Solitary Hill. In the Ming Dynasty, there was a bridge connecting the two islets. At present, there is only the Large Solitary Hill, which is more than 40 meters higher than the surface of the lake, covering an area of about 50 hectares with caves.

在湖的周围，有许多旅游景点。西面是尖山，状如玉笋，雄伟峻峭。在东侧，有若干温泉，当地称为热水塘，水温在40℃左右，是沐浴、疗养的理想之地。在东北面，有回龙山，此山如大象长鼻，故称象鼻岭。在湖的最南端，有一条长达1公里的河流，连接着抚仙湖和临近的江川星云湖。引人注目的是，两湖的鱼游到星云和抚仙湖交汇处，从未越过俯视湖水的界石点，此石由此被称为"界鱼石"。在"界鱼石"西侧100多米处，有一座雕刻精美、建于明朝天顺四年（1460年）的海门桥。在湖中心的西南面，曾有两座小岛，名大孤山和小孤山。明朝曾有一座桥，把两岛连接起来。目前仅存大孤山，面积约50公顷，山上有岩洞，比湖面高出40多米。

However, the Fuxian Lake is known far and wide mainly for its discovery of the ruins of underwater artificial buildings in 1992. So far, the verified ruins cover an area of 2.4 square kilometers, where there are eight main buildings, including two tall terraced buildings and one circular building. One of the tall terraced buildings consists of three storeys. Its first storey is 60 meters wide, the second storey is 32 meters wide, the third storey is 18 meters, and the entire building is 16 meters in height. In addition, according to sonar scanning images, its steps are found neat and symmetrical. The other terraced building is 21 meters high and magnificent. It has five storeys. The first storey is 63 meters wide, the second storey is 48 meters wide and the fifth storey is 27 meters wide. The third and fourth storeys collapsed badly, and the width can't be accurately measured. Between the two buildings there is a flagstone road, which is more than 300 meters long and 5 to 7 meters wide, and is paved with slabs of different shapes. In addition to the ruins of the ancient city, people have also found various geometric patterns of flat-shaped human faces, numbers similar to Arabic numerals, as well as the symbols of ancient Roman letters, such as "0," " 1," "Y and "I".

然而，抚仙湖之所以闻名遐迩，主要是因为 1992 年发现了水下人工建筑遗迹。目前，已经探明的面积达 2.4 平方公里，其中有 8 座主要建筑，包括两座高层阶梯状建筑和 1 座圆形建筑。其中 1 座高层阶梯状建筑共分 3 层，底部宽 60 米，第二层宽 32 米，顶层宽 18 米，整个建筑高 16 米。此外，从声呐扫描图图像看出，其台阶整齐对称。而另 1 座阶梯状建筑高 21 米，气势恢宏。它上下共 5 层，第一层宽 63 米，第二层宽 48 米，第五层宽 27 米；三四层倒塌严重，宽度无法准确测量。在这两座建筑之间还有一条石板路，长 300 多米、宽 5~7 米，用不同形状的石板铺成。除了古城遗迹外，还发现了各种各样的几何图案，"扁形人面图案"、类似阿拉伯的数字，以及古罗马字母的符号，如："0""1""Y""I"。

According to historical documents, there have been three ancient cities in the history of Chengjiang County. The earliest one was called Yuyuan. Later, it disappeared mysteriously from the historical documents. Why did Yuyuan ancient city disappear? What is the connection between the underwater buildings in Fuxian Lake and the ancient Yunnan civilization in history? Some experts tend to believe that the ancient underwater buildings might be the Yuyuan ancient city. They think that the discovery of the Fuxian underwater ruins will help to unravel the mystery of the ancient Yunnan civilization.

据史料记载，澄江县历史上出现过三座古城。最早的一座叫俞元。后来，它从史书上神秘地消失了。俞元古城为什么消失了？抚仙湖水下建筑与古滇文明在历史上有什么关联呢？有些专家认为古代水下建筑可能是俞元古城，抚仙湖水下遗址的发现将有助于揭开古滇文明的谜团。

Well, so much for the brief introduction to the Fuxian Lake. Today, our tour of the lake is like this: we begin with a hike in the Bijia Hill, where we go and see the Husband-and-Wife Tree, the Jade-Cloud Pavilion, the Green-

Wave Pavilion, Guanyin Temple, and the Temple of Fortune. After taking photos with the 100-Year-Old Auspicious Turtle and taking a panoramic view of the entire lake, we will make our way to the Dragon King Temple, the Banyan Bay and the caves. At about 1:30 p.m., we will experience a boat cruise on the lake. At 4:30 p.m., we will take our minivan back to Kunming. Note that the lake is vast, so be aware of high tides while strolling along the lake. The water level varies greatly when the tides rise and fall.

好了，抚仙湖的简介到此为止。今天，我们游览线路是：徒步登笔架山，游览夫妻树、玉烟亭、碧波亭、观音寺、财神寺；与百年神龟拍照，俯览整个湖面全景；之后，再去龙王寺、榕树湾、地洞；下午1:30，坐船在湖上游览；4:30，乘坐面包车返回昆明。抚仙湖宽广，在岸边散步时，要注意湖水涨落潮，在湖水涨落潮时水位变化很大。

16

Colorful Sand Forest in Luliang County
陆良彩色沙林

Luliang Colorful Sand Forest is one of the highly recommended and important tourist attractions in Yunnan Province. It is located 18 kilometers south of Luliang County, 40 kilometers away from the Stone Forest and 130 kilometers away from Kunming. The sand forest occupies an area of 25 square kilometers and the protection zone covers 52.8 square kilometers, The scenic area is divided into the Cuan Culture Section, the Natural Landscape Section, the Sand Sculpture Competition Section and the Forest Park Section. There are many attractions in the sand forest. Our trip route will be like this: we go to watch the wonders of the sand forest, view the works of sand sculptures and visit the state-level forest park on Wufeng Hill. The whole trip takes about three hours. Well, I'd like to remind you of the following points: don't scribble in the Colorful Sand Forest; don't climb the sand sculptures; and don't get into enclosure places while taking photos.

陆良彩色沙林是云南省重点推荐的旅游景点之一。它位于陆良县城以南18公里，距石林40公里、昆明130公里。沙林占地25平方公里，保护区面积52.8平方公里，景区分为爨文化片区、自然景观片区、沙雕赛区和森林公园片区。沙林景点众多。我们此次旅游线路是：游彩色沙林，观沙林奇观，欣赏沙雕作品，游五峰山国家级原始森林公园。整个旅程大约需要三小时。好了，提醒大家注意以下几点：不要在彩色沙林里乱刻乱画；不要攀爬沙雕；照相时，不要进入围栏。

Yunnan Province 云南省

Sand Sculpture

　　Geological surveys found that the Luliang Colorful Sand Forest was formed about 340 million years ago. Between the Pliocene epoch and the early Pleistocene period, this area became a faulted basin due to the Himalayan tectonic movement and crustal rifting, and a large delta was thus formed at the southern end of the basin, where colorful quartz grains of sand were deposited from the block masses of Niutou Hill. Later, due to the crust uplift movement and the constant erosion of lake waves, rains and rivers, the delta became a lake, and finally developed into the today's colorful sand forest.

　　地质考察发现,陆良彩色沙林形成于3.4亿年前。在上新世至更新世时期早期阶段,受喜马拉雅构造运动和地壳断陷作用的影响,这一地区成为断陷盆地,盆地南端形成了一个大的三角洲,来自牛头山古陆的各色石英砂粒沉积于此。后来,由于地壳抬升运动,以及湖泊波浪、雨水和河流的不断侵蚀,三角洲变成了湖积,最终形成了现在多姿多彩的彩色沙林。

Today, the Luliang Colorful Sand Forest has higher tourism geographical research value. It is a rare natural wonder in the world and a desert in the oasis. It is the world's largest colorful sand sculpture theme park, much like a world of dreams, where the sand sculptures have various postures and different expressions. It is said that this was once the hometown of Meng Huo, the head of the southern ethnic minorities during the Three Kingdoms Period, and the Cuan culture that was widely developed in the southern region during the Southern and Northern Dynasties originated here. In addition, in this scenic area, there is a national primeval forest park, ancient battlefields sites, the ten-thousand-*mu* (667 hectares) grassy hill, and clear, sweet springs. There are other interesting attractions around it, including the Xichong Lake with a smooth surface like a mirror, the Cuan Long Yan Stele which was inscribed on the list of national key cultural relics protection units in 1961, and a number of classical buildings constructed for the shooting of more than two dozen large-scale movies and television series, such as the *Romance of the Three Kingdoms* and *the Journey to the West*. Here you can ride a horse, take a sedan chair or chariots, drive a speedboat, enjoy the Cuan's ancient music and participate in other recreational activities.

今天的陆良彩色沙林具有较高的旅游和地理研究价值。这是世界罕见的自然奇观，是绿洲中的沙漠，是世界上最大的彩色沙雕主题公园，那里的沙雕千姿百态，如同梦幻世界似的。传说，这是三国时期南方少数民族首领孟获的故乡，南北朝时期南部地区广为发展的爨氏文化就发源于此。景区内有国家级原始森林公园、古战场遗址、万亩草山、清澈甘冽的神泉。景区周围还有其他景点，如：水面平静如镜的西冲湖泊、1961年列入全国重点文物保护单位名录的《爨龙颜碑》，以及为拍摄《三国演义》《西游记》等二十多部大型影视剧而修建的许多古典建筑。在这里，可以骑马、乘轿、坐战车、驾快艇、听爨氏古乐、参加丰富多彩的娱乐活动。

Of course, the main attraction is the Colorful Sand Forest itself. According to folklore, the colorful sand forest was the incarnation of a black dragon. It was killed by an evil dragon for saving people. His flesh and blood became red sand, his skin turned into white sand, his scales changed into black sand, and his tendons and bones grew into rugged rocks. Within its perimeter, the sand forest appears in different colors, including red, yellow, white, blue and others, all of which are composed of more than 40 well-spaced attractions, notably with its unique sand groups, sand peaks, sand columns, sand beaches, and sand caves. Different sand forest objects take on different shades of colors at different time, making these objects look like wonderful landscape paintings. Such unique scenery will remain in the memory of tourists long after their tour of the forest. In addition, in the sand forest there are numerous springs, where water gurgles or slowly permeates into the vicinity and distance. If tourists stand barefoot in a sand brook, they will experience the water silently washing the sand under their feet. These springs add a unique charm to the sand forest. Besides, there are many wild animals and plants in the forest. The main wild lives include multiple-colored snakes, multiple-colored tiny frogs and multiple-colored butterflies. The other lives are otters, barking deers, foxes, pangolins, hares, weasels, squirrels, owls, woodpeckers, pheasants, turtledoves, mynas, doves, swallows, yellow duck, etc. As for plants, they feature orchids, azaleas, camellias and matsutake. At present, due to its close to the Cuan Long Yan Stele, Zhongnan Hill and Wufeng Hill, forest has formed a touring circle of Luliang County, together with Yufeng Hill, Zhongnan Hill, the Thousand-Buddha Pagodas and other attractions.

当然，最吸引人的是彩色沙林。根据民间传说，彩色沙林原是黑龙的化身，它为拯救百姓而被恶龙杀死。红沙是黑龙的血肉，白沙是黑龙的肌肤，黑沙是龙鳞，嶙峋的崖石是龙筋龙骨。在所占区域里，沙林显现出红、黄、白、蓝等不同颜色,并组成了40多处错落有致的景点,独特的沙群、沙峰、沙柱、沙滩、沙洞特别引人注目。时间不同,不同的沙林物体呈现出不同深浅的色彩,让这些物体似乎成了一幅幅美妙的山水画,久久地留在游客的记忆里。此外,沙林多处有泉水,潺潺流出,由近及远,缓缓浸渗;游客如果静站在沙溪间,会感觉溪水静静地冲刷着脚下的沙子;泉水为沙林增添了独特的魅力。除此之外,沙林,还有众多的野生动植物。主要的野生动物有七彩小蛇、七彩小蛙、七彩蝴蝶;还有水獭、麂子、狐狸、穿山甲、野兔、黄鼠狼、松鼠、猫头鹰、啄木鸟、野鸡、斑鸠、八哥、鸽子、燕子、黄鸭,等等。植物以兰花、杜鹃、茶花、松茸为特色。目前,由于沙林与爨龙颜碑、终南山、五峰山相毗邻,已与玉峰山、终南山、千佛塔等景点共同组成陆良县旅游环线。

In 2000, the Colorful Sand Forest was listed as a national 3A-level tourist attraction. In 2003, it was updated as a national 4A-level tourist attraction. Since 2001, the forest has successfully hosted the International Colorful Sand Sculpture Conferences five times. In July 2004, the International Sand Sculpture Association awarded the Colorful Sand Forest the titles of the "China International Colorful Sand Sculpture Global Promotion Center" and the "World Colorful Sand Sculpture Exposition Garden". Well, my brief introduction to the Colorful Sand Forest is over. Now please follow me to the forest for sightseeing!

2000年,彩色沙林被列入为"国家AAA级旅游景区",2003年成为"国家AAAA级旅游景区"。自2001年以来,彩色沙林已经成功举办了五届国际彩色沙雕大会。2004年7月,国际沙雕协会授予彩色沙林"中国国际彩色沙雕全球推广中心"和"世界彩色沙雕博览园"的称号。好了,彩色沙林的简介到此结束,请随我游览彩色沙林吧!

Yunnan Province
云南省

Temple of Confucius in Jianshui County
建水文庙

Jianshui Temple of Confucius is located in the northwest of Jianshui County, about 300 kilometers away from Kunming. The Temple of Confucius, also known as the Confucian Temple, was built almost all over the country in ancient times, as it was an important place for worshipping Confucius and popularizing Confucianism. According to historical records, there were about 1,560 Temples of Confucius at the level of province, prefecture or county in the Ming Dynasty, and in the Qing Dynasty, the number of temples rose to more than 1,800.

建水文庙位于建水县县城西北，距昆明约300公里。文庙又称孔庙，在古代几乎遍布全国各地，是祭祀孔子，推广儒教的重要礼制性地方。据史料记载，明代全国就有府、州、县三级文庙，约1560所，清代则增至1800多所。

Jianshui Temple of Confucius was built in 1285, covering an area of 114 *mu* (7 hectares). Its existing scale and architectural standards rank second only to the Temple of Confucius in Qufu and the Temple of Confucius in Beijing. Our tour route goes like this: we first enter the entrance gate of the temple (Archway of Supreme Harmony and Vitality), walk through the Ritual Gate and pass along the Righteousness Path. Then we follow the route that leads through the Semicircular Platform-Shaped Square, until we reach the Lingxing Gate (Front Portal of the Temple). Afterwards, we go to the Wenchang Hall, the Dacheng Hall (variously translated as "Hall of Great Achievement", "Hall of Great Completion", or "Hall of Great Perfection") and the Chongsheng Shrine that honors the ancestors of Confucius, as well as the fathers of the Four Correlates and Twelve Philosophers. Our tour lasts about 60 minutes. For the tour of the temple, please follow me, as I will further interpret some inscriptions, horizontal plagues, poetic couplets and paintings. I hope that my interpretation will be of great help to your tour of this place of historic interest.

建水文庙始建于1285年，占地114亩（7公顷），其现存规模及建筑水平，都仅次于曲阜孔庙和北京孔庙。今天我们参观线路是：首先步入文庙大门（太和元气坊），穿过"礼门"，沿着"义路"坊前行；然后再穿过半圆形月台广场至棂星门；最后走进文昌阁、大成殿和崇圣祠。参观时间约60分钟。请跟我一同参观文庙，我将继续讲解有些题词、匾额、对联、绘画，希望我的讲解对你们参观这座名胜古迹大有帮助。

Here, the Temple of Confucius faces south and has six courtyards. Greenness was everywhere, and age-old trees look solemn. Its construction fully follows the standard pattern of the Temple of Confucius in Qufu. Along the north-south axis stands the Lingxing Gate, the Dacheng Portal, the Xianshi Hall, the Chongsheng Shrine and other buildings. Originally, there were 37 main buildings in total. Although four of them were destroyed, the other buildings are still intact. Behind the Panchi is the Semicircular Platform Square, on which stand giant stones vividly engraved into a dragon, tiger, unicorn, lion and elephant. Those stone-carved animals stand upright on the bases of the archway, guarding the wooden arch way with three-tier-eaves. On the either side of the archway are the mural walls made with bricks and bracket sets covered with green glazed tiles. Above the walls are the 3-tier-Xieshan roofs with overhanging eaves upturned at the end of eaves and glazed tiles seemingly rolling upward. It is worth noting that other archways, such as the Archway of the Supreme Harmony and Vitality, the Ritual Gate and the Righteousness Path have similar architectural styles, prominently creating an imaginary space for the gathering of archways of the ancient temple.

这里的文庙坐北朝南，有六个院落；翠绿遍地，古木庄严肃穆。其建筑完全依据曲阜孔庙的风格规制建造，中轴线上矗立着棂星门、大成门、先师殿、崇圣祠等建筑。最初，主要建筑共有37座，现在除了其中4座被毁以外，剩余的仍然完好无损。泮池后是半圆形月台广场，那里矗立着雕刻得栩栩如生的龙、虎、麟、狮、象巨石。这些巨石高踞于坊座上，拱卫着木构架的三檐牌楼。牌楼两侧为壁画墙，砖砌成斗，覆以碧瓦；墙上方是三重檐歇山顶，檐牙高翘，碧瓦看似向上起伏。值得注意的是，"太和元气""礼门""义路"等其他牌楼都具有相似的建筑风格，为古庙牌楼神奇聚合创造出想象的空间。

Undoubtedly, the grand Dacheng Hall is the most attractive place in the temple and also the main building constructed on the temple's marble terrace. Its Xieshan roof is structured with a single layer of eaves, nine ridges and yellow glazed tiles. Under the eaves stand 22 extended-eave pillars, each being five-meter in length and carved out of a single piece of stone. In the center of the main hall is placed with a dragon throne, where the statue of Confucius is enshrined. In addition, the facade of the hall is partitioned into five compartments by pillars, with a total of 22 carved partition doors. Of these doors, the central compartment have six partition doors, each being carved with a dragon among clouds. The carvings make up a picture of which the "six dragons have an audience with Confucius". Inside the hall, there are many plaques and statues. Most of the plaques were inscribed by the emperors of the past dynasties, including eight imperial inscriptions written by the Qing emperors. These gilded inscriptions, either glorify or highly respect Confucius, such as Kangxi's "An Exemplary Teacher for All the Ages", Yongzheng's "No Such Saint like Confucius since the Dawn of Time", Qianlong's "Confucius Being Side by Sides with Heaven and Earth". As for the statues in the hall, they are all celebrities who have contributed to the promotion of Confucianism, such as the Twelve Sages of Confucianism. Their statues are prominently placed on the east and west sides of the hall, with six on each side. The east and west wings of the hall are dedicated to Confucian's sages and scholars. According to the record by Sima Qian, Confucius said, "The disciples who received my instructions, and could themselves comprehend them, were seventy-seven individuals. They were all scholars of extraordinary ability." It is so called that Confucius had three thousand students, but that only seventy-two mastered what he taught.

毫无疑问，在文庙里宏丽的大成殿是最吸引人的地方，也是在文庙大理石台阶上修建的主体建筑。其歇山顶上单檐九脊，琉璃黄瓦，屋檐下矗立着22根外檐柱，每根长5米，为整块石雕成。殿内正堂置龙宝座，供奉着孔子塑像。大殿正面五个开间，共有22扇雕花隔扇门，其中明间六扇各雕一条云龙，雕刻构成了"六龙捧圣"的景象。大殿里有很多字匾和塑像。字匾大多为历代皇帝所题，其中包括八块清代帝王御题。这些贴金匾皆赞孔尊孔，如：康熙的"万世师表"、雍正的"生民未有"、乾隆的"与天地参"。这里的塑像，雕刻的都是对弘扬儒教做出贡献的名人，如：孔门先贤十二哲，他们的塑像安放在大殿东西两侧，一边六座。东西厢房是祀奉孔子的先贤先儒的场所。据司马迁记载，孔子说："受业身通者七十有七人，皆异能之士也。"所谓的，孔子弟子三千，贤人七十二。

At present, the Temple of Confucius in Jianshui is a National Key Cultural Relic Protection Unit and a National 4A-level Tourist Attraction. Every year in spring and autumn, a grand music and dance will be performed in the temple's Dacheng Hall as part of the ceremony to commemorate Confucius. In addition, every year on the first day of the first month of the lunar calendar, festival activities are held in the temple, where numerous people come from far and wide, piously worship Confucius and experience Confucian culture and etiquette. Well, so much for my brief introduction to Jianshui Temple of Confucius. Please come with me for the tour of the temple and experience the traditional Confucian culture.

目前，建水文庙为"全国重点文物保护单位"，也是"国家AAAA级旅游景区"。每年春秋两季，文庙大成殿要举行祭孔乐舞。此外，每年农历正月初一，举行游文庙活动，许多人从四面八方赶来，虔诚地祭拜孔子，感受儒家文化和礼仪。好了，讲解到此结束，请随我参观建水文庙，去体验儒家传统文化。

⑱
Dinosaur Valley in Lufeng County
禄丰恐龙谷

The World Dinosaur Valley is located in Lufeng County, Yunnan Province, 80 kilometers away from Kunming. On the east side of Lufeng County, there is a hill whose stratum is the Mesozoic Jurassic strata and a large number of dinosaur fossils have been unearthed. Thus, this hill is named as the Dinosaur Hill, and Lufeng County becomes known far and wide in the world for its dinosaur fossils.

世界恐龙谷位于云南禄丰县，距昆明80公里。在禄丰县城东侧，有一座小山，其地层为中生代侏罗纪地层，并出土了大量的恐龙化石。这座山因此而得名恐龙山，禄丰县因其恐龙化石而闻名世界。

In history, Lufeng dinosaur fossils have shocked the world twice. In 1938, Mr. Yang Zhongjian, the founder of Chinese paleobiology and the father of dinosaur research, unearthed China's first dinosaur skeleton fossils in Lufeng. The fossils were named "Lufengosaurus Huenei Young". The samples of the dinosaur fossils were displayed to the public after being mounted in Chongqing, thus making Lufeng become known worldwide as the "Hometown of Chinese Dinosaur".

历史上，禄丰恐龙化石曾两次引起世界震撼。1938年，我国古生物学奠基人、恐龙研究之父杨钟健先生在禄丰发掘出了中国第一条恐龙骨骼化石，取名叫"许氏禄丰龙"。这些恐龙骨骼化石的标本在重庆装架后对外展出，禄丰由此成为闻名世界的"中国恐龙原乡"。

In 1995, a burial site of dinosaur fossils was found in A'na Village, Chuanjie Town, Lufeng County. As a result, this site became the location of the current "World Dinosaur Valley". After the three years of excavation efforts by paleobiologists from China and the United States, this place now has been identified as the world's largest dinosaur burial ground, where more than one hundred dinosaurs from the late Middle Jurassic were buried there. Accordingly, this site is also known as the "Treasure House of Dinosaur fossils".

1995年，在禄丰川街乡阿纳村地界，发现了一处恐龙骨骼化石掩埋点，由此成为现在"世界恐龙谷"的所在地。经过中美两国古生物工作者三年的发掘工作，这个地方被确定为世界上迄今最大的一处恐龙埋葬地，中侏罗纪晚期的上百条恐龙就埋藏于此，故此处又称之为"恐龙化石宝库"。

The World Dinosaur Valley mainly consists to the "Dinosaur Site Zone for Scientific Investigation and Sightseeing" and the "Jurassic World Tourist Zone". Among them, the key scenic spot is the "Large Site of the China Lufengosaurus Valley". There, the Site No.1 Hall is the dinosaur burial site, which contains a 160-million-year-old geological section dating back to the late Middle Jurassic. This section is 15 meters in height, 40 meters in width and 83 meters in length. Part of the section has been excavated, revealing about 20 dinosaurs' fossils, as well as the fossils of snake-necked turtles. From October 1997 to October 1999, the paleobiologists from China and the United States carried out excavations there five times. Totally, they dug two exploration pits, covering the excavated area of 512 square meters. 12

dinosaurs fossils, five snake-necked turtles fossils and a wealth of the fossils of fish scales, fish bones, snails, ostracodas and bivalves were unearthed. These unearthed fossils, named the Chuanjie dinosaur fauna, lived in the late Middle Jurassic. In 2002, paleobiologists dug another exploration pit on the west side, covering an excavated area of about 120 square meters. Their purpose was to confirm how many dinosaur skeletons had been buried in the dinosaur burial site. In the end, they ascertained that more than 600 dinosaurs fossils were still buried under the unexcavated section. Also, they found the fossils of stegosaurus, small ornithopods and other species. The Site No.2 Hall displays more than 60 Lufengosaurus skeletons, which set up a Guinness World Record for their numbers. Following are several major features of the Lufeng Dinosaur Site. 1. In Lufeng, the unearthed dinosaurs lived between 135 million and 180 million years ago, spanning the Triassic, Jurassic and Cretaceous eras, while the Jurassic fossils remain the most complete. 2. The complete rate of Lufeng dinosaur fossils is very high. Even the small caudal vertebra, phalanges and ribs are well preserved, and their bone patterns look quite clear. 3. The fossil burial area is very concentrated, with hundreds of dinosaurs fossils buried under the rock stratum within the area of 10,000 square meters. 4. There are numerous species and genera. Research shows that only in the Dawa Dinosaur Hill alone there are as many as 34 species of dinosaurs from 25 different genera that have been excavated. Accordingly, the construction of the scenic zone of the World Dinosaur Valley started in March 2007 and opened to the public on April 18, 2008 after its completion. The scenic zone recreates the lost Jurassic world dinosaur valley, while providing tourists with a joyful experience of walking into the dinosaur kingdom, where they travel through the Jurassic world and witness the millions-of-years-old wonders in the world.

世界恐龙谷主要由"恐龙遗址科考观光区"和"侏罗纪世界旅游区"

组成。其中,重点游览区为"中国禄丰恐龙谷大遗址"。在那里,遗址第一馆是恐龙埋葬地,馆内有一段1.6亿年前的中侏罗纪晚期的地质剖面,其高15米、宽40米,长达83米。部分剖面已被发掘,裸露出约20具恐龙骨骼化石和蛇颈龟化石。1997年10月到1999年10月,中美两国古生物工作者在这里进行了5次发掘工作,共挖探坑两座,发掘面积512平方米,出土了12具恐龙化石、5具蛇颈龟化石,以及大量的鱼鳞、鱼骨、螺、介型类、双壳类化石。这些发掘的化石被命名为川街恐龙动物群,其生存年代为中侏罗纪晚期。2002年,古生物工作者又在西侧开挖了一座探坑,发掘面积约120平方米,目的是确定恐龙掩埋点埋藏了多少恐龙骨骼。最终,古生物工作者确定了600多具恐龙化石仍埋在未挖掘的剖面下。此外,他们还发现了剑龙类、小型鸟脚类和其他物种的化石。遗址第二馆展示了60多具禄丰龙骨架,其数量创吉尼斯世界纪录。以下是禄丰恐龙遗址的几大特点:1. 在禄丰,发现的恐龙生存距今1.35亿年—1.8亿年,纵跨三叠纪、侏罗纪、白垩纪三个时代,而侏罗纪时代的化石最为完整;2. 禄丰恐龙化石完好率相当高,即使是小的尾椎、趾骨、肋骨也保存得很好,骨纹很清晰。3. 埋藏区域非常集中。在这1万平方米范围内,有几百只恐龙化石埋在岩层下。4. 种属分类众多。研究表明,仅大洼恐龙山发掘的恐龙就达25属34种之多。为此,世界恐龙谷景区于2007年3月开工,2008年4月18日建成开放。景区重现了失落的侏罗纪时代的世界恐龙谷;与此同时,景区也为游客提供走进恐龙王国的快乐体验,穿越侏罗纪世界,目睹亿万年前的世界奇观。

Well, so much for my introduction to the World Dinosaur Valley. Now please follow the local tour guide for the tour of the valley. Our tour route goes like this: we pose for photos at the entrance, and then we view the sculptures named the Grand Powerful Dominators and the High-Rise Dinosaur Columns. Afterwards, we walk along the Jurassic plank path before the tour of the Jurassic Castle, the Dinosaurs Campus and the

Dinosaur Grand Ruins. Our tour takes about 2.5 hours. Let's get moving now!

  好了，世界恐龙谷的介绍就到此为止，现在请随当地导游游览恐龙谷吧。我们行走的线路是，在大门入口处留影拍照，然后去参观一代霸主雕塑和龙柱擎天；之后过侏罗纪栈道，再游览侏罗纪城堡、恐龙大本营、恐龙大遗址。参观时间约两个半小时。现在我们出发吧！

Yunnan Province
云南省

19
Puzhehei Scenic Area
普者黑景区

Puzhehei Scenic Area is located 13 kilometers away from the seat of Qiubei County in Wenshan Zhuang and Miao Autonomous Prefecture of Yunnan Province. The scenic area has been designated as a national 5A-level tourist attraction, a national-level wetland park, and the sole pilot of the tourist circular economy in Yunnan Province. In addition, it has been included in the list of the first group of provincial-level whole-region tourist demonstration zones in Yunnan.

云南文山州普者黑景区,位于云南省文山壮族苗族自治州丘北县境内,距丘北县城13公里。普者黑国家风景名胜区是国家AAAAA级旅游景区、国家湿地公园、全省唯一的旅游循环经济试点、全省首批省级全域旅游示范区。

So far as we know, the scenic area covers a total area of 388 square kilometers, with the core scenic places spanning 15 square kilometers. Within the scenic area, there are 258 scenic attractions, each with its own distinctive features. In addition, there exist 312 isolated hill or mountain peaks scattered throughout the area like numerous stars, 83 karst caves in a variety of positions or postures, and 54 lakes interconnected with one another. Furthermore, the scenic area includes the 40,000 *mu* (2,666.67

hectares) of wild-lotus waters, 13-kilometer long Grand Canyon, 3 kilometers of the mysterious Tea Horse Route, 60,000 *mu* (4,000 hectares) of plateau karst wetlands, as well as the diverse customs of the Zhuang, Miao, Yi and other ethnic nationalities in this area.

据了解,景区总面积388平方公里,核心景区面积15平方公里。景区内共有258个景点,各具特色。此外,312座孤峰星罗棋布,83个溶洞千姿百态,54个湖泊相连贯通。景区还有4万亩野生荷花水域,13公里的壮观大峡谷,3公里的神秘茶马古道,6万亩高原喀斯特湿地,以及区域内壮、苗、彝等少数民族的多彩风情。

In the scenic area there exist numerous major attractions, including Pucaotang Pier, Shede Grassland, Bailong Lake Scenic Site, Puzhehei Karst National-level Wetland Park.

景区内景点众多,主要包括蒲草塘码头、舍得草场、摆龙湖景区、普者黑喀斯特国家湿地公园。

The Pucaotang Pier is a low-lying structure built in the water and joined to the land at one end, for the use of tourist boats to facilitate passengers to get on and off. The pier is surrounded by the karst landscape, which looks like a scroll painting. Shede Grassland is renowned for its five wonders, namely the grassland, plateau scenery, famous local products, rich ethnic customs, and the revolutionary base area established by the local Communist Party from October 1946 to March 1949. It covers an area of more than 100,000 *mu* (6,666.67 hectares), which is the largest grassland in Yunnan Province and is hailed as "little Shangri-La" in the Wenshan Zhuang and Miao Autonomous Prefecture. Bailong Lake is an artificial reservoir built in 1958 and also referred to the "Red Flag Reservoir". With a water surface area of 3 square kilometers, the reservoir serves as the irrigation source for over 3.1 million *mu* (206,666.67 hectares) of farmland in the county, thus earning it the nickname "Mother River" of the people of Qiubei.

蒲草塘码头是一处低矮建筑，一端与陆地相连，供游船使用，方便游客上下船；码头四周，喀斯特地貌风景如画卷。舍得景区以五绝而著称，即草场、高原风光、名优特产、民族风情，以及当地共产党组织在1946年10月至1949年3月建立的革命根据地。舍得草场面积达10多万亩，是云南省最大的草场，被誉为文山壮族苗族自治州的"小香格里拉"。摆龙湖属于人工水库，修建于1958年，也称"红旗水库"。水库面积3平方公里，承担着全县310多万亩农田的灌溉，因此也被称为丘北人民的"母亲河"。

Among these numerous attractions, Puzhehei Karst National-level Wetland Park deserves special mention. In 2011, the park was approved for pilot construction by the State Forestry Administration, and in 2015 it was listed by the State Forestry Administration as one of China's 22 key national-level wetland park construction projects.

在众多景点中，普者黑喀斯特国家湿地公园尤为值得一提。公园于2011年经国家林业局批准试点建设，2015年被国家林业局列为中国22处国家重点湿地公园建设项目之一。

The wetland park is located 3 kilometers north of the seat of Qiubei County. It covers a planned area of 1,107.4 hectares and forms a diverse ecological system of lakes, rivers, isolated peaks, peak forests and peak clusters. This region features karst lake groups and a unique natural landscape. Scattered throughout the wetland are numerous karst caves, which collectively form an extensive cave network.

湿地公园位于丘北县城以北3公里处，规划面积1107.4公顷，是由湖泊、河流、孤峰、峰林、峰丛等构成的复合生态系统，有喀斯特湖群和独特的自然景观；喀斯特洞穴遍及湿地，形成了宏大的洞群。

Every year in July, August and September, 40 *li* (20 kilometers) of waters encircles isolated peaks within the wetland park, where the waters cover over ten thousand *mu*, stretching as far as the eye could see; lotus leaves seem to blanket the entire sky; pink lotus flowers exude delicacy and charm, while white ones emanate elegance and refinement. At this time of the year, tourists from all over the country flock to the wetland park, where they can not only enjoy the distinctive landscape and idyllic scenery, but also actively engage in a lively and interesting "water battle", a way to achieve more intimate contact to the green mountains and waters.

每年七八九月，40里的水路环绕着湿地公园内的座座孤峰，水域面积达万余亩，一望无际；荷叶接天蔽日，粉色荷花娇艳迷人，洁白荷花优雅大方。每年这个时候，全国各地游客涌向湿地公园，他们在欣赏独具特色的山水田园风光的同时，还积极参与生动有趣的"打水战"，与青山绿水更亲密地接触。

In addition, the wetland park is abundant in bird resources. At the migratory bird base, nearly 10,000 migratory birds leave early in the morning and return late at night. Tourists leisurely stroll or take a battery car ride, while observing the scene of thousands of water birds flying together—a scene reminiscent of the artistic conception interwoven with birds soaring in the sky and human wandering through painted landscapes.

此外，湿地公园鸟类资源丰富。在候鸟基地，近万只候鸟早出晚归。游客们或悠闲漫步，或乘坐电瓶车，观赏着万千水鸟齐飞的景象，领略鸟在天上飞、人在画中游的美景。

Following the broadcast of the TV series *Life After Life, Blooms Over Blooms*, Puzhehei Scenic Area has emerged as Yunnan's latest tourist hot spot, alongside Kunming, Dali and Lijiang. A visit to the Puzhehei Scenic

Area to enjoy its earthly paradise and stay in local-themed folk houses has gained popularity among tourists.

随着电视剧《三生三世十里桃花》的播出，普者黑景区成为云南继昆明、大理、丽江之后的另一旅游新热点。到普者黑景区享受人间仙境，住当地特色民居，成为游客的热门选择。

Well, so much for my brief introduction to Puzhehei Scenic Area. Today's tour route includes visits to Shuangjiashan Pier, Puzhehei Xihuang Wetland, and back to Shuangjiashan Pier. You will board on an electric bamboo-raft boat for a 50-minute excursion. Those interested in engaging in the "water battle" had better come with water guns, water basins, raincoats and life jackets when boarding.

好了，普者黑风景名胜区就介绍到这里。今天的游览线路：双甲山码头—普者黑西荒湿地—双甲山码头。我们将乘坐电动竹筏船，游览时间为50分钟。喜爱打"水战"的游客，请在登船前准备好水枪、水盆、雨衣和救生衣。

Guizhou Province
贵州省

贵州省《导游服务能力》考试大纲

01. Qingyan Ancient Town
青岩古镇 /105
02. Yangming Cultural Park in Xiuwen County
修文阳明文化园 /110
03. Tianhetan Scenic Area
天河潭景区 /114
04. Huangguoshu Waterfalls Scenic Area
黄果树大瀑布景区 /118
05. Longgong Caves in Anshun
安顺龙宫风景名胜区 /123
06. Fanjingshan Nature Reserve
梵净山自然保护区 /128
07. Zhusha Old Town
朱砂古镇 /133
08. Zhangjiang Scenic Area in Libo County
荔波樟江景区 /137
09. Chishui Danxia Scenic Area
赤水丹霞 /142
10. Zunyi Conference Site
遵义会议会址 /147
11. Hailongtun Fortress
海龙屯 /153
12. The Center of the Tea Sea in Fenggang County
凤冈茶海之心 /157
13. The Tea Sea in West China
西部茶海 /161
14. Shuanghe Karst Cave in Suiyang County
绥阳双河洞 /166
15. Zhijin Cave in Bijie
毕节织金洞 /170
16. Baili Azalea Scenic Area
百里杜鹃景区 /174
17. Thousand Households Miao Village in Xijiang
西江千户苗寨景区 /179
18. Zhenyuan Ancient Town
镇远古镇 /184
19. Wanfeng Forest Scenic Area in Xingyi
兴义万峰林景区 /190
20. Yeyuhai Scenic Area
野玉海 /195
21. Guizhou Third Line Construction Museum
贵州三线建设博物馆 /199
22. Ancient Ginkgo Scenic Area in Tuole Village
妥乐古银杏 /204
23. Qianling Mountain Park
黔灵山公园 /208
24. Jiaxiu Pavilion
甲秀楼 /213
25. Sidonggou Scenic Area
四洞沟风景区 /217
26. Tianlong Tunpu Old Town
天龙屯堡古镇 /223
27. Culture of Miao Ethnic Minority
苗族文化 /227
28. Culture of Dong Ethnic Minority
侗族文化 /232
29. Culture of Buyi Ethnic Minority
布依族文化 /237

（注：根据2024年全国导游资格考试大纲，贵州省外语类考生景点讲解范围包括01-22共计22个景点，其余为补充内容。）

01

Qingyan Ancient Town
青岩古镇

Qingyan Ancient Town, located in the southern suburb of Guiyang City, is one of the four ancient towns in Guizhou Province. In September 2005, the ancient town was listed as the second batch of famous historical and cultural towns in China. On February 25, 2017, it was classified as a national 5A-level tourist attraction.

青岩古镇，是贵州四大古镇之一，位于贵阳市南郊。2005年9月，古镇被列为第二批中国历史文化名镇；2017年2月25日，该镇被评为国家AAAAA级旅游景区。

This ancient town was built in the eleventh year of Hongwu reign of the Ming Dynasty (1378). Originally, it was a military defense work, but gradually became a mountainous military town, known as "the Southern Gate" of Guiyang.

古镇始建于明洪武十一年（1378年）。最初，这是一座军事防御设施，后演化为山地兵城，称之为贵阳"南大门"。

If you climb up a hill not too high at the edge of the town, you can get a bird's eye view of the whole town, which is built on an uneven hillside. Seen from the hill, the layout of the entire town offers a three-dimensional beauty that is difficult to see elsewhere.

如果爬上镇边一座不算太高的山坡，便可以鸟瞰全镇。小镇建在高低不平的坡面上。从山上俯瞰，整个小镇的布局给人一种在别处难以看到的立体美感。

Many of the buildings in the ancient town have a deep historical background. The historical spots can be seen wherever you are in the town. Specifically, there are nine monasteries by the names of Longquan, Ciyun, Guanyin, Chaoyang, Yingxiang, Shoufo, Yuantong, Fenghuang and Lianhua. There are eight temples by the names of Yaowu, Heishen, Chuanzhu, Leizu, Caishen, Huoshen, Sunbin and Dongyue; there are five pavilions by the names of Kuiguang, Wenchang, Yunlong, Sangong and Yuhuang. In addition, the town has Zhao Yijiong's Official Residence, Qingyan Academy of Classical Learning, the Longevity Palace and Shuixing Tower.

在古镇，许多建筑的历史底蕴深厚，古镇胜迹随处可见。具体来说，有九寺，即：龙泉、慈云、观音、朝阳、迎祥、寿佛、圆通、凤凰和莲花；有八庙，即：药五、黑神、川主、雷祖、财神、火神、孙膑和东岳；有五阁，即：奎光、文昌、云龙、三宫和玉皇。小镇还有赵以炯府、青岩书院、万寿宫和水星楼。

Historically, there were once eight stone memorial arch-gates located inside or outside the four gates of the town. Now, only three arch-gates are in existence. One, known as the Filial Piety Arch for Zhou Chaozhong's Wife and Wang's Daughter-In-Law, is located outside the south gate; another one, known as the Longevity Arch for Zhao Lilun, is situated inside the south gate; and the third one, known as the Longevity Arch for Zhao Caizhang, stands outside the north gate.

历史上，古镇四门内外，曾有八座石刻牌坊，现仅存三座。一座位于南门外，名"周王氏媳刘氏节孝坊"；另一座位于南门内，名"赵理伦百寿坊"；还有一座位于北门外，名"赵彩章百寿坊"。

The Longevity Arch for Zhao Caizhang was built in the 19th Daoguang year of the Qing Dynasty (1839). The Longevity Arch for Zhao Lilun was built in the 23rd Daoguang year of the Qing Dynasty (1843), and the Filial Piety Arch for Zhou Chaozhong's Wife and Wang's Daughter-In-Law was built in the 8th Tongzhi year of the Qing Dynasty (1869). The architectural layouts of the three arch-gates are basically the same, and they belong to the architectural style of arch-gates in the Qing Dynasty. Specifically, each arch-gate faces north. It is 9.5 meters high and 9 meters wide. More impressively, the arch-gate has no foundation trench, but is supported by four pillars that stand upright on the ground.

"赵彩章百寿坊"建于清道光十九年（1839年）；"赵理伦百寿坊"建于清道光二十三年（1843年）；"周王氏媳刘氏节孝坊"建于清同治八年（1869年）。三座牌坊的建筑造型基本相同，属清朝牌坊建筑风格。具体来说，每座面北背南，高9.5米，宽9米。更令人惊奇的是，三座牌坊都没有基槽，全靠四根竖立在地上的柱子支撑着。

Of these arch-gates, the Longevity Arch for Zhao Lilun is considered to be a rare masterpiece of art. At that time, Zhao Lilun's family had great power and influence in the town, so his arch-gate was set up in the most prosperous area. Compared with the other two arch-gates, its workmanship is exquisite and the decoration is elegant and rich. On the beam right in the middle of the arch-gate, there is a hollow-out sculpture called "Double Dragons Fighting for Treasure". On both sides of the horizontal plaque are the pad stones, which are sculpted into the double-hundred-fruit columns.

Above the plaque are five trapezoidal pad stones, with "the Statue of the Dragon and Turtle" sculpted in the middle, inside which are embedded with two characters "Li Bian" that literally means "establishment of the plaque". Four other stone columns on the left and right are sculpted with reliefs of Chinese mythological figures. In addition, there are many prismatic patterns on the arch-gate, as well as the sculptures of double turtles and hundred fruits. All of these are symbols of longevity. Also, the image of the stone lions on the pillars is completely different from that seen elsewhere. These four lions appear to be descending the mountain, with their heads down and their feet upward. The male lions are playing treasures, while the lionesses are holding her cubs. This lion sculpture is considered to be "the masterpiece of stone carving". For these facts, this arch-gate has now become a favorite among photographers.

在这些牌坊中,"赵理伦百寿坊"被认为是不可多得的艺术精品。当时在镇里,赵理伦家族的权势和影响力很大,牌坊建立在最繁华地段。与其他两座牌坊相比,其做工精细,装饰典雅丰富。在牌坊正中间的横梁上,有"二龙抢宝"空雕;横匾两侧垫石,为空雕双百果栏;横匾上方为五块梯形石墩,正中间镌"龙鳌图",里面还嵌有"立匾"两个字。左右两边的四块石墩,皆有中国神话人物浮雕。此外,石坊有不少的棱柱形图案和"双鳌百果"雕塑,皆是象征长寿。石柱上的石狮也与各地狮子造型截然不同。此处的四只狮子像是下山而来,头朝下,脚朝上;雄狮压宝,母狮抱崽。这种狮子造型被誉为"石雕杰作"。由于这些特点,这座牌坊现在已经成为摄影师们最喜爱的建筑。

Well, so much for my brief introduction to the ancient town. Of course, there are other scenic attractions, such as the Side Street, Wenchang Pavilion, Ciyun Temple and the Longevity Palace. For those who plan to go to Qingyan Ancient Town, please take a bus at the Guiyang City Passenger

Station. It is better to visit the ancient town in the afternoon, because it will be less crowded and a tour of the town will be quiet and enjoyable.

　　好了,古镇的介绍到此结束。当然,镇上还有其他的景点,如:背街、文昌阁、慈云寺、万寿宫。凡是想去青岩古镇的游客,请在贵阳市客运站乘车前往。游玩古镇最好在下午,可以避开人潮,安静愉快地游览古镇。

02

Yangming Cultural Park in Xiuwen County
修文阳明文化园

Yangming Cultural Park, located in Xiuwen County, is a cultural-oriented tourism park. The park started its construction in August of 2014 and was officially open to the public in October 2016.

阳明文化园位于修文县,是一座文化旅游园区。该文化园于2014年8月动工建设,2016年10月正式对外开放。

Up to now, the park covers an area of more than 3,500 *mu* (233 hectares). The construction of the core scenic sites has been basically completed, including the Square of Knowledge-Action Unity, the Arch-Gate of Knowledge-Action Unity, the Mind-Heart Pool, the bronze statue of Wang Yangming, Hengnan-Yunxuan Business Center, the Tourist Service Center, the Memorial Hall of Wang Yangming, and Longgang Academy of Classical Learning. Through the integration of culture and tourism, the park is not only an important platform to promote Yangming culture, but also has become a tourist destination. In September 2017, Yangming Cultural Park was listed as a national 4A-level tourist attraction.

截至目前,园区占地3500余亩(233公顷)。核心景区已经基本建成,包括"知行合一"广场、"知行合一"牌坊、正心池、阳明先生铜像、"衡南云轩"商业中心、游客服务中心、王阳明纪念馆、龙岗书院等。通过文旅融合，园区不仅是弘扬阳明文化的重要平台，也成为旅游目的地。2017年9月，阳明文化园被评定为国家AAAA级景区。

The core attraction, of course, is Yangming Cave. When Wang Yangming was exiled to Longchang (Xiuwen County today), he lived here and worked as a postal clerk in charge of postal general affairs. Wang, official career had ups and downs. When he went through a bad patch, he suffered two months in prison and a beating of 40 strokes followed by exile in Guizhou. When he arrived at Longchang, he had nowhere to live. Then, he moved to Longgang Hill and resided in a cave with a flat floor and plenty of space. After Wang resided here, the cave was named Yangming's Xiaodongtian, commonly known as Yangming Cave. Outside the cave, there is a stone stair flanked by two towering ancient cypresses, which are believed to have been planted by Wang Yangming himself. On the upper left of the cave entrance, Wang also built a small pavilion and planted some bamboo around it.

当然，阳明洞是核心景点。王阳明贬谪至贵州龙场（今修文县城）为驿丞时，曾居于此洞。王阳明的仕途并非一帆风顺。在他处于人生低谷之时，他被囚狱两月，杖四十，随后贬谪至贵州。初到龙场，王阳明居无处所。而后，他搬到龙岗山，住在一处地面平坦、空间宽广的山洞里。王阳明在此居住后，山洞就称为"阳明小洞天"，俗称"阳明洞"。洞外有一石阶，两侧有两棵参天古柏，据说是王阳明亲手种植。他还在洞口左上方修建一座小亭，并栽竹四周。

While Wang Yangming was in exile in Longchang, his essential insight came suddenly after a period of his intense thought. His experience has often been likened to the sudden enlightenment sought by Chan Buddhists. In history, it is called "Enlightenment in Longchang". Wang Yangming followed this up by stating that knowledge and acting were inseparable from each other, and that a "spontaneous understanding" was the best guide for conduct. Wang Yangming believed in the Learning of the Mind, the way to advance in understanding of the world was through the discovery of one's own mind, by a process of meditation and contemplation similar to Buddhist practice.

王阳明在龙场谪居期间，经过一段时间潜心"悟道"，之后突然洞悉事物的本质，此番经历常会使人联想起禅宗的顿悟，史称之"龙场悟道"。王阳明认为，知行合一，不可分离；"良知"是行为的最好指南。王阳明信仰"心学"；如果要提高对世界的理解，就得从自己内心寻找，像佛教修炼那样冥思苦想。

Wang Yangming's theory originated in Guiyang and later spread all over the country, even to Korea, Japan and other countries. Accordingly, scholars at home and abroad regard Longchang as the Sacred Yangming Land. The Song and Ming dynasties were another heyday of ancient Chinese philosophy, and its theoretical speculative level surpassed the study of Confucian classics in the Han and Tang dynasties. Undoubtedly, Yangming's theory is regarded as the last pinnacle of Chinese Confucianism, and Yangming Culture is thus known as the treasure of Chinese culture.

王阳明学说起源于贵阳，后来传遍全国，甚至传到韩国、日本等国家。因此，中外学者都把龙场视为"阳明圣地"。宋明历代是中国古代哲学的又一鼎盛时期，其理论思辨水平超过了汉唐时期的经学研究。毋庸置疑，阳明学说被视为中国儒学的最后巅峰，"阳明文化"则是中国文化的瑰宝。

In 1551, 23 years after Wang Yangming's death, Zhao Jin, the grand coordinator of Guizhou, transformed Longgang Academy into Wang Yangming Ancestral Hall, and Yangming Cave thus became an important memorial site. Later, in the 19th Jiaqing year of the Qing Dynasty (1814), Yangming Shrine was built at the foot of Fufeng Hill in the east of Guiyang. In 2006, Yangming Cave was put on the list of the national key cultural relic protection units. So far, there are 43 cliff inscriptions in the cave, dating from the Ming and Qing dynasties to the Republic of China, with different calligraphic styles, such as cursive script, regular script, official script or seal script. At present, Yangming Cave is a good place for academic studies on Yangming doctrines. Also, it is a popular destination for men of letters and scholars who are interested in studies of Wang Yangming's theory.

1551年,即王阳明死后23年,贵州巡抚赵锦将龙岗书院改建为"王文成公祠",阳明洞也因此成了王阳明的重要纪念地。后来,清嘉庆十九年(1814年)在贵阳城东扶风山麓修建了阳明祠。2006年,阳明洞被列为全国重点文物保护单位。迄今为止,阳明洞有明、清、民国年间的摩崖石刻43幅,书法各具风格,有行书、楷书、隶书、篆书。目前,阳明洞是研究阳明学说的好场所,也是研究王阳明理论的文人雅士的向往之地。

Well, so much for my brief introduction to Yangming Cultural Park. We will spend half a day in the park. If you have enough time, you can also go and visit some other historical sites, such as Longgang Academy of Classical Learning, Helou Mansion, Junzi Pavilion and so on. Have a pleasant tour!

好了,阳明文化园的介绍到此结束。我们将在公园里逗留半天。如果你们有时间的话,也可以去参观一些其他历史遗迹,如:龙岗书院、何陋轩、君子亭。祝游览愉快!

③
Tianhetan Scenic Area
天河潭景区

Tianhetan Scenic Area is about 24 kilometers away from the downtown Guiyang, covering a total area of 15 square kilometers in Shiban Town, Huaxi District.

天河潭景区距离贵阳市中心约24公里,景区位于花溪区石板镇境内,总面积15平方公里。

Tianhetan Scenic Area is a typical karst natural landscape with a landform characterized by tortuous river valleys and steep ravines. Specifically, it is a truly picturesque combination of mountains, water, caves, pools, waterfalls, natural bridges and canyons. The caves are hidden in the mountain, while water flows in the caves; the mountain remains secluded and quiet, and the sound of water gurgling is heard everywhere; the pools are blue, with water overflowing into the shape of waterfalls. Due to these facts, the Tianhetan is reputed as "a unique place in central Guizhou" and "the concentrated bonsai of Guizhou landscape".

天河潭景区是典型的喀斯特自然景观,河谷曲折,沟壑险峻。特别是景区完美地融合了山、水、洞、潭、瀑布、天生桥和峡谷。洞穴隐于山,洞中水流动;山空寂静,处处闻水声;水潭碧蓝,溢水成瀑。天河潭由此被誉为"黔中一绝""贵州山水浓缩盆景"之称。

In 2008, Tianhetan Scenic Area was officially put into the list of the national 4A-level tourist attractions. Then, the Tianhetan began to upgrade its core scenic sites, with the goal of making the Tianhetan a national 5A-level scenic area. After years of efforts, Tianhetan had new attractions and facilities have been added to Tianhetan, including the Tourist Service Center, the Square of the Sun, the Street of Guiyang Stories, Binshui Recreational Area, and the Five-color Flower Sea.

2008年，天河潭风景区正式进入国家AAAA级旅游景区行列。此后，天河潭就以创建国家AAAAA级景区为目标对核心景区进行改造提升。经过多年的努力，天河潭新增了新的景点和设施，如：游客服务中心、太阳广场、贵阳故事街、滨水休闲区、五色花海等。

Here is a brief introduction of the main attractions concerned:

以下是主要景点的简介：

The Water-View Show adopts sound, light, electricity and other high-tech means to make the water move with music and even dance rhythmically as the water transforms itself into different patterns or postures, just like the performance of "water ballet" or the images of folk dance. Wolong Waterfalls are more than 20 meters wide and more than 10 meters high, which look like a water dragon in the sky. During the season of high water, the waterfalls cascade turbulently from a height above the beachhead. Shibang Beach is a place where the spring water flows out from the caves, forming two different kinds of scenery, one being dynamic, and the other static. Around the scenery stand corridors and pavilions amidst lush plants or on the cliffs. Such a wonderful place can be called the Land of Idyllic Beauty.

水秀景观采用声、光、电等高科技手段，让水随着音乐而动，甚至有节奏地舞动起来，同时变化成形态各异的图案或姿态，呈现出如"水上芭蕾""民族歌舞"的表演模式。卧龙飞瀑宽二十余米，高十余米。卧龙飞瀑就像一条天上的水龙；每到丰水季节，瀑布从滩头高处倾斜而下，气势汹涌。石蚌滩是山洞泉水汇聚之处，从而形成动、静两种景色；景观周围有走廊与楼榭，掩映在繁茂植物中，或矗立在悬崖之上。这样的佳境可称之为"世外桃源"。

Tianhetan Scenic Area contains water caves and dry caves, among which Kongling Cave is a water cave, and Yinhe Palace is a dry cave. Kongling Cave is accessible by boat. Once you enter the cave, you will find yourself as if in a wonderland. The cave is about 1,200 meters long, with its highest point exceeding 50 meters. In addition, its underground river is 31 meters in depth. Stalactites, stalagmites, stalagnates and other karst landscape can be seen everywhere in the cave. One of the attractions is called "the Carp Jumping Dragon Gate". According to legend, there was a scholar who just passed by here when he suddenly saw a one-meter-long carp jumping out of the water. At the same time, the carp nodded to the scholar three times and then plunged back into the water. It was in the same year that the scholar succeeded in the imperial examinations. Yinhe Palace is a dry cave with three layers. Inside the cave, there is a natural stone bridge, which seems to be extraordinary work made by the spirits. The bridge lies between two cliffs. Under the bridge is an unfathomable pool. In addition, the cave is covered with stalactites of various forms, among which the famous ones include "Monkeys Grasping for the Moon" and "the Chamber of Scriptures".

天河潭景区有水洞和旱洞，其中崆灵洞为水洞，银河宫为旱洞。崆灵洞可以乘船进入。进入洞内，仿佛置身于仙境。该洞全长约1200米，最高处50余米，暗河水深处31米。洞内随处可见石钟乳、石笋、石柱等喀斯特景观。其中一处取名"鲤鱼跳龙门"。传说,有一位学子路过此地,突然看见一条一米长的鲤鱼跃出水面,对他点头三次,然后又跳回水里。就在这一年,此人成功中举。银河宫为旱洞,分为三层。洞内有一座天然石桥,堪称鬼斧神工。这座桥坐落悬崖之间,桥下是深不可测的水潭。洞内四处是千姿百态的钟乳石,著名的有"猴子捞月""藏经阁"。

Well, so much for my brief introduction to Tianhetan Scenic Area. Today, our tour route is from Wolong Pool to Mengcao Garden, via Shibang Beach – the Water Cave – Jiudao Bends and the Dry Cave. Please make sure to follow your group when touring the caves, otherwise it's easy to get lost.

好了,天河潭景区讲解到此结束。我们今天游览路线是卧龙潭—石蚌滩—水洞—九道弯—旱洞—梦草园。游览溶洞时,请务必跟随旅行团,否则容易迷路。

04

Huangguoshu Waterfalls Scenic Area
黄果树大瀑布景区

Huangguoshu Waterfalls Scenic Area is located 128 kilometers from Guiyang and 45 kilometers southwest of Anshun. The waterfalls were admitted into the list of the first batch of the National Key Scenic Sites. In March 2007, the scenery was listed as a 5A-level tourist attraction by China National Tourism Administration. Huangguoshu Waterfalls, the number one tourist attraction in Guizhou, remain as the centerpiece surrounded by other huge waterfalls, caves and karst complex, covering several sub-scenic sites, such as Shitouzhai Scenery, Tianxingqiao Scenery, Dishuitan Falls, Doupotang Falls and Langgong Scenery. In the 1980s, the local people started developing this area. Their preliminary attempt was to tap the region's hydropower potential. As a result, they found about 18 waterfalls, four subterranean rivers and 100 caves, many of which are now gradually opening to tourists.

黄果树大瀑布景区距贵阳市128公里，安顺市西南45公里，是全国第一批国家重点风景名胜区。2007年3月，它被国家旅游局评定为AAAAA级旅游景区。黄果树瀑布是贵州第一胜景，地处中间地带，四周环绕着其他大瀑布、洞穴、岩溶，覆盖了好几处附属景区，如：石头寨景区、天星桥景区、滴水滩瀑布景区、陡坡塘景区、郎宫景区。20世纪80年代，当地人开发此地，最初打算利用该地区的水力发电资源，结果发现了约18座瀑布和4条地下河流、100个洞穴。目前，这些发现正逐步向游客开放。

Guizhou Province
贵州省

Today, we first go for a view of the Huangguoshu Waterfalls and then move to the Doupotang Falls and the scenery of Tianxingqiao. We enter through the scenery entrance and descend a short flight of stairs to the Rhinoceros Pool where the waterfall drops in. Afterwards, we walk into the Water-Curtain Cave, stay there for a while before departing from there. Then, we cross the Water Suspension Bridge, climb the stone steps and exit from the entrance. I'd like to advise you to wear hiking boots or sneakers for easy walking on steep stone steps. In addition, please take your umbrella or raincoat, as we will traverse the Water-Curtain Cave. As you know, the water mist at the mouth of the cave may soak your clothes.

今天，我们先去看黄果树瀑布，然后再去陡坡塘瀑布和天星桥景区。我们从景区大门进去，沿着一段不长的阶梯而下，到瀑布跌落处——犀牛潭。然后，进"水帘洞"，在洞里停留一会儿就离开，过水上吊桥，拾梯而上，出景区大门。我建议大家穿上登山鞋或运动鞋，以便在陡峭的石路上行走。另外，备好雨伞或雨衣，在穿越水帘洞时，水雾可能会弄湿衣服。

Huangguoshu Waterfall

The Huangguoshu Waterfall is China's largest waterfall and one of the famous waterfalls in the world. Its actual height is 77.8 meters, the width is 101 meters, and the fall of water that falls into the Rhinoceros Pool is 74 meters. There are many legends about the origin of its name. One legend says, "A long time ago, local peasants, who resided near the waterfalls, liked growing yellow-fruit trees (Huangguoshu). Gradually these trees developed into a large yellow-fruit orchard beside the waterfalls, and the waterfalls were thus called Huangguoshu Waterfalls (Waterfalls of the Yellow-Fruit Trees).

黄果树瀑布是中国第一瀑布，也是世界上著名的大瀑布之一。瀑布实际高度为77.8米，宽101米，落差74米，落水跌入犀牛潭。关于其名字由来，有许多传说。其中一个故事讲到：以前，瀑布附近的农民喜欢种黄果树。这些树木在瀑布旁边渐渐地形成了一大片黄果园，而这座瀑布也因此被称为黄果树瀑布。

The Huangguoshu Waterfall is the highlight of the tour in this area. There are other attractions around it. In front of the waterfall is a deep cave canyon, to the left are cliffs where age-old forests grow, to the right is the Travertine Slope and the Stalagmite Hill. At the foot of the waterfall are the Rhinoceros Pool and the Horse-Hoof Pool. A pavilion, called Guanputing (Pavilion of Viewing Waterfalls), stands on a high cliff on the other side of the waterfall. It is an excellent spot, where visitors can gain a panoramic view of the waterfall flowing directly into the Rhinoceros Pool. A couplet written on the pavilion reads, "The white-color water looks like cotton fabrics; it doesn't need a string-bow to fluff it up, but it spreads widely by itself. The misty rainbow appears like silk brocade; it doesn't need a loom to shuttle itself, for its shape is natural." As the water rushes from the top of the cliff down to the Rhinoceros Pool, the scenery of the waterfall changes constantly. In winter when the flow of water becomes a trickle, the waterfall falls down gently and looks charmingly pretty. In summer and autumn, especially during the rainy seasons when the discharge of water increases greatly, the waterfall presents a spectacular wonder of which the roaring sound of waterfall produces breathtaking momentum and can be heard in distance. Sometimes, as the water hits the ground, it immediately splashes high up into the air, and its mist often shrouds a village and streets nearby. When the sun shines, visitors often see golden glows that emerge in the mist. Such sights seem so unreal, and the entire village and streets seem to be in golden color, forming an unusual scene widely known as the "Silver Rain Spraying Golden Streets". At the foot of the waterfall is the Rhinoceros Pool, where a multi-color rainbow often emerges among splashed water-drops. As the viewer moves, the rainbow follows and changes unpredictably. Behind the waterfall is a recess inside the cliff. It is known as the Water-Curtain Cave, which is approached by a slippery wade across the Rhinoceros Pool. The cave is 134 meters in length, with six "windows", three cave-springs, and six passageways. Behind the six "windows" in the cave, visitors can watch the cascading water. If the visitor looks out of the cave windows as the sun sets in the west, they will find out pleasant sights of which a rainbow curls up around the Rhinoceros Pool, the sunset clouds look colorful and are rising slowly, and bright redness flourishes on the top of the cliffs. Such a scene is widely referred to as "Viewing the Sunset from the Water-Curtain Cave".

　　黄果树瀑布是此地游览的重点。周围还有其他景点：瀑布前面是一条很深的溶洞峡谷，左为悬崖峭壁、古木森森；右为钙华坡、石笋山；瀑布脚下为犀牛潭、马蹄潭。在瀑布对岸，有观瀑亭，矗立在高崖上。这是观看瀑布的绝佳地点，可以在此看到瀑布直泻犀牛潭的。观瀑亭上有对联道："白水如棉，不用弓弹花自散；虹霞似锦，何须梭织天生成"。瀑布从悬崖顶端奔泻至犀牛潭，瀑布的形态不断变化。冬天，流水变成涓涓细流，轻轻下泻，妩媚秀丽。夏秋之时，尤其在雨季的时候，水量大增，瀑布呈现出壮观的景象，瀑布的轰鸣声撼天动地，令人惊心动魄，在远处也听得见。有时候，瀑布激起，水液飞溅，抛入空中，水雾常常弥漫附近寨子和街市。当艳阳高照之时，常常可以看到水雾里映出金色的光芒，似真似幻，街道似乎覆盖上了一片金色，形成了远近闻名的"银雨洒金街"的奇景。瀑布脚下是犀牛潭，那里的水花飞溅，缤纷彩虹常常出现在水花之间，随人移动，变幻莫测。瀑布后绝壁上有一凹洞，称"水帘洞"，蹚过湿滑的犀牛潭便可到达洞口。"水帘洞"洞穴长134米，有六个洞窗、三股洞泉、六条通道。游人可以在六个洞窗内观看飞流直下的瀑布。每当日薄西山，凭窗眺望，美景映入眼帘：犀牛潭里彩虹缭绕，云蒸霞蔚，苍山顶上绯红一片，这便是著名的"水帘洞内观日落"。

Apart from the Huangguoshu Waterfall, some other water falls are worthy of viewing. These include the Doupo tang Falls, one kilometer upstream of the Huangguoshu Waterfall; the Luositan Falls, one kilometer downstream of the Huangguoshu Waterfall; and the Yinlianzhuitan Falls and the Dishuitan Falls, eight kilometers downstream of the Huangguoshu Waterfall. Well, so much for my introduction to the Huangguoshu Waterfall. Now let's enter the entrance of the scenery, where we are scheduled to spend one hour and a half touring the Huangguoshu Waterfall before making a trip to the other falls nearby.

除了黄果树大瀑布外，还有其他瀑布也值得观赏，诸如：位于黄果树瀑布上游1公里处的陡坡塘瀑布、在黄果树瀑布下游1公里处的螺丝滩瀑布、在黄果树瀑布下游8公里处的银链坠潭瀑布和滴水滩瀑布。好了，黄果树大瀑布介绍到此为止。我们现在进入景区大门吧，在黄果树大瀑布景区逗留一个半小时，然后再去附近其他瀑布。

05
Longggong Caves in Anshun
安顺龙宫风景名胜区

Longgong Caves (Dragon Palace) are about 27 kilometers southwest of Anshun and 116 kilometers away from Guiyang. In 1984, the Longgong Caves were open to public. In 1988, the caves were admitted into the second batch of the National Key Scenic Sites. In 2007, it was listed as a 5A-level tourist attraction.

龙宫风景名胜区位于贵州省安顺市西南27公里处，距离贵阳116公里。龙宫风景名胜区于1984年对外开放，1988年被评为第二批国家重点风景名胜区，2007年被评为AAAAA级旅游景区。

Longgong Caves look like a huge network across 20 hills. The scenery mainly includes the Central Scenic Section, the Xuantang Pool, the Youcai Lake and the Xianrenqing Valley, with a series of spectacular underground karst caverns, caves and waterfalls as the principle attractions. The features of the Longgong Caves are as follows. ① In the Longgong Caves, the water-filled karst cavern is 15 kilometers long and is considered the longest karst cavern in China. ② The Guanyin Cave is China's largest cave temple, where all the halls are natural karst caverns, with 32 artificially-carved statues of Buddhas, among which the Guanyin Statue is 12.6 meters highs. In the main hall there exists a natural stalactite that looks like Guanyin in spirit. ③ The

Longmen (Dragon's Gate) Waterfall is considered the largest cave waterfall in the country. It is more than 50 meters high and 26 meters wide. ④ The water in the Xuantang Pool flows clockwise, day and night without stop.

龙宫像一个巨大的网络，穿越20座山脉。景区以一系列壮观的地下溶洞、洞穴、瀑布为主体，主要包括中心景区、漩塘、油菜湖和仙人箐。龙宫有以下特色：①龙宫水溶洞长达15公里，为国内之冠。②观音洞是国内最大的洞中寺院，所有的殿堂都是天然溶洞，有32尊人工雕刻佛像，其中观音像高达12.6米，主殿上有一种天然钟乳石，神似观音。③龙门飞瀑为国内最大的洞中瀑布，高50余米，宽26米。④龙宫漩塘，池水顺时针方向旋转，昼夜不停。

Among the numerous scenic spots in the Longgong Caves, the waterfilled karst cavern is particularly impressive. It is the most exquisite product of nature over tens of millions of years, with the fantastic formations of different stalactites shaped like an underground crystal palace. The water-filled cavern is five kilometers long. Its underground river divides the five-kilometer water cavern into five sections, which are known as the first, second, third, fourth and fifth dragon palaces respectively. The First Dragon Palace, located between the Tianchi Pool (Heavenly Pool) and the Bangke Rock (Clamshell Rock), is the lowest submerged section of the underground river, with a total length of 840 meters. In this section, large amount of stalactites vary in size. Some of them hang their heads downwards from the ceiling of the cavern, some heads touch the surface of the underground water, and some others grow downwards along the cavern walls. The longest diameter in the section is 40 meters and the shortest diameter is two meters. Its maximum height is up to 110 meters, while the minimum height is no more than 2 meters with a space that only allows a guided boat to pass by. The First Dragon Palace is divided into five cavern halls due to the space of the cavern and the width change of the river. The first hall is partially submerged, with more than a dozen stalactites hanging down from the roof of the cavern. These stalactites are exactly like the image of dragons, so the first hall is named the "Qunlong Yingbin Ting"(Hall of the Group of Dragons Welcoming Guests). The second hall is a splendid grand hall, where stalactites appear in different shapes, hanging from the roof of the cavern or grow on the cavern walls, just like true-to-life stalactite walls, so this hall is called the "Fudiao Bihua Ting"(Relief Fresco Hall). The other three halls are called the "Wulong Hubao Ting"(Hall of the Five Dragons Protecting Treasures), the "Shuijinggong Ting"(Hall of the Crystal Palace) and the "Gaoxia Yougu Ting"(Hall of High Gorges and Valleys) respectively. The Hall of the Crystal Palace occupies a space of more than 4,000 square meters with a water depth of 26 meters. The Hall of High Gorges and Valleys, also known as the Underground Lijiang River, is about 100 meters high and 200 meters long. The water in the halls remains cool and flows gently, while stalactites intersect one another, just like a forest.

在龙宫景区众多的景点中,龙宫水溶洞尤为引人注目。它是大自然经过几千万年精工雕琢而成的精品,钟乳景观千奇百怪,形似地下水晶宫殿。水溶洞总长度约为5公里。暗河水流把5公里长的水溶洞分为5段,分别称为一、二、三、四、五进龙宫。一进龙宫位于天池与蚌壳岩之间,是龙宫地下暗河的水平面最低伏流段,总长840米。在宫内,许多钟乳石大小不一,有的高悬空中,有的下接水面,还有的沿洞壁向下生长。洞体最宽达40米,窄处却只有2米,最高度达110米,最低处仅容引导船通行。因洞体和水流的宽窄变化,一进龙宫又分为5个洞厅。第一厅部分被淹没了,10条钟乳石从洞顶悬垂下来,酷似龙形,由此称为"群龙迎宾厅"。第二厅是一处辉煌宏大的厅堂,石钟乳形态各异,悬挂在洞顶,或长在洞壁上,像栩栩如生的钟乳石壁,故称之为"浮雕壁画厅"。其余的三个洞厅分别为:"五龙护宝厅""水晶宫殿厅""高峡幽谷厅"。"水晶宫殿厅"面积4000多平方平,水深26米。"高峡幽谷厅"又称为地下漓江,高约100米,长约200米。洞中水清洌,水流平缓,钟乳石交错如林。

The Second Dragon Palace, about 100 meters away from the exit of the First Dragon Palace, is over 540 meters in length. The whole palace is divided into four halls, with a 22-meter corridor connecting its third and fourth halls. This section is not only accessible by boat, but also walkable for visitors along some cavern trails. At present, the third, fourth and fifth palaces are not open to the public. So far as I know, in these palaces, there are stalactites all over with beautiful shapes. The landscape appears spectacular.

二进龙宫距一进龙宫出口约100米。该水洞长540多米,整个洞穴分为四个洞厅,三厅与四厅间有22米的廊道相通,洞内可以通船,人们还可以沿着一些洞厅小道穿行。目前,三、四、五进龙宫尚未开放。据我所知,在这些洞厅里,钟乳石遍布,造型优美,景观壮丽。

The Longgong Caves is cool in summer and warm in winter. It is suitable for year-around travel due to the temperature inside the caves. The water in the Longgong Caves flow through dozens of hills. They suddenly emerge from the surface of one small hill, then disappear underground and eventually merge into ponds and cascade downwards. Such a phenomenon is like a magic dragon that moves forward, appearing at one moment and disappearing next. Therefore, every gear on the 2nd day of the 2nd month of the lunar calendar, locals hold traditional ritual activities to honor the magic dragon and pray for good weather, peace and health.

龙宫水溶洞冬暖夏凉,洞内温度适宜全年旅游。龙宫的水流流经几十座山峰,忽而从一座小山地表流出,忽而潜入地底,最终聚而成潭,又瀑布般向下飞泻。这样的现象宛如游走的神龙,见首不见尾。由此,每年农历二月初二，当地居民都要举办传统的颂龙典礼活动，以祈求风调雨顺、平安健康。

  Well, so much for the my brief introduction to the Longgong Caves. Today we will take a guided boat to tour the central scenic section of the Longgong Caves, then go to the Second Dragon Palace and the scenic spot of the Dragon's Gate Waterfall, and finally pass the Qunfang Valley to the central section of the Xuantang Pool. The whole trip takes about half a day.

  龙宫的讲解就到此结束。今天我们将乘坐引导船先游览龙宫中心景区，然后前往二进龙宫、龙门飞瀑景区，最后经群芳谷到达漩塘中心区。整个游览大约需要半天时间。

Fanjing Mountain Nature Reserve
梵净山自然保护区

Fanjing Mountian Nature Reserve mainly covers Mt. Fanjing, the Taiping River and other natural landscape. With a total area of 567 square kilometers, the reserve is 2,572 meters above the sea level, 21 kilometers long from east to west and 27 kilometers wide from south to north. In addition, it is connected with Jiangkou, Yingjiang and Songtao, the three counties in Tongren of Guizhou. This area is the most important protected section in Guizhou, providing habitat for more than half of the province's protected plants and two-thirds of its protected animals. In 1986, it was listed as a National Nature Reserve. In the same year, it was included in the International Network of Biosphere Reserves.

梵净山景区主要由梵净山、太平河等自然景观组成。自然保护区总面积567平方公里，海拔2572米，南北长约27公里，东西宽约21公里，位于贵州铜仁市的江口、印江、松桃三县交界处。该区域是贵州省最重要的保护区，为全省一半以上的保护植物和三分之二的保护动物提供了栖息地。1986年，梵净山被列为国家级自然保护区，同年又入选国际生物圈保护区网。

Mount Fanjing is considered the first mountain in Guizhou. Prior to the Tang Dynasty, according to relevant textual researches, the mountain was called Sanshangu, Chenshan or Siqiongshan. It has been called Fanjingshan since the Ming Dynasty. Fanjing refers to "the state of Nirvana silence (wantaj-nirvanam), a condition beyond the limits of space and time, and life and dearth", and its name originated in the 16th century when the mountain became an important Buddhist shrine and dedicated to Maitreya, one of Bodhisattvas commonly referred to as "Pusa" in Chinese.

梵净山是贵州的第一山。根据相关考证,梵净山唐朝以前称"三山谷""辰山""思邛山",明代以后称"梵净山"。"梵净"是指超越时空和生死的涅槃寂静的境界,其名源于16世纪,此山当时已经成为重要的佛教圣地,为弥勒菩萨道场。

Mount Fanjing has a unique landscape, where peaks rise one higher than the other, dense forests cover everywhere and rare plants and animals are numerous. It intersects with a range of natural landscapes: spectacular hills and rocks, unique trees and flowers, rare animals, pleasant water and ancient monasteries. Here, it is suitable for sightseeing in four seasons on the mountain. In spring, azalea flowers are in blossom, turning the mountain into a blaze of colors; in summer, the vast forests are ideal places to escape the heat; in autumn, red leaves are pleasing to look at; in winter, thick snow covers spectacular peaks and rocks, giving them different shapes.

梵净山风光神奇,层峦叠嶂,森林茂密,珍稀动植物众多;各种自然景观与之交融:奇山、奇石、奇树、奇花、奇兽、奇水、奇庙!在这里,游览梵净山,四季皆宜。春天,杜鹃盛开,姹紫嫣红;夏天,莽莽林海是避暑消夏的理想场所;秋天,红色的秋叶赏心悦目;冬天,大雪覆盖奇峰怪石,显现出不同的姿态。

Golden Summit

Mount Fanjing has three golden summits. The Red-Cloud Summit is the essence of the mountain. To the left is the Age-Old Golden Summit, also known as Mt. Yuejing, 2,493 meters above the sea level. To the right is the third golden summit, the highest peak of the mountain, known as the Fenghuang Ridge, or the Ridge of Phoenix at 2,572 meters above the sea level. The Red-Cloud Summit looks like an isolated, towering rock peak, with its top that remains cloudy all year round. Every time when the sun rises, the surrounding clouds become brilliant and its summit is blazed with golden color. This cloud-wrapped peak is 94 meters in height. A path, made of hundreds of stone steps, leads from the bottom of the peak to its top and finally reaches the Multi-Layer Mushroom Rocks. The top of the isolated peak splits into two parts. Between the two parts is a cliff canyon known as the Jindao Gorge, which is about 20 meters in width. A bridge, known as Tianxianqiao, spans over the canyon and connects the two split huge rocks. On each of the two rocks stands a temple, one dedicated to Śākyamuni, and the other to Maitreya Buddha. As you stand on the summit, you can experience the primordial and mysterious nature of the temples hidden in the mountains. You can also see the scenery that disappears and reappears among clouds around. For instance, the Rock of the Prince and the Rock of Scripture Depository stand comfortably among the lush greenery; the Phoenix and the Xianguo hills are clustered by colorful floating clouds. Fortunately, you can see the Halo of Buddhism, also known as the Glory of Fanjing, which appears as a multicolored ring of light in the sky, with the shadow of the viewer in the middle of the ring. Besides, you can sit there happily all day long, watching the ever-changing sea of clouds that drift in and out of the sunlight like waves in the sea. Clouds may rise slowly, filling the sky. They may plunge into deep canyons like huge surging waves. They may crash into the cliffs or hide the mountain, making the peaks look like isolated islands.

梵净山有三座金顶。"红云金顶"是梵净山的精华所在。红云金顶左边为老金顶，又称月镜山，海拔2493米；右边是第三座金顶，为梵净山主峰，称为凤凰岭，海拔2572米。红云金顶看似一座孤立突兀的石峰，山顶常年云雾缭绕。每当日出，周围的云朵灿烂夺目，山顶闪耀着金色的光芒。这座云雾缭绕顶峰高94米。有一条由几百块石阶铺成的小道，从峰底通往峰顶，之后到达多层蘑菇岩。孤峰山顶裂为两半，中间是绝壁峡谷，名为"金刀峡"，宽约20米。一座名为天仙桥横跨峡谷，连接着两块裂开的巨石。在两巨石上各矗立着一座庙宇，一座供奉释迦佛，另一座供奉弥勒佛。站在峰顶，你可以体验到藏匿于深山中庙宇的古朴与神秘。你还可以观望周边云中时隐时现的景色，如：太子石、藏经石舒适地矗立在郁郁葱葱的绿树间；霞云飞彩簇拥着凤凰山、献果山。如若运气好，你还会看到佛光，又称为"梵净宝光"，像多彩的光环，出现在空中，在环影中还呈现出观看者的影子。此外，你可以整天开心地坐在那里，观赏变幻莫测的云海，像大海上的波浪在阳光下漂移。云海可能会慢慢升腾，遍及天际；它们可能会像滔滔巨浪那样跌入深谷；也可能会撞击悬崖，或淹没山峦，使山峰看起来像座孤岛。

Well, so much for my introduction to the Fanjing Mountain Nature Reserve. Today, our tour route goes like this: we start from the entrance of the reserve and take a reserve-van to Yu'ao and then take a cable-car from Yu'ao up to the Wanbao Rock, where there are only about 600 steps to reach the Golden Summit. If you have more energy to spare, you can hike up to the Age-Old Summit. Here are a few things to watch out for. Be sure not to look at the scenery while walking, and not to walk while looking at the scenery. The Golden Summit is a relatively small area. When the tour is over, please go down the mountain as soon as possible. We will meet you at the parking lot at 3 o'clock in the afternoon.

好了，梵净山介绍到此为止。今天，我们行走的线路是：从保护区的入口处出发，乘坐保护区车至鱼坳，再从鱼坳登索道缆车到万宝岩，步行约600步至金顶。体力好的，可以再登老金顶。注意：走路不看景，看景不走路；金顶上面积比较小，参观后，请尽快下山。下午3点在车场集合。

Zhusha Old Town
朱砂古镇

Zhusha Old Town is located in Wanshan District, Tongren City, Guizhou Province. Covering an area of 3.57 square kilometers, it was once the largest mercury deposit in China and the core area of mercury mines in Guizhou. However, over the past years, the mercury resources have become depleted. Faced with the depletion, local people have made full use of the natural landscape, tapped the mining culture and developed a new-type of tourism, successfully transforming the old town into a tourist destination for both domestic and foreign tourists.

朱砂古镇位于贵州省铜仁市万山区，总面积3.57平方公里。这里曾经是中国规模最大的汞矿地，也是贵州汞矿的核心区。然而，在过去的年月中，汞矿资源已经枯竭。面对枯竭困境，当地人充分利用自然景观，挖掘矿山文化，开发新型旅游，使其成功转型为国内外游客的旅游胜地。

Zhusha Old Town is rich in tourism resources. The 970-km mercury-mine tunnel, known as the Underground Great Wall, is considered to be the longest tunnel in the world. At present, the old tunnel sites have been repackaged with modern high-tech means, and the tunnels have been transformed into a fascinating landscape, such as the Dreamlike Time Tunnel, the Colorful Ink Paintings, as well as the Exciting Journey Through the Veil of Time.

朱砂古镇旅游资源丰富。970公里的汞矿矿道,有着"地下长城"的美誉,是世界上最长的矿道。目前,景区运用现代高科技手段,对矿道遗址全新包装,把矿道打造成了精彩的景观,如:梦如幻般的时光隧道、色彩斑斓的水墨丹青、激情穿越时空。

As visitors enter the mines, they will find yourself as if in a wonderland. Nearby are small bridges, under which are streams, where fish swim happily. In the distance, colorful lights are mysteriously overflowing. As you move along the tunnel, the light images vary through the delightful illusion. Outside the mercury tunnels, glass-bottomed walkways and glass-bottomed over-bridges have been built along the cliffs, allowing visitors to enjoy the historical culture and the natural scenery of the mountains.

游客进入矿洞,仿佛置身于仙境。近处,小桥流水,鱼儿游乐。远处,灯光五彩缤纷,溢彩神秘;在矿道,步移景异,幻化莫测,令人欣喜。在汞矿矿道外,沿悬崖峭壁修建了玻璃栈道和玻璃天桥,可让游客欣赏到历史文化和山上的自然风光。

In 2001, the locals carried out a large-scale restoration of the mercury mine sites and old buildings in the old town. As a result, a large number of historical sites have been preserved, including the Heidongzi, Xianrendong and Yunnanti and other ancient mining sites, as well as the Apartment Buildings for Soviet Union Experts, Yuanyang Building, Xiangqian Mercury Mining Company and the British-French Mercury Mining Company. Their efforts aim not only to create a nostalgic town that recalls the unforgettable years from the 1950s to the 1970s, but also to make it an ideal place for leisure, vacation and sightseeing.

2001年,当地人对汞矿遗址和古镇旧建筑进行了大规模的修复工作,由此保存了大量的历史遗迹，包括黑硐子、仙人硐、云南梯等古代采矿遗址，还有苏联专家楼、鸳鸯楼、湘黔汞矿公司和英法水银公司。其目的不仅要打造一座怀旧小镇，追忆20世纪50至70年代的难忘岁月，而且要使之成为休闲、度假、观光的理想场所。

Entering the old town, all you can see are Chairman Mao's quotations written on the walls of the Soviet-style buildings, a post office, grain and cooking-oil stores... The neighborhoods where the families of the former mercury miners lived remain the same as before. There, old objects such as thermoses, kettles, barn lamps, sewing machines, bicycles and so on are typically placed in the houses to remind visitors of the old days. Particularly, the eye-catching architecture is the grand auditorium, the canteens of the people's commune and the apartment buildings for the Soviet Union experts. In addition, the echoes of the once inspirational slogans and classic revolutionary songs resonate, taking visitors back to the extraordinary years between the 1950s and 1970s. During that period, when the national economy was in dire straits, Guizhou mercury mines adopted the unconventional and intensive mining methods, over-fulfilling their tasks month after month and setting new industrial highs year after year.

进入古镇，目之所见是苏式建筑墙上的毛主席语录、邮局、粮油店……以前汞矿职工家属住宅区仍然如旧。在那里，房屋里通常放置着保温杯、水壶、马灯、缝纫机、自行车等老物件，让游客恍若想起过去的日子。格外醒目的建筑群有大礼堂、人民公社食堂、苏联专家楼。此外，曾经鼓舞人心的口号和经典的革命歌曲在回荡，把游客带入20世纪50至70年代的不平凡的岁月。当时，国民经济处于极度困难时期，贵州汞矿采取了超常规、集约化开采方式，月月超额完成任务，年年创造产业新高。

The construction and development of Zhusha Old Town and mercury mining in Guizhou Province is a typical epitome of the development history of Chinese mining industry. Due to the protection and development of the existing mines and cultural relics in the old town, the number of tourists in the scenic area continues to rise, thus driving the whole Wanshan District to glow with new vitality. In 2006, the town was listed as a national cultural relic protection unit. In 2012, it was listed in the Tentative List of China's World Cultural Heritage. In May 2014, it was classified as a national 4A-level tourist attraction.

朱砂古镇和贵州省汞矿的建设和发展，是中国矿业发展史上的典型缩影。由于对古镇现有矿山和文物的保护与开发，景区游客人数不断上升，从而带动整个万山区焕发出新的活力。2006年，古镇被列入国家重点文物保护单位，2012年被列入《中国世界文化遗产预备名录》，2014年5月被评为国家AAAA级旅游景区。

Well, so much for my brief introduction to Zhusha Old Town. In a few minutes, we will start our excursion, which will take four hours. Please make sure to follow the group as a local tour guide will accompany us and give a detailed account of the town's history and culture.

好了，朱砂古镇的介绍到此结束。我们很快就要开始游览了，时间为四小时。请务必随团同行，有当地导游陪同，他还要详细介绍小镇的历史与文化。

⑧ Zhangjiang Scenic Area in Libo County
荔波樟江风景区

Zhangjiang Scenic Area, around 314 kilometers from Guiyang, is located in Libo County south of Guizhou. In this scenic area, ridges and hills stretch incessantly, and rivers and streams flow in all directions. The scenery, dominated by the vast forests and waterscapes of Zhangjiang water system, presents the perfect unity and charm of the karst forest ecological environment, which is interwoven with the unique, elegant, primitive, wild, rugged, and tranquil natural beauty. In addition, the Bouyei, Yao and Miao ethnic minorities live around the scenic area, and visitors can immediately feel the integration of local ethnic culture, customs and landscapes.

荔波樟江风景区位于贵州南部的荔波县，距贵阳市约314公里。风景区峰峦叠嶂，溪流纵横，以樟江水系的水景和浩瀚的森林为主体，呈现出喀斯特森林生态环境的完美统一和神奇魅力，与奇、峻、古、野、险、幽的自然美景交织在一起。此外，风景区四周居住着布依族、瑶族、苗族少数民族，游客会立刻感受到当地民族文化、风土人情、山水风光的融合。

The scenic area is mainly composed of three scenic sections: the Daqikong Scenic Section (Large Seven-Arch Bridge Section), the Xiaoqikong Scenic Section (Small Seven-Arch Bridge Section) and the Shuichunhe Gorge (Gorge of the Shuichun River). The Daqikong Scenic

Section is named after a large seven-arch ancient bridge, which is located in the scenic area. This section is mainly composed of primitive forests, canyons, and underground rivers and lakes. The main scenic spots include the Large Seven-Arch Ancient Bridge, the Mengtan Pool (Pool of Dreams), the Shanshen Gorge (Gorge of the Hill Deity) and the Tiansheng Bridge. Typically, within the gorge there stand towering cliffs, which are connected by countless stalactites and layers of green forests.

荔波樟江区风景区主要由大七孔、小七孔、水春河峡谷三个景区组成。大七孔景区是以位于景区的一座大七孔古桥而命名的，景区以原始森林、峡谷、伏流、地下湖为主体，主要景点有大七孔桥、梦潭、山神峡、天生桥。其峡谷峭壁耸立，连接着无数钟乳石和层层翠林。

The Shuichunhe Gorge, located in the upper reaches of Zhangjiang River, is actually a canyon, with steep peaks facing each other and the dense shade of trees obscuring the sun. The river in the upper reaches remains calm, and many tourists usually like to go boating on the river or stroll along the paths by the river to enjoy the surrounding scenery. However, as the water flows downstream, it immediately becomes turbulent and rolls down over rapids. The lower reaches are an ideal place for surfing and rafting.

位于樟江上游的水春河峡谷实际上是一条峡谷，其险峰对峙，浓荫蔽日。水春河上游清幽宁静，许多游客往往会在河上荡舟，或沿着河边小路漫步，观赏周边的景色；然而，河水到了下游，则湍流翻卷，奔驰急流，是冲浪、漂流的理想之地。

The Xiaoqikong Scenic Section is located in a deep valley, which is one kilometer wide and 12 kilometers long. It is a national 4A-level tourist attraction and a world heritage site. It is named after a small seven-arch bridge built over Xiangshui River (River of Sound water) in the Daoguang years of the Qing Dynasty. The whole scenery integrates hills, rivers, forests, caves, lakes and waterfalls. The Hanbi Pool remains graceful and tranquil. The Laya Waterfalls provides a view of water gushing downwards. The Sixty-Eight-Level Cascades look like the stage tier upon tier. The Guibei Hill is covered with primitive forests, and the Wild Boar Woods feature the karst funnel forest. In addition, the Water Forest allows streams to crisscross. The Yuanyang Lake is inlaid with dense forests. The Wolong Pool appears blue and deep, and the Xiangshui River passes through the scenic area. In particular, the Guibei Hill, the Wild Boar Forest, the Water Forest and the Yuanyang Lake are regarded as the pride of the Zhangjiang Scenery in Libo County. Over Guibei Hill extensively grows wild Guibei bamboo, a kind of monstera deliciosa. There, rocks appear towering, grotesque peaks look rugged, vines are twining, and age-old trees reach into the sky. The Karst Funnel Forest, also known as the Wild Boar Forest, once had many wild boars running about in its territory. There, the forest densely extends layer by layer from the bottom of the karst funnel to the edge of the distant hills. As for the Water Forest, it belongs to the unusual type of the water forest belt of the karst landform. There, hundreds of woods, including more than a dozen exotic trees, all grow on underwater stones and take root in riverbeds through the stones. Stones are in the water, on the stones grow trees, and the trees take root in the water. So by a look at the forest from a distance, it looks like a forest floating on water. The Yuanyang Lake is composed of two large lakes and four small lakes, presenting a wonderful water network, where the lakes are quite and peaceful. Waterways extend in all directions and various colorful plants grow around the lakes. While boating on the lakes, visitors usually feel as if they live in complete isolation from the outside world.

小七孔景区位于宽仅1公里、长12公里的幽深山谷里,是国家

AAAA级旅游景区，也是世界自然遗产。景区名字源于清朝道光年间在响水河上修建的一座小七孔古桥。整个风景区集山、水、林、洞、湖泊和瀑布于一体，涵碧潭柔美恬静，拉雅瀑布飞流狂泻，六十八级瀑布层层叠叠，原始森林覆盖龟背山，野猪林像喀斯特漏斗森林。此外，水上森林溪水纵横交错，鸳鸯湖上镶嵌着茂密的森林，卧龙潭水蓝深邃，响水河流经整个风景区。尤其是龟背山、野猪林、水上森林、鸳鸯湖，是樟江风景区的精华。在龟背山上漫山野生着无数龟背竹；在那里，岩石高耸，怪石嶙峋，藤萝缠绕，古木参天。喀斯特漏斗森林也称野猪林，曾经有许多野猪在林间奔突；那里的丛林密集，重重叠叠，从漏斗底部延伸到遥远的山沿。水上森林属于罕见的喀斯特地貌水林带。那里的成百上千的树木，包括十多种珍奇树木，都生长在水中的顽石上，又透过顽石扎根于河床。石在水中，石上有树，树植于水，所以远远望去，宛如是漂浮在水面上的森林。鸳鸯湖是由两个大湖、四个小湖组成，呈现出一个奇妙的水网。那里的湖面幽静，水道四通八达，各种五颜六色的植物生长在湖泊周围。游客在湖中荡舟之时，常常会有一种与世隔绝的感觉。

So much for the introduction to the Zhangjiang Scenic Area. Today, we are going to tour the Scenery of the Xiaoqikong and Daqikong sections. We first enter the Xiaoqikong Scenic Section from its west gate, where we take a battery vehicle to visit such places as the Wolong Pool, the Yuanyang Lake, the Cuigu Waterfall, the Water Forest and the Xiaoqikong Bridge. Then, we take a carriage to the gate of the Daqikong Scenic Section, where we walk through the primitive forests, gorges and underground rivers. The whole trip takes about three hours. I'd like to advise you to bring sandals or slippers in case we wade through some water-filled paths, while visiting the Daqikong Scenic Section.

好了，樟江景区介绍到此为止。今天，我们将游览小七孔景区和大七孔景区。我们先从小七孔景区西门进小七孔景区，在景区内乘坐电瓶车，游览卧龙潭、鸳鸯湖、翠谷瀑布、水上森林、小七孔桥；然后乘马车到大七孔景区入口处，在那里步行游览原始森林、峡谷、地下河道。游览时间共 3 小时。建议大家最好带上凉鞋或拖鞋，因为在游览大七孔景区时，有些地方要蹚水而行。

Chishui Danxia Scenic Area
赤水丹霞

Danxia is a term in geography. It refers to the "red stone conglomerate" that forms isolated peaks or steep, grotesque rocks due to long periods of weathering and water erosion. As for Chishui Danxia, it is located in the south of Chishui City, Guizhou Province. It covers a total area of 36.3 square kilometers, with grotesque and beautiful Danxia landforms, clusters of waterfalls, sea-like bamboo forests, lush spinulosa-fern plants and vast forests.

丹霞是地理学上的术语，意指"红色砂岩经长期风化和水蚀，而形成的孤立的山峰和陡峭的奇岩怪石"。赤水丹霞位于贵州省赤水市南部，总面积36.3平方公里，区内瀑布成群、丹霞奇丽、竹林似海、桫椤繁茂、森林壮阔。

Chishui Danxia is a representative of Danxia landform in early-adolescence. It is considered to be the largest and most beautiful Danxia landform in China. The development of its formation can be roughly divided into four stages, namely, palaeolake deposition, uplift and denudation, very young Danxia and adolescent Danxia. On August 2, 2010, Chishui Danxia, along with other famous Danxia landforms, such as Mount Langshan in Hunan, Mount Danxia in Guangdong, Taining in Fujian, Mount Longhu in Jiangxi and Mount Jianglang in Zhejiang, was inscribed on the World

Heritage List under the name of "China Danxia".

赤水丹霞是青年早期丹霞地貌的代表，是全国最大、最美丽壮观的丹霞地貌，其形成大致可以分为四个阶段，即：古湖沉积期、抬升剥蚀期、幼年丹霞期、青年丹霞期。2010年8月2日，赤水丹霞与湖南崀山、广东丹霞山、福建泰宁、江西龙虎山、浙江江郎山等著名丹霞地貌组合成为"中国丹霞"，被列入《世界遗产名录》。

Prior to the 1920s, there were few sightseeing records of Chishui Danxia landform. After the 1930s, relevant records appeared one after another. Since the 1980s, a system of demarcating relevant landscape protection areas within Chishui Danxia landform has been gradually established, forming a tourist destination with Danxia landform, waterfalls, bamboo seas, lush spinulosa-fern plants and virgin forests as its main features. In addition, this area is combined with historical sites related to the Long March and other local cultural relics. Successively, Chishui Danxia Tourist Area has been approved as the national tourist attraction, national geopark, national forest park, as well as the nature reserve of China.

20世纪20年代以前，几乎很少有赤水丹霞地貌的观赏记录。30年代以后，相关记录才陆续问世。80年代以后，在丹霞地貌范围内逐步建立了制度，规划了相关景观保护区界，形成了以丹霞地貌、瀑布、竹海、桫椤、原始森林为主要特色的旅游地。同时，该地区还融合了长征历史遗址和其他地方文物古迹。该旅游地先后被批准为国家级风景名胜区、国家地质公园、国家森林公园、中国自然保护区。

Chishui Danxia Tourist Area is divided into two parks, namely, Datong–Bing'an Park and Lianghekou–Yuanhou Park.

赤水丹霞旅游区分为两个园区，即：大同—丙安园区、两河口—元厚园区。

Datong–Bing'an Park is divided into three scenic sections, namely, Sidonggou Scenic Section, Yangjiayan Scenic Section and Bing'an Scenic Section. The park is mainly composed of Danxia landform, waterfalls and relict plants, with main attractions, such as Danxia cliffs, Danxia pillars, Tiansheng Bridge (Danxia Stone Arch) and waterfall landscape (Sidonggou Waterfall Group, Baizhangwulian Waterfalls and Yangjiayan Waterfalls). In addition, there are many historical and cultural resources, including Bing'an Ancient Town and the old sites where the Red Army crossed Chishui River for four times.

大同—丙安园区分为四洞沟、杨家岩和丙安三个景区。该园区由丹霞地貌、瀑布、孑遗植物组成，主要景点有丹霞崖壁、丹霞石柱、天生桥（丹霞石拱）、瀑布景观（四洞沟瀑布群、百丈五连瀑布、杨家岩瀑布）。此外，园区历史文化资源丰富，有丙安古镇、红军四渡赤水旧址等。

Lianghekou–Yuanhou Park is divided into two scenic sections, namely, Shiziyan Scenic Section and Guiyuanlin Scenic Section. This park is also mainly composed of Danxia landform, waterfalls and relict plants, with main attractions, such as Danxia cliffs, Danxia pillars, Danxia peaks, waterfalls (Panlong Waterfall Group, Changshuiyan Waterfalls, Baizhangya Waterfalls, etc). In addition, the park has paleo-collapse deposits, as well as lakes and marshes.

两河口—元厚园区分为两个景区，即：狮子岩景区和桂园林景区。该园区同样由丹霞地貌、瀑布、孑遗植物组成，主要景点有丹霞崖壁、丹霞石柱、丹霞石峰、瀑布景观（盘龙瀑布群、昌水岩瀑布、百丈崖瀑布等）。此外，园区还有古崩塌堆积体和湖沼景观。

Among many attractions, Sidonggou Waterfall Group is particularly impressive. The waterfall group refers to the four falls located along a

4-kilometer-long stream valley in Sidonggou Scenic Section. The first waterfalls are called the Water-Curtain-Cave Falls, behind which is a natural stone cave, known as the Water-Curtain Cave Heaven. The waterfalls are 37.5 meters wide and 31 meters high, creating a thunderous sound and imposing vigor. The second waterfalls, called the Moon-Pool Falls, are 42 meters wide and 10 meters high, looking like a silvery half moon. Under the waterfalls is a deep pool, which is like a full moon. The third waterfalls, called the Flying-Frog-Cliff Falls, are 26 meters high and 43 meters wide. The waterfalls are divided into two parts by a stone in the shape of a frog, making an image of "the snake and frog splashing in the water". The fourth waterfalls, 60 meters high and 23 meters wide, are the largest falls among Sidonggou Waterfall Group. The thunderous roar of the waterfalls deeply touch the hearts of visitors, even when they are standing more than 100 meters away. The fast-flowing waterfalls, which plunge over the cliffs, generate a large amount of flying water droplets. Within 30 or 40 meters of the waterfalls, the camera lens will be completely covered by dense droplets, making it impossible to take pictures. All the four waterfalls are in different shapes and poses. Zhao Puchu, a master of calligraphy, once visited Sidonggou Scenic Section. After his visit, he wrote down four Chinese characters "Si Dong Xian Jing", meaning Four Waterfalls in Wonderland.

在众多景点中，四洞沟瀑布群尤为值得提及。瀑布群指的是四座瀑布，位于四洞沟景区一段约四公里长的溪谷间。一洞叫"水帘洞瀑布"，瀑布后面是天然石穴，取名"水帘洞天"；瀑布宽37.5米、高31米，声若雷鸣，气势万钧。二洞叫"月亮潭瀑布"，瀑布宽42米、高10米，像银色半月；瀑布下是深潭，则像一轮满月。三洞叫"飞蛙崖瀑布"，瀑布高26米、宽43米；瀑布被石蛙一分为二，构成一幅"蛇蛙戏水图"。四洞叫"白龙潭瀑布"，是四洞沟瀑布群中最大的瀑布；瀑布高60米、宽23米；即使站在100多米之外，雷鸣般的轰鸣声常让人感到震撼；飞湍的瀑流从悬崖直冲而下，形成大量的飞沫；在距离瀑布三四十米的地方，密集的水滴会打湿相机镜头，根本无法拍照。四座瀑布以不同的形态出现在游客面前。书法大师赵朴初曾游览四洞沟风景区。游览之余，他挥毫写下"四洞仙境"四字。

Well, so much for my brief introduction to Chishui Danxia Scenic Area. It is suitable to visit Chishui Danxia in all seasons, and summer is the high season. Local travel agencies are always ready to recommend one-day, two-day or multi-day tours of Chishui Danxia. For example, if visitors have only two days available, it is recommended to go to Sidonggou Scenic Section and Bing'an Ancient Town on the first day, and then go to the Great Waterfalls and Yanziyan National Forest Park on the second day. Since most of the scenic sites are mountainous area with slopes and narrow roads, please wear comfortable hiking shoes when starting out trips.

好了，赤水丹霞景区讲解到此结束。赤水丹霞游览四季皆宜，夏季是旅游旺季。当地的旅行社随时会向游客推荐赤水丹霞一日游、两日游，或多日游的旅游线路。例如，如果游客只有两天空闲时间，建议第一天去四洞沟景区和丙安古镇，第二天去大瀑布和燕子岩国家森林公园。景点多在山地，坡多路窄，出发时请穿上舒适的徒步鞋。

⑩ Zunyi Conference Site
遵义会议会址

Zunyi Conference Site is around 160 kilometers away from Guiyang City and about five kilometers southwest of the Zunyi railway station on the Ziyi Road. Apart from the visit to the Zunyi Conference Site, we will also visit the Former Site of the General Political Department of the Red Army, the Former Place of the Soviet National Bank, and Comrade Mao Zedong's Former Residence when the Zunyi Conference was in session. Please walk with me, and I will give you a detailed account of the history related to the site. The whole trip takes one hour and a half.

遵义会议会址距贵阳市大约160公里，位于遵义火车站西南5公里处的子尹路上。今天，我们除了参观会议会址，还要去红军总政治部旧址、苏维埃国家银行旧址，以及毛泽东同志在遵义会议期间的住所。请跟我来，我边走边详细介绍与会议地址有关的历史。整个行程需要一个半小时。

English Tour Guide for *Yunnan, Guizhou, Sichuan and Chongqing* | 云贵川渝英语导游讲解词

Zunyi Conference Site

Here we are at the entrance of the Zunyi Conference Site. Originally, it was the private residence of Bo Huizhang, the second division commander of the 25th army of the Kuomintang army. The site construction is a two-storey wood-and-brick building, with the length of 25.19 meters and the height of 12 meters. Constructed in the early 1930s, the building remained as the city's most magnificent architecture in the 1930s. Its entrance gate faces the street. On the two sides of the gate, there used to be eight stores, which belonged to Bo Huizhang's family. In the middle of the stores is a decorated archway. Right in the middle under the eaves of the archway hangs a huge plaque with six huge gilded characters "Zun Yi Hui Yi Hui Zhi"(Zunyi Conference Site). It was written by Mao Zedong in November 1964, and the characters are vigorous.

现在，我们到了遵义会议会址入口处。这原是国民党军第25军第二师师长柏辉章的私邸，会址建筑是一幢砖木结构两层楼房，长25.19米，通高12米。该楼房建于20世纪30年代初，是当时最宏伟的建筑。会址

大门临街，门两侧曾经为八间铺面，为柏辉章的商店。铺面居中是一座牌楼，牌楼屋檐下正中高悬巨匾，匾上刻有六个巨大的金色汉字"遵义会议会址"，这是毛泽东于1964年11月题写的，字字苍劲有力。

The Zunyi Conference was held in Zunyi of Guizhou. It was a very important enlarged meeting convened by the Political Bureau of the Central Committee of the Communist Party of China (CPC). In the CPC history, the conference was a crucial turning point. In January 1934, the Fifth Plenary Session of the Sixth Central Committee of the CPC was held in Ruijin of Jiangxi. After the session, the implementation of the Wang Ming's policy of the "Left" Adventurism had been further strengthened in the CPC various tasks, as well as the base areas. This kind of the wrong leadership caused great losses to the revolutionary forces, resulting in the shrinking of the revolutionary bases and the failure of the Fifth Counter-Campaign Against Encirclement and Suppression. Under these circumstances, the Central Red Army had to retreat from Jiangxi in October 1934 and began the world-renowned Long March. However, on the initial stage of the Long March, Bo Gu and other leaders made a military mistake, adopting the tactics of flightism, which once again caused heavy losses to the Red Army. At the critical moment of the revolution, the CPC Central Committee accepted Mao Zedong's correct opinion, abandoned the plan to advance to Western Hunan and marched towards Guizhou instead. In January 1935, the Red Army arrived at Zunyi. On January 15, the CPC Central Committee held an enlarged political bureau conference in a meeting room on the second floor of this residential building. The conference aimed to solve the extremely urgent military issues. Mao Zedong made an important speech at the conference, criticizing the "Left" leaders' mistakes in the military line. The conference corrected military mistakes of the "Left" adventurism and adopted several important resolutions. Thus, the Zunyi Conference ended the domination of Wang Ming's "Left" adventurism in the Central Committee of CPC and established a new central leadership with Mao Zedong as the core. At such a crucial moment, the conference saved the Party and the Red Army. From then on, the Chinese revolution advanced along the road of victory. Accordingly, the Zunyi Conference is a monument in the history of the Chinese revolution, and Zunyi City also becomes known far and wide for the Zunyi Conference.

遵义会议在贵州遵义召开，这是中共中央政治局召开的一次极为重要的扩大会议。在中国共产党历史上，这次会议是一个生死攸关的转折点。1934年1月，中共六届五中全会在江西瑞金召开。会后，在中国共产党和根据地的各项工作中，王明"左"倾冒险主义变本加厉地推行。这种错误的领导使革命力量损失惨重，造成革命根据地日益萎缩，导致第五次反"围剿"失败。这种情况迫使中央红军于1934年10月撤出江西，开始了举世闻名的长征。长征初期，博古等领导人在军事上又犯了逃跑主义错误，使红军再次蒙受重大损失。在革命的紧急关头，党中央接受了毛泽东的正确建议，放弃向湘西进军的计划，转而向贵州进军。1935年1月，红军到达遵义。1月15日，中共中央在这栋住宅的二楼会议室召开了政治局扩大会议，解决迫在眉睫的军事问题。毛泽东在会上做了重要发言，他批评了"左"倾领导在军事路线上的错误。会议纠正了"左"倾冒险主义在军事上的错误，并通过了多项重要决定。遵义会议结束了王明"左"倾冒险主义在中共中央的统治，确立了毛泽东在中共中央和红军的领导地位。在这样的关键时刻，会议挽救了党和红军。从此以后，中国革命沿着胜利的道路前进。遵义会议是中国革命史上的一座丰碑，遵义市也因遵义会议而远近闻名。

Guizhou Province
贵州省

Here we are at the meeting room. It used to be the host's small living room. The room is rectangular with an area of 27 square meters. Basically, the interior furnishings are what they looked alike at the time of the conference. In the center of the ceiling hangs a kerosene lamp hooded by a flouncing lampshade. The west wall is a glass window with pieces of glass embedded in the wooden frame. There are two wall cabinets on the east wall, and one of which is embedded with a full-length mirror. Besides, there is a wall clock on the same wall. In the center of the room there is a chestnut-colored rectangular table, surrounded by 20 folding armchairs for the conference participants. These armchairs are made of wooden frame and woven with rattan. Under the table is a charcoal-burning brazier, which was used for heating in those days.

好了，我们到了遵义会议的会议室。这原为房主的小客厅。会议室呈长方形，面积27平方米。室内陈设基本上是当年开会时的原貌。天花板中央挂着一盏煤油灯，上面罩着荷叶边灯罩；西壁是玻璃窗，木制框架内嵌有一排排玻璃；东壁有两个壁柜，其中一个壁柜上嵌着一面穿衣镜。此外，东壁还有一台挂钟。屋子中央有一张栗色的长方桌，四周围着20张折叠式扶手椅，供参会人员使用。扶手椅是木制的，用藤条编织而成。长方桌下有一个烧炭的火盆，为当时取暖所用。

After the founding of New China, people began to restore this site to its original status. In October 1955, it was officially open to the public. In March 1961, the State Council added the Site of the Zunyi Conference to the list of the first batch of the National Key Cultural Protection Units. In December 2005, it became a national 4A-level tourist attraction. In addition, it remains as a national attraction of the red tourism. Well, so much for my brief introduction to the Zunyi Conference Site. Now let's move to the Exhibition Hall of the Zunyi Conference Site.

中华人民共和国成立后,会址的原状得以恢复。1955年10月,会址正式对外开放。1961年3月,国务院公布遵义会址为全国第一批重点文物保护单位。2005年12月,会址成为国家AAAA级景区。此外,会址还是全国红色旅游经典景区。好了,遵义会议会址的讲解结束,现在我们一道去会址的陈列馆吧。

⑪ Hailongtun Fortress
海龙屯

Hailongtun Fortress, located at the top of Mount Longyan, is about 28 kilometers northwest of Zunyi City, Guizhou Province. It is the ruins of a Tusi fortress dating back to the Song and Ming dynasties.

海龙屯位于龙岩山巅，距离贵州省遵义市西北约28公里，是一处宋明时期的土司城堡的遗址。

Hailongtun Fortress is the best preserved military fortress in China and one of the most complete medieval military fortresses in the world. During the Wanli period of the Ming Dynasty (1573–1620), Hailongtun Fortress was the main battlefield, which was known as the "Battle of Pingbo". The largest and most deadly battles took place here at the same time.

海龙屯是我国目前保存最完整的军事古堡，也是世界上最完整的中世纪军事城堡之一。明代万历年间（1573—1620），海龙屯是"平播之役"的主战场，规模最大、伤亡最惨重的战役同时发生在这里。

Hailongtun Fortress was the last stronghold of the Yang's 700-year rule in Bozhou. According to historical document, Yang's ancestral home was Taiyuan of Shanxi. At the end of the Tang Dynasty, Yang Rui led an army into Bozhou to recover the land occupied by the Nanzhao army. In the Southern Song Dynasty, Yang Can, the 13th ruler of the Yang's regime, unified Bozhou militarily. During the Wanli period of the Ming Dynasty, Yang Yinglong, the 29th ruler of the Yang's regime, rebelled. In order to resist the government forces, he mobilized his servants and craftsmen to expand the fortress on Mount Longyan. Meanwhile, he had his men construct nine passes at the front and rear of the mountain. In addition, around the top of Mount Longyan, which was 5,000 meters long and 5,000 meters wide, he built three walls, including an earthen wall and a moon-shaped wall to protect the fortress and strengthen the defense. Inside the fortress, new buildings were constructed, such as multi-story buildings, an ancestral clan shrine, warehouses, barracks and water dungeons. The stone walls were connected to the main gates, the bridleways joined with one another, and fortress battlements stretched for more than five kilometers along the mountain. However, as the Ming army approached Bozhou and besieged the fortress for a long time, it became the main battlefield. Finally, along with the end of Yang's rule in Bozhou, the fortress lost its previous glamour.

海龙屯是播州杨氏政权七百年统治的后期据点。据文献记载，杨氏祖籍是山西太原。唐末，杨瑞率兵入播，收复南诏军占据的土地。南宋，杨氏第13代播州统治者杨粲在军事上统一了播州。明万历年间，杨氏第29代统治者杨应龙起兵造反，遂调集役夫工匠，扩建龙岩屯上的城堡，筑前后九座关隘，以抵抗官兵。此外，他在长宽各5000米的龙岩山顶围筑土城、月城等三重城墙，用于保护城堡和加强防御。城堡内还建造了新的建筑，如：楼房、家庙、仓库、兵营、水牢。石墙与关隘相连，与马道互通，城堞随山势绵延5000余米。然而，随着明军逼近播州，并持久围困城堡，海龙屯成为主战场。最终，随着杨氏在播州统治的终结，城堡也失去了昔日的风采。

Since then, for more than 400 years, Hailongtun Fortress has been lying quietly on the Mount Longyan. At present, it has become an important historical place of interest in Qianbei. Within a radius of five kilometers, there are a number of historical sites, such as Tongzhu Pass, Tiezhu Pass, Feilong Pass, Feifeng Pass, Chaotian Pass, Feihu Pass, Wan'an Pass, Xiguan Pass, Yunfeng Tower, as well as the water dungeons, the gold treasury house, the silver treasury house, gunpowder pools, an embroidery building, the drill ground and other sites.

自从那时起，400多年来，海龙屯默默无闻地静卧于龙岩山上。如今，此地成了黔北的重要的历史名胜。在方圆5公里内，有铜柱关、铁柱关、飞龙关、飞凤关、朝天关、飞虎关、万安关、西关、云凤楼，以及水牢、金库、银库、火药池、绣花楼、校场坝等遗址。

Hailongtun Fortress was originally a Tusi town, which integrated the passes, military fortresses, mountains with Tusi headquarters. The highest point of the fortress is 1,354 meters above the sea level, while the lowest is at altitude of 974 meters. The flat ground around the fortress is about 1.59 square kilometers. At that time, it was constructed by combining the experience of the Yang's mountain fortress defense with the popular urban construction concept in the Central Plains. For example, the central axis was symmetrical, and the main hall was in the middle, all of which indicated the elements of the architectural concept of the Central Plains. The Yang's experience in the construction of the defensive fortress even influenced the building of the Diaoyu Town in Hechuan County, as well as the construction of many fortresses and villages in that area during the Ming and Qing dynasties. From this point of view, Hailongtun Fortress can be regarded as an outstanding example of mountain architecture in Southwest China.

海龙屯原是集关、堡、山、土司衙署于一体的土司城，屯上最高点海拔1354米，屯下海拔974米，屯顶平阔，面积约1.59平方公里。当时的修建融合了杨氏山城防御的经验，以及中原普遍流行的筑城理念。如：中轴线对称、正堂居中，这些显示了中原建筑理念的元素。杨氏城堡防务建设的经验甚至影响了合川钓鱼城的修建，以及明清时代该地区许多堡寨的建设。从这个角度上讲，海龙屯可以说是中国西南山地建筑的杰出典范。

In addition, Hailongtun Fortress has witnessed the evolution of the Jimi System to the Tusi Chieftain System and then to the Bureaucratization of Native Officers. Particularly, it witnessed the glory and demise of the Bozhou regime under the Yang's leadership. Therefore, from the perspective of archaeology, the excavation of Hailongtun Fortress is of great historic significance for the study of the Tusi Chieftain System in Southwest China. In 1982, Hailongtun Fortress was listed as a cultural relic protection unit at provincial level. In 2001, it was classified as a national key cultural relic protection unit. In 2015, it was officially listed as the World Cultural Heritage Site by UNESCO.

此外，海龙屯见证了由"羁縻之制"到"土司制度"，再到"改土归流"的演变过程，尤其见证了杨氏家族统领下播州的辉煌与覆灭。因此，从考古学角度上讲，海龙屯的发掘对研究我国西南土司制度具有重要的历史意义。1982年，海龙屯被列为省级文物保护单位，2001年晋升为全国重点文物保护单位，2015年被联合国教科文组织正式列为世界文化遗产。

Well, so much for my introduction to Hailongtun Fortress. The following is our schedule for tomorrow. Gather in Zunyi Tourist Center at 9:30 a.m. and go to Hailongtun Fortress by bus. Arrive at the site at 10:30 and return to Zunyi Tourist Center at 2:30 p.m. Wish you all a pleasant journey!

好了，海龙屯的介绍到此结束。以下是明天的日程安排。上午9点半在遵义游客集散中心集合，乘车前往海龙屯；10点半到达观光地点；下午两点半返回遵义游客集散中心。祝大家游览愉快！

The Center of the Tea Sea in Fenggang County
凤冈茶海之心

The Center of the Tea Sea is located in Yong'an Town, Fenggang County, Guizhou Province. The center has been classified as a national 4A-level tourist attraction and also has won the following titles, such as the National Demonstration Site of Agricultural Tourism, the National Demonstration Site of Rural Tourism and Leisure Agriculture (new forms of agricultural production and management) and one of the Top Ten Agricultural Tourism Attractions in Guizhou.

茶海之心位于贵州省凤冈县永安镇境内,是国家AAAA级旅游景区,并荣获以下多项称号:"全国农业旅游示范点""全国休闲农业与乡村旅游示范点""贵州十佳农业旅游景区"。

The center covers an area of 69 square kilometers, where an average altitude is 1,000 meters, and an average annual temperature is 14℃. There is no severe cold in winter, nor extreme heat in summer. Here, the tea plantations form a fine contrast with the pine forests, that is, tea plantations are in the forests, the forests grow in the tea plantations, and teahouses can been seen everywhere.

景区占地面积为69平方公里,平均海拔1000米,年均气温14℃,冬无严寒,夏无酷暑。茶园与松林交相辉映,茶中有林、林在茶中、茶庄随处可见。

As is known to all, pleasant climate and environment are the basic requirements for the production of high quality tea. The soil of local tea plantations is rich in zinc and selenium, which is called by the medical community "the king of anti-cancer" and "the star of longevity". As a result, the scenic site has become the unique main production area of Fenggang Zinc-Selenium Tea in China, and this kind of tea has also won the reputation of "Longjing Tea in the east and Fenggang Zinc-Selenium Tea in the west". In 2013, Fenggang Zinc-Selenium Tea was listed as China's well-known trademark. In 2015, it won the Gold Prize of the Chinese Famous Tea in the Centennial World Expo in Milan, Italy.

众所周知,优异的气候与环境是出产优质茶叶的必要条件。当地茶园的土壤富含锌和硒元素。在医学界,硒被称为"抗癌之王""长寿之星"。由此,景区成为全国绝无仅有的凤冈锌硒茶的主产区,而这种茶也赢得了"东有龙井,西有凤冈"的美名。2013年,凤冈锌硒茶被列为中国驰名商标,2015年荣获意大利米兰百年世博中国名茶金奖。

As early as in August 2010, a statue of Lu Yu was built on Xianren Ridge in Fenggang County. Lu Yu, a tea expert in the Tang Dynasty, is widely known for his *Classic of Tea*, the first monograph on tea in the world. In history, he is honored as the "Tea Immortal" or the "Tea Sage". Every year on the 19th day of the second month of the lunar calendar, tea growers and tourists from all over the country will gather here to hold a grand tea ceremony to commemorate Lu Yu and pray for a bumper tea harvest.

早在2010年8月,凤冈县在仙人岭山上就建起了陆羽塑像。陆羽,唐代茶学家,因著世界第一部茶叶专著《茶经》而闻名于世。历史上,他被誉为"茶仙""茶圣"。每年农历二月十九,茶农们和四面八方的游客会齐聚在这里,举行祭茶大典,纪念陆羽,为茶叶丰收祈福。

If tourists are in the Center of the Tea Sea, they will truly feel their completely close to nature. Around them are tea plantations, which stretch along the hills and seems to be covered in layers of greenery. The Sightseeing Cableway has a total length of 780 meters and a height difference of 170 meters. While overlooking the boundless Tea Sea from the cableway, you can feel the "terrestrial surface radiation" brought by the vitality of the Tea Sea. The site called the Nine Forts and the Thirteen Bends is not the tea sea as imagined, but a mixture of tea plantations and pine forests, where villages and farmhouses are overshadowed by lush greenery. After the rain, if you stand on the viewing platform on Xianren Ridge, you will find that a panorama of the tea plantations will be clearly visible, much like a magnificent light-ink landscape painting.

游客如果置身于茶海之心，会真正感受到与自然完全亲近。周围皆是茶园，依山绵延，绿色似乎重重叠叠。观光索道全长780米，高差170米，从索道上俯瞰无边的茶海，会感到茶海的活力所带来的"地面辐射"。被称为九堡十三弯的景点并不是想象中的茶海风景，而是茶林与松林相互交错，村庄与农家绿荫掩映。雨后，站在仙人岭的观景台上，茶林全景清晰可见，犹如一幅博大精深的淡墨山水画。

Of course, in the scenic site, learning to pick and process tea may be of great interest to tourists. They usually rent tea-picking tools and go to the designated tea plantations, where local tea pickers will teach them in detail how to pick tea and find single-bud leaves, one bud with two leaves, or a bud with three leaves. It is said that one *jin* (0.5 kilogram) of tea needs the amount of nearly 10,000 tea buds, so it can be seen that the tourists can experience the pickers' hard work in tea plantations. Back at the teahouse from the plantations, the tourists will be arranged to process their picked leaves. Under the guidance of local tea masters, they will spread out the fresh leaves for a period of time, then place the leaves in a large, deep iron pot and dry them by hand. The temperature in the pot is about 25℃. If time permits, the tea masters will also teach them how to grind or roll the leaves into a certain shape. Many tourists will be happy to take home the tea they have processed.

当然,在景区游客可能对学习采茶和制茶很有兴趣。他们通常租用采茶工具,然后去指定的茶园。在那里,采茶农会详细地讲解如何采茶,如何找到单芽、一芽二叶、一芽三叶的茶叶。据说,一斤(0.5千克)茶叶需要近一万粒茶芽。游客可以体验采茶农在茶园的辛苦劳动。从茶园返回茶庄后,当地制茶师傅会安排游客加工采摘的茶叶。在他们的指导下,游客将鲜叶摊放一会儿,然后把茶叶放在既大又深的铁锅里,手工杀青鲜叶,铁锅温度大约在25℃。如果时间容许,制茶师傅还会教如何采用"压"或"卷"的方式给茶叶造型。许多游客很乐意把自己加工的茶叶带回家。

Well, so much for my brief introduction to the Center of the Tea Sea. We will soon go to the scenic site. The highlights of our tour will be the sightseeing of Xianren Ridge, as well as the tea picking and processing. Wish you all a pleasant journey!

好了,茶海之心的介绍到此结束。我们很快就要启程去景区,旅行的亮点将是游览仙人岭和参加采茶加工活动。祝大家游览愉快!

The Tea Sea in West China
西部茶海

In Qianbei there is a sea of tea, which covers an area of about 20 square kilometers in Yongxing Town, Meitan County. This site is a tea-themed agricultural sightseeing park and a demonstration area of tea-culture tourism, known as "the Tea Sea in western China".

黔北高原有一片茶海，位于湄潭县永兴镇境内，面积约20平方千米。这片茶海是以茶叶为主题的农业观光公园，也是茶文化旅游示范区，被誉为"中国西部茶海"。

This area is characterized by low and hilly terrain, where dark green rows of tea plantations extend along the hills and uplands. As a breeze blows, it is difficult to distinguish whether it is the breeze blowing, or the chanting of tea trees.

该地区为低矮丘陵地貌，茶林沿着山丘和高地顺势延伸，一行行，一色深绿。微风吹过，很难分清是风的吹拂，还是茶树的吟唱。

Now, the Tea Sea in West China has not only become the major industry in Meitan County, but also a famous eco-tourism attraction in southwest China. In spring, tea plantations are dyed green; in summer, the hills and uplands are verdant; in autumn, the valleys are shrouded with frost;

in winter, the Tea Sea is covered with snow. The Tea Sea has its own beauty in four seasons, just like a group of huge painted screens, making the scenic area crowded with tourists all year round.

现在，西部茶海不仅成为湄潭县的主要产业，还成为西南地区著名的生态旅游景点。春天，茶树染绿；夏天，山峦和高地葱茏；秋天，山间披霜；冬天，茶海被雪覆盖。茶海四季各有风韵，如一组巨大的彩绘屏风，吸引无数游人前来参观。

In the scenic site of the Tea Sea, bicycle trails crisscross, allowing tourists to cycle anywhere in the tea plantations. When they get tired of cycling, they can park their bicycles on the hillside and have a rest for a while.

在茶海景区，自行车道纵横交错，游客可以骑自行车在茶林间穿梭。如果骑车骑累了，可以停靠在山坡上休憩片刻。

The Tea Sea is also a favorite place for photographers. Every year around the Tomb Sweeping Festival many photographers gather here. At the same time, tea plantations become very lively, for tea pickers, male and female, old and young, are busy picking tea with baskets on their backs.

茶海也是摄影家喜欢的地方。每年清明节前后，很多摄影师都会聚集于此。与此同时，采茶人不分男女老少，背着篮子，忙着采茶，茶海变得热闹起来。

In the Tea Sea, there is a tall building called "Tea Sea Viewing Tower", which is located on the highest terrain of the scenic site. Usually, tourists climb to the top floor to enjoy panoramic views of the undulating Tea Sea from all sides. Meanwhile, the tower seems to be bathed in green waves, which will make them feel completely relaxed and happy.

在茶海，有一座高楼，取名"观海楼"，位于景区最高处，游客通常会登上楼顶，一览四面涌动起伏的茶海全景。同时，塔楼仿佛沐浴在绿色的波浪中，让游客感觉心旷怡然。

In 1937, Zhejiang University moved to West China and stayed in Meitan County for seven years. While Zhejiang University was in Meitan County, some of the professors formed a group called "the Meijiang Poetry Recitation Club", where they would drink tea and write poems in their spare time. In their poems, there are some beautiful expressions or phrases, which have become the true portrayal of the eight scenes of the tea areas in Meitan County today. These include "Ladling out Greenery Beyond the River", "Houses on the Purple-Myrtle Hill", "Sunset at the Rainbow-Shaped Bridge", "Leaning on Tung Trees and Waiting for the Moon to Rise", "Fishing in the Willow Shadow", "Listening to the Sound of Spring Water in the Bamboo Pier", "Lotus Platform and Willow Waves" and "Pine Paths Shaded at Noontime". The westward move of Zhejiang University has enriched the cultural connotation of the Tea Sea and tea products in Meitan County.

1937年，浙江大学西迁，在湄潭县办学7年。浙江大学在湄潭县办学期间，一些教授创建了一家叫"湄江吟社"的社团，闲时品茗作诗。在这些诗歌里，有些优美的词句如今已经成了湄潭县茶区八景的真实写照，如："隔江挹翠""紫薇山馆""虹桥夕照""倚桐待月""柳荫垂钓""竹坞听泉""莲台柳浪""松径午荫"。浙江大学的西迁丰富了湄潭茶海和湄潭茶产品的文化内涵。

In recent years, Meitan County has reshaped its local tourism industry with the theme of "one city, one museum, one kettle, one festival, one meeting, one institute, and one village". The "one city" refers to the "West Tea City", which is the largest tea market in Guizhou and even in

Southwest China. It also functions as a special economic and cultural park that integrates tea-related production, processing, scientific research, trade, culture and tourism. The "one museum" refers to Guizhou Tea Cultural and Ecological Museum. The "one kettle" refers to the large tea kettle located in Xianhu Hill. The tea kettle is believed to be the largest tea kettle in the world, as it is 52 meters high and 17.8 meters in diameter. The "one festival" and the "one meeting" generally refer to the large-scale tea culture activities held during the marketing of spring tea in Meitan County. These activities have exerted far-reaching influence and achieved good results. The "one institute" refers to Guizhou Tea Research Institute, which was established in Meitan County in 1939. Through decades of development, the institute has made great contributions to the growth and development of tea in Meitan County. The "one village" refers to Hetaoba Village, known as the No.1 Tea Village in China. The village is located in the southeast corner of the county seat, covering an area of 12 square kilometers. So far, the village owns 4,200 *mu* (280 hectares) of tea fields, every household in the village is engaged in tea plantations, and the courtyards of tea growers are all hidden in the tea gardens or under the shade of trees, just like a picture of leisurely free and well-off land.

近年来，湄潭县已形成了"一城、一馆、一壶、一节、一会、一所、一村"的旅游格局。"一城"，即"西部茶城"，是贵州乃至西南地区最大的茶叶大市场，也是集茶叶生产、加工、科研、贸易、文化、旅游为一体的特色经济文化园区。"一壶"，是位于仙壶山上的大茶壶；此壶高52米，直径17.8米，为世界上最大的茶壶。"一节""一会"，通常指的是湄潭县曾在春茶上市期间举办的大型茶文化活动；这些活动影响深远，取得了良好效果。"一所"，是1939年在湄潭县建立的贵州茶叶研究所；经过几十年的发展，该所为湄潭县茶叶的生长与发展做出了巨大贡献。"一村"，即"核桃坝村"，素有"中国茶第一村"之称；该村位于县城东南角，面积

12平方千米；到目前为止，全村拥有茶园4200亩（280公顷），村里家家户户种茶，茶农庭院隐于茶林树荫里，犹如一幅闲适富足的园地。

Well, so much for my brief introduction to the Tea Sea in West China. Tomorrow, we will visit the scenic site. The route is from China's Tea Sea to the West Tea City via Meitan Tea Sea Ecological Park, the Tea Culture Park where the world's largest kettle is located, Xiangshan Exposition Park of Tea Plants and the Central Hall of Guizhou Tea Cultural and Ecological Museum.

好了，西部茶海介绍到此结束。明天我们将去景区游览，游览旅游线路是：中国茶海—湄潭茶海生态园—天下第一壶茶文化公园—象山茶植物博览园—贵州省茶文化生态博物馆中心馆—西部茶城。

Shuanghe Karst Cave in Suiyang County
绥阳双河洞

Shuanghe Karst Cave is located in Wenquan Town, Suiyang County, Guizhou Province. This scenic site has the largest cluster of karst caves in China, and Shuanghe Karst Cave is believed to be the world's longest dolomite cave and the world's largest lapis lazuli cave. At present, the scenic site has been listed as a national 4A-level tourist attraction and a national geological park.

双河洞位于贵州省绥阳县温泉镇境内。双河洞景区拥有中国最大的溶洞群,而双河洞是"世界上最长的白云岩洞穴""世界上最大的天青石洞穴"。目前,该景区为国家AAAA级旅游景区,是国家地质公园。

The total length of Shuanghe Karst Cave is 70.502 kilometers, which are layered into three layers, with a total of 97 sub-caves, including eight main sub-caves. These sub-caves are shown to be very concentrated. Some of them are bordered, so to speak, even adjacent to each other, some have caves overhead or below, some have caves inside, and some are watery or dry. The temperature in the sub-caves is generally constant throughout the year, ranging from 13°C to 15°C, making the sub-caves the best place for sightseeing.

双河洞总长度达70.502公里,分三层,共97个溶洞,其中主溶洞8个。

这些洞穴非常集中。洞靠洞，洞边洞，洞上有洞，洞下有洞，洞中套洞，水洞旱洞。洞里的温度一年四季都很稳定，在13℃到15℃之间，非常适宜旅游观光。

At the bottom layer there flow three underground rivers, which are so deep that the river bottom can't be seen. When torrential floods occur in the surrounding mountains, the underground rivers remain clear, while the rivers on the ground become muddy. At the confluence of these rivers, it will present a distinct picture of which one half of the confluent flow is clear and the other half is turbid.

最底层有三条地下河，水深不见底。山洪暴发时，地下河依然清澈，地上的河流则变得浑浊。在河流的汇合处，呈现出清晰的画面，汇合之水半是清澈半是浑浊。

However, what is impressive is the scenery inside Shuanghe Karst Cave. For example, there is a narrow sub-cave named the Grape Gully. Its walls extend tens of meters and are covered with stone grapes, looking crystal clear. Beyond the Grape Gully is the Lotus Pond, where pieces of natural stone lotus leaves float on the clear water. The light from a flashlight can go straight through the water to the bottom. Jinghua Cave is 13 kilometers long, with helictits, a kind of spiral or twisted upward stalactites. These helictits look transparent and exquisite, much like snow trees or silvery flowers. Among the karst cave cluster, the most delicate and ingenious is Guihua Cave, with helictits covering a total area of 5,000 square meters. In this crystal world, the ceiling and ground are milky white, much like a crystal palace. Images in the cave are in all shapes and forms. Some look like rare birds or animals who seem to be chasing each other. some resemble wandering immortals or sword women, floating in the air.

然而，令人叫绝的是双河洞内的景观。例如，有一座狭窄的溶洞叫"葡萄沟"，洞壁延伸数十米，上面覆盖着石葡萄，显得晶莹透亮。过了葡萄沟，便是"荷花池"，清澈的水面漂浮着片片天然的石头荷叶，手电筒发出的光线可以直透水底。晶花洞长13公里，洞内的卷曲石，通体透明别致，如雪树银花。溶洞群中，最精致巧妙的是桂花洞。洞中的卷曲石总面积达5000平方米。在这个晶体世界里，洞顶洞底一片乳白，像一座水晶宫。溶洞里的造型千姿百态；有的如奇禽异兽，奔突追逐；有的如游仙侠女，漂浮在天。

In addition, waterfalls provide a perfect backdrop for the cave cluster. Some waterfalls are on the ground, some are hidden underground, some flow all year round, and some others are non-perennial. Shigao Cave is actually a water curtain cave, with 300-meter-high waterfalls hanging over its entrance, like an upside down silvery chain. Between Shigao and Luojiao caves, there is a huge karst funnel with a depth of over 130 meters. There, waterfalls plunge straight down to the bottom of the funnel, just like a dragon moving swiftly into the sea. Longtangzi is also a deep-cut funnel surrounded by high mountains, with waterfalls rushing down from a relative height of more than 200 meters, like a jade dragon descending from the mountains.

此外，瀑布与溶洞群交相辉映。有的瀑布在地面上；有的藏于地下；有的终年瀑水不断；还有的是季节性的。石膏洞实际上是一座水帘洞，300米高的瀑布悬在洞口，犹如倒挂银链。在石膏洞与罗教洞之间，有一处巨大的喀斯特漏斗，深度130余米，飞瀑直泻斗底，犹如奔龙入海。龙塘子也是一处深切割漏斗，四周皆是高山，飞瀑从200多米的相对高度悬垂而下，好似玉龙下山一般。

Since 1987, geological and cave experts from Guizhou and other provinces, together with experts from France, Japan, Italy, the United

States and many other countries, have conducted several joint scientific investigations in Shuanghe Karst Cave. At the beginning, the cave was found to be only seven kilometers long. However, as the investigations progressed, the length of the cave continued to extend, setting Asia's new record for the length of caves. So far, the cave has become a karst cave system that integrates tourism, cave exploration and scientific research.

自 1987 年以来，来自贵州和其他省的地质、洞穴专家与法国、日本、意大利、美国等国的专家一起对双河洞进行了多次联合科学考察。最初，人们发现双河洞长度只有 7 公里。然而，随着调查的进行，双河洞的长度不断延伸，创下了亚洲洞穴长度的新纪录。迄今为止，双河洞成了一座集旅游观光、洞穴探险、科学研究于一体的洞穴系统。

Well, so much for my brief introduction to Shuanghe Karst Cave. At present, the whole area becomes a scenic site due to the cluster of caves, forests, mountains and rivers. So far as I know, Suiyang County will further strengthen the protection and development of the cluster of the karst caves, aiming to build a 5A-level cave scenic site, so that more tourists at home and abroad can better enjoy the scenery and mysterious charm of Shuanghe Karst Cave.

好了，双河洞的介绍到此结束。目前，整个区域因溶洞群、森林、山脉、河流而成了风景名胜区。据我所知，绥阳县将进一步加强保护和发展溶洞群，旨在打造 AAAAA 级溶洞景区，以便让更多的国内外游客领略双河洞风光及其神秘的风姿。

15

Zhijin Cave in Bijie
毕节织金洞

Zhijin Cave, formerly known as Daji Cave, is located in Guanzhai Town, 23 kilometers northeast of Zhijin County in Guizhou Province. Zhijin Cave is 6.6 kilometers long, with a maximum width of 175 meters and a relative height difference of over 150 meters. The whole cave is composed of upper, middle and lower layers, where there are more than 40 kinds of deposits in the cave, such as stalagmites, stalagnates, clints and others, forming karst landscapes in thousands of postures.

织金洞，原名打鸡洞，位于贵州省织金县城东北23公里处的官寨乡。织金洞长6.6公里，最宽处175米，相对高差150多米。全洞有上、中、下三层，洞内有石笋、石柱、石芽等四十多种堆积物，形成了千姿百态的溶洞景观。

The most striking features of Zhijin Cave can be summed up in three words: hugeness, uniqueness and completeness. The "hugeness" refers to the great size and grandeur of the cave. The "uniqueness" refers to the typical shape of scenery and space, like the underground heavenly palace. The "completeness" refers to a variety of landscape, which include the key forms and categories of the major karst caves in the world. Those who have visited the cave often praise it as "one of the wonders on the earth", "the underground treasure house of art in the universe", "the first cave under heaven", or "the king of karst caves".

织金洞最显著的特征可以用三个字概括：大、奇、全。"大"指的是织金洞规模宏大，气势宏伟。"奇"指的是景物及空间造型的独特形状，像似地下天宫。"全"指的是景观形态的多样性，囊括了世界主要溶洞的主要形态和类别。凡是参观过织金洞的人，通常会赞其为"地球上一大奇观""宇宙的地下艺术宝库""天下第一洞""溶洞之王"。

According to different landscapes and features, Zhijin Cave is divided into a number of scenic sections that include 47 halls and more than 150 scenic spots. The scenic sections are named the Welcome Hall, the Sutra Lecture Hall, the Snow Incense Palace, the Longevity-Deity Hall, the Moon Palace, the Miraculous Mist Hall and so on.

根据不同的景观和特点，织金洞分为若干景区，有47个厅堂、150多个景点。景区命名为迎宾厅、讲经堂、雪香宫、寿星宫、广寒宫、灵霄殿等。

The Miraculous Mist Hall is considered to be one of the most beautiful scenic sections in the cave. On either side of the cave walls hang giant curtains that are brightly colorful and dozens of meters wide, just like those of heaven. In the center of the hall is the Yaochi, the abode of immortals, where there is a towering column, which looks exquisitely carved. Especially, a cluster of snow-white drip stones occupies the largest space in the hall, presenting wonderful landscapes by the names of the Jade Emperor, the Ornamental Columns, the Red-crowned Crane, the Jade Dragon, the Goddess and Snakes, and so on.

灵霄殿是洞中最美的景区之一。洞壁两侧垂下色彩鲜艳、几十米宽的巨型石幔，宛若天宫幔幕。大殿中央是"瑶池"，池中的"擎天一柱"看似雕刻精美。特别是雪白的滴石群落占地最大，呈现出美妙的景观，其名曰："玉皇大帝""华表""仙鹤""玉龙""神女与蛇"等。

The Moon Palace is one of the largest scenic sections, with a total area of more than 50,000 square meters. The palace is high and spacious, and karst deposits take shape of dozen-meter-high "peaks". Some "peaks" are as steep as sharp cuts, some stretch uninterrupted, some look like flower clumps, and some seem to have luxuriant foliage. Between the "peaks" is open flat ground, interspersed with lakes and marshes. In the center of the scenic section there stands a "suoluo tree" that reaches the top of the cave. On the "tree" there grows stone lucid ganoderma in layers. In the depths of the scenic section, there is a translucent opalescent crystal in the shape of flower blossom. Such an image, known as "silvery rain tree", stands 17 meters high on a white jade plate. Another important image is the "Overlord Helmet", which has two halberd-shaped stalagmites growing side by side on circular karst deposits. In addition, there are some other spectacular attractions by the names of "the Mysterious Buddha", "Chang'e Flying to the Moon", "the Underground Capital of Stars", "the Tropical Rainforest", and so on.

广寒宫是规模最大景区之一，总面积5万多平方米。洞厅高大宽敞，喀斯特沉积物形成了一座座十几米高的"山峰"。有的陡峭如削，有的相接连绵，有的像花团锦簇，有的似枝繁叶茂。在"山峰"之间为空阔平川，点缀着湖泊和沼泽。景区中心有株"梭罗树"，直指洞顶，"树"身上石灵芝层层叠叠。在景区深处，有一株开花状的、半透明乳白色结晶体。此景物被称为"银雨树"，高17米，竖立在白玉盘中。另一重要景物是"霸王盔"，其物有两支戟形石笋，并靠生长在圆形喀斯特堆积物上。此处，还有其他壮观的景点，如："神秘大佛""嫦娥奔月""地下星都"以及"热带雨林"。

In Zhijin Cave, aesthetic terms corresponding to specific landscape can be found everywhere. For example, specific "magnificent" landscape can be denoted by particular phrases, such as "silent mountains", and "golden pagodas and forest sea"; the phrases such as "silvery rain trees", and the "overlord helmet" are used to refer to "magical" landscape; and other phrases such as "stone bamboo gardens", and "stone flowers in full bloom" are used to describe "beautiful" landscape. The debate about morphological comparisons has long been of interest among linguists and tourists alike. In many other karst caves, aesthetic terms are also used to refer to indicative landscape, but their morphological comparisons are inevitably more far-fetched. However, in Zhijin Cave, this is not just an aesthetic coincidence. Their landscape has achieved the unity of form and spirit, so that their use of aesthetic terms illustrates a good case in point.

在织金洞里，随处可以找到与具体的景观对应的美学术语。例如，具体表达"壮美"的景观，就有特定的词组，如"寂静群山""金塔林海"；"银雨树""霸王盔"等术语用来表达"神奇"的景观；还有"石竹园""石花斗奇"等术语用来形容"美"景物。关于形态比较的争论，一直是语言学家和游客们感兴趣的话题。在许多溶洞中，美学术语也被用来指定景物，但其形态比较难免牵强附会。不过在织金洞，这并不仅仅是审美上的偶然巧合，而是景观达到形神兼备，所用的美学术语恰到好处。

Well, so much for my brief introduction to Zhijin Cave. When touring of Zhijin Cave, you should pay attention to the following matters. The tour of the cave takes about three hours. When taking photos in the cave, be careful to avoid touching sedimentary rocks, as they are very fragile. Warm clothes are necessary in the cave, and be careful when walking on the slippery trails.

好了，织金洞的讲解到此结束。在游览织金洞时，需要注意如下事项：整个游览大约需要三小时。洞中拍照时，注意避免触碰到路边沉积岩，它们很脆弱。另外，在洞穴里要穿暖和的衣服，道滑要小心行走。

16

Baili Azalea Scenic Area

百里杜鹃景区

Baili Azalea Scenery is located at the junction of Dafang and Qianxi counties. It is about 155 kilometers away from Guiyang, Guizhou Province, with a total area of 600 square kilometers. This is a narrow hilly area about 50 kilometers long and 1.2 to 5.3 kilometers wide. It has all 5 subgenus and more than 60 species of azaleas in the world. So far, this hilly area is the largest natural azalea forest in China. Here, "different kinds of azaleas bloom on a tree." That is to say, several different species of azaleas bloom on the same tree. Even azalea flowers of seven species grow on the same tree.

百里杜鹃景区位于大方、黔西两县交界处，距贵州省贵阳市155公里，总面积600平方公里。这是一片长约50公里、宽1.2至5.3公里的狭长丘陵地带，拥有全世界杜鹃花全部5个亚属和60多个品种。迄今为止，这片山地是中国面积最大的原生杜鹃林。在这里，"一树不同花"，即有几种不同品种的杜鹃花生长在同一棵树上，甚至同一棵树上还有七种杜鹃花。

According to legend, a long time ago, Dafang and Qianxi were very desolate. There was a Yi couple living on one side of the hill, and a Miao couple living on the other side. They worked hard year after year, hoping to leave behind happiness for their future generations. Unexpectedly, they

Guizhou Province
贵州省

became sick from overwork and died one after another. Their children buried their bodies at the foot of the barren hill. After a few years, their remains turned into inexhaustible coal, and beautiful azaleas grew on the ground.

相传很久以前,大方和黔西一带非常荒凉,有一对彝族夫妇住在山的这边,一对苗族夫妇住在山的那边。他们年复一年辛勤劳作,希望给子孙后代留下幸福。不料,他们积劳成疾、相继去世。他们的子女便将他们的遗体埋葬在这贫瘠的山坡下。若干年后,他们的遗体变成了取之不尽的煤,地面上长出了美丽的杜鹃花。

The Baili Azalea Scenery is in a warm temperate zone with humid monsoon climate. There is no severe cold in winter and no scorching heat in summer, so it is known as the "Earth Ribbon", the "Kingdom of Azaleas", the "Health Blessing Place" and the "Cool and Refreshing World". Accordingly, it is listed as a national 5A-level tourist attraction. In addition, it has been crowned with such titles as the National Eco-tourism Demonstration Zone, the Only Azalea National Forest Park in the World and the National Nature Reserve.

在百里杜鹃景区,冬无严寒,夏无酷暑。景区属暖温带湿润季风气候,享有"地球彩带、杜鹃王国、养身福地、清凉世界"之美誉。百里杜鹃风景区是国家AAAAA级旅游景区。此外,景区还获得了"国家生态旅游示范区""世界唯一的杜鹃花国家森林公园""国家自然保护区"等称号。

At present, the Baili Azalea Scenery is mainly divided into the Jinpo Scenic Section and the Pudi Scenic Section. Characteristically, the terrain of the Jinpo Scenic Section is undulating and magnificent, while the Pudi Scenic Section appears small, beautiful and exquisite. Every year from late March to May, the Azalea Festival is held in the scenic area, where all kinds of azaleas are in full bloom. At the same time, in addition to viewing azaleas in full bloom, you can also participate in the Chahuajie (Flower Arrangement Festival of the Yi Nationality) and the Tiaohuapo (Flower Jumping Slope Festival of the Miao Nationality). It is really a beautiful picture of "Peaks overlap in thousands, and coal is buried underground. Azaleas bloom extensively like the sea, and the whole hills are filled with exotic fragrance."

现在，百里杜鹃景区主要分为金坡景区和普底景区。金坡景区地形连绵起伏、气势宏伟。普底景区纤细小巧、秀丽玲珑。每年3月下旬至5月，风景区内会举办杜鹃花节，各种杜鹃花竞相怒放，漫山遍野。这时候，除了观赏杜鹃争艳，还可以参加彝族插花节、苗族跳花坡，真是好一幅"千峰叠起嶂，乌金地下埋，杜鹃花似海，满山留异香"的美丽画卷。

There are many scenic spots in the Baili Azalea Scenery as follows. The azaleas in Baihuaping are colorful and diverse. It is said that every year when the flowers bloom, the fairies in the heaven will secretly come down to enjoy flowers, and sing and dance with the girls and boys among flowers. Therefore, this scenic spot has become an ideal place for the Flower Arrangement Festival of the Yi Nationality and the Flower Jumping Slope Festival of the Miao Nationality. In the Jinjiqing(Golden Pheasant Valley), the azalea plants grow large and dense, with the clusters of pink charming azaleas (rhododendron agastum), white or yellowish azaleas (rhododendron irroratum), great white azaleas (rhododendron decorum) and bright red azaleas (rhododendron delavayi). Standing on the Lansheng Peak, you will find the delavayi azaleas the most attractive. They are in brilliant red, bright pink, light red, pinkish red, or soft red. When the breeze blows, the delavayi azaleas take on a dazzling color, like rolling fire-dragons or rising flames. The delavayi azalea plants grow tall and have layers of dense flowers and many plants each have more than three hundred flowers. The branches are covered with clusters of flowers, like burning flames, reflecting the sky, the earth, the faces of tourists and the hills around. The delavayi azalea is also known as the Maying Flower or Soma Flower. Legend has it that the blood of Soma girl became holy flowers. In Jinpoling, flowers look very beautiful. Some hills are dressed up as red as the morning glow, as bright as a blaze of colors. Some hills appear white, as if they were clothed with snow. Some other hills are covered with azaleas of every kind, like brocades. Whenever the sun sets, the afterglow of the setting sun makes the hills red, so this place is called Jinpoling or the Golden Slope Ridges. The Shuhua Peak (Counting-Flower Peak) is the best scenic spot for viewing flowers, showing the scale and impressiveness of azaleas in the Baili Azalea Scenery. The Wucailu (Multicolored Path) is a scenic spot, where the azalea species are relatively concentrated and complete. In the blooming season, fallen petals are scattered on the Multicolored Path, where visitors walk on the uneven flagstone paths, and flowers constantly stroke their faces, as if they were walking among colorful clouds.

景区有很多景点。百花坪的杜鹃花五彩缤纷，多种多样。相传每年百花盛开时，天宫仙女会偷偷下凡赏花，与花丛中的姑娘小伙对歌跳舞。这里因此就成为每年彝族的插花节、苗族跳坡节的理想场所。锦鸡箐的杜鹃，树大林密，交织丛生着粉红色的迷人杜鹃、鹅黄色的露珠杜鹃、大白杜鹃，以及深红色的马缨杜鹃。站在览胜峰上，游客会发现马缨杜鹃最引人注目，亮红、水红、淡红、肉红、粉红。微风吹拂，马缨杜鹃花呈现出耀眼的色彩，像翻滚的火龙，如升腾的烈焰。马缨杜鹃树身高大，花冠浓密，多的有三百花朵。枝头上覆盖着簇簇鲜花，像燃烧的火焰，映红了天、映红了地、映红了游人的脸、映红了四周的山。马缨杜鹃又叫"马缨花""索玛花"。传说是索玛姑娘的鲜血变成的圣花。在金坡岭，花朵特别漂亮，有的山装点得若朝霞一样红，鲜艳光亮；有的山一片雪白，银装素裹；还有的山百花齐放，繁花似锦。每当太阳西下，落日余晖使整座山火红一片,故此地被称为"金坡岭"。数花峰是观花的最佳景点,展现出百里杜鹃的规模、气势。五彩路是杜鹃花品种比较集中、齐全的景点;盛花季节,落花散落在五彩路上,游客在高低不平的石板路上漫步,鲜花不断拂面而来,犹如行走在彩云之间。

If we walk to the scenic spots, we can hardly cover all the spots in one day. So, we will take a sightseeing van to visit five or six scenic spots. It will take about half a day. When we are in the second scenic spot, we can have something to eat, such as the baked food in a pan, cakes and sweetmeats, and glutinous rice cakes stuffed with bean curd. These are local flavor snacks. Well, so much for my introduction to the Baili Azalea Scenery. Now please follow the local guide for sightseeing.

如果在景区步行游览,一天的时间也难逛完景区。所以,我们将乘坐观光车,参观五六个景点,约半天的时间。在第二个景点,大家可以吃些东西,有烙锅、茶食、糍粑包豆腐,这些是当地的风味小吃。好啦,百里杜鹃景区简介到此结束,现在请大家随当地导游游览吧!

Thousand-household Miao Village in Xijiang
西江千户苗寨景区

Xijiang Thousand-household Miao Village, is 260 kilometers away from Guiyang and located in the folds of the Leigong Hills of Leishan County in Guizhou Province. It is composed of more than ten sub-villages and is considered the largest Miao village in China.

西江千户苗寨,距离贵阳市约260公里,位于贵州省雷山县雷公山麓洼地之处,由十余个自然村寨组成,是中国最大的苗族聚居村寨。

A View of Xijiang Miao Village

The Xijiang Miao nationality constitutes an important part of the Miao community in Qiandongnan, and its 99.5% of its villagers are of the Miao nationality. In history, Xijiang served as a main settlement for the fifth large-scale migration of the Miao people. In the Han Dynasty, this place was called Jijiang. In the Yongzheng's reign of the Qing Dynasty, it was still called Jijiang, but it sounded different with different tones and used a different character. In the period of the Republic of China, the local gentry changed the name of Jijiang to Xijiang.

西江苗族是黔东南苗族的重要组成部分，村寨苗族人口占99.5%。在历史上，西江是苗族第五次大迁徙的主要集结地。此地在汉朝称为"鸡江"，清朝雍正时期称"鸡讲"；民国时期，当地绅士将"鸡讲"改为"西江"。

There are some interesting sights to explore in the Xijiang Miao community. The first one, ascend onto the Observation Platform to enjoy a panoramic view of the Miao village, which is located in a natural basin, surrounded by green paddy fields, and wooden houses are built on the hillside. The second one, take a photo on the Bridge of Wind and Rains. Such a bridge is composed of the top covered bridge, a pavilion, towers and gates, where people can take a walk or have a rest. The third one, take a look at how local craftsmen make silver head-crowns, horns or phoenixes, as the village is known for its silver products. The fourth one, observe the embroidery patterns stitched on Miao women clothes in the village, as the embroidery is the most important part of their clothing. The fifth one, watch the Miao dance performances, such as the copper-drum dance, the bench dance and the golden pheasant dance. The sixth one, taste the Miao cuisine and enjoy the Miao toast songs.

在西江苗寨，主要看点如下：①登观景台，一览苗寨全景；苗寨坐落在自然盆地,周边为翠绿稻田,木屋依山而建;②在风雨桥留影,这座桥由廊桥、亭、塔、门组成,人们可以在上行走,也可以在那里休息;③观看当地工匠制作银冠、银角、银凤雀,村寨的银制产品远近闻名;④观看村寨苗族女子服装上的刺绣图案,刺绣是她们服装的最主要部分;⑤观看苗族舞蹈表演,如:铜鼓舞、板凳舞、锦鸡舞;⑥品尝苗家风味餐,领略苗族敬酒歌。

Well, compared with other sights in the village, the stilted houses of the Xijiang Miao community is particularly impressive. This type of the architecture originated from the southern style of pole-supported residential dwellings, which can be traced back to ancient times. These stilted houses are connected with each other and built along a slope of 30 to 70 degrees, covering a large part of land that integrates with the surrounding mountains and rural landscape. These houses remain solid and strong. Designers and builders create a multiple structure, with rectangles, triangles and rhombuses neatly combined to form a three-dimensional space system. These stilted houses are mainly made of wood. Generally, this type of the architecture has a *xieshan*-style roof that slopes down from both sides, with the roof eaves that extend beyond the high walls on either side of the houses. All the roofs in the village, except for a few fir barks, are covered with gray tiles. On the roof ridge, there is a pattern of "Longji" (Dragon Backbone) made of tiles. The end of the pattern is gently turned up, and the center is decorated with "Longbao" (Dragon Treasure). If you look at the "Longbao" from a distance, it looks like an eagle ready to fly off the ridge. Usually, the stilted house is a three-storey building. The first floor is used to store production tools and fertilizers or as a small area of enclosure for keeping poultry and livestock. The second floor is divided into a living room, bedrooms and a kitchen. The third floor is mainly used to store grains, animal fodder and living materials.

There is a curved balustrade-style balcony on the second floor, where Miao women like to sit there to take a rest or embroider. This place is called "Mei Ren Kao (Beauty Backrest)".

当然,与苗寨其他景点相比,西江苗族吊脚楼尤其值得一提。这种建筑源于远古南方干栏式的民居建筑,吊脚楼栋栋相连,在30至70度的斜坡上建造,连成了一大片,与周围的山脉和田园风光融为一体。这种建筑坚固牢实。设计和建造者们创造出多重结构组合,将长方形、三角形、菱形巧妙地组合成三维空间体系。吊脚楼主要由木头建成。一般来讲,这种建筑有歇山顶,房屋上部为前后两坡,屋檐伸出房屋两侧的高墙。村寨所有的屋顶,除少数杉木皮覆盖外,全是青瓦盖顶。在脊梁上,有用瓦块砌成"龙脊"图案。图案末端翘起,中间饰以"龙宝",远远看去就像一只欲飞的雄鹰。通常,吊脚楼为三层楼。底层用于存放生产工具和肥料,或用作饲养家禽和牲畜的小区域。第二层用作客厅、堂屋、卧室和厨房。第三层主要存放谷物、饲料等生产和生活用品。二楼上有一种曲形栏杆式的阳台,苗族妇女喜欢坐在那里休息或刺绣,此处取名为"美人靠"。

In 1992, the Xijiang Miao Village was listed as a Provincial Cultural Heritage Site. In 2004, it was included in the list of the First Provincial-Level Key Ethnic-Nationality Villages and Small Towns for Protection and Development. In November 2005, the "China Nationalities Museum—Xijiang Thousand-Household Miao Village Hall" was established. Since then, the Xijiang Miao Village has become known far and wide, and the number of tourists coming for sightseeing is increasing.

西江苗寨于1992年被列为省级文物保护单位,2004年被列为全省首期村镇保护和建设项目重点民族村镇;2005年11月,"中国民族博物馆西江千户苗寨馆"在此建成。自此,西江苗寨广为人知,前来观光的游客也日益增多。

Well, so much for my introduction to the Xijiang Miao Village. We will soon start our tour of the village. Please follow the signs along the way. These signs indicate where to ascend the Observation Platform, observe the stilted houses, and watch the Miao singing and dancing performances. At 5:30 p.m., we will have a meal of the Miao cuisine and then return to Guiyang by bus. The Xijiang Miao Village is an ethnic-nationality village. No matter wherever you are in the village, please respect their religion and customs.

好了，西江苗寨简介到此结束，我们将很快开始游览苗寨。请沿着指示牌行走，这些指示牌会告诉你们在哪里登观景台，看吊脚楼群，观看苗族歌舞表演；下午5点半品尝苗家风味餐，然后乘车返回贵阳。西江苗寨是少数民族村寨，请尊重当地的宗教和风俗。

18
Zhenyuan Ancient Town
镇远古镇

Zhenyuan Ancient Town is a well-known town in Zhenyuan County of Qiandongnan Miao and Dong Autonomous Prefecture in Guizhou Province. It is located at a bend in the Wuyang River. The turquoise stream of river splits the town into two parts. The old town on the north side, traditionally called Fucheng, is a fascinating maze with cobblestone streets, while the new town, known as Weicheng, is on the south bank. The river meanders through the city in the shape of an "S". Seen from a distance, it looks like the symbol of Taichi, so Zhenyuan is also known as the Ancient Town of the Eight Trigrams.

镇远古镇是贵州省黔东南苗族侗族自治州镇远县的名镇。它位于舞阳河的转弯处，蓝绿色彩带似的河水把小镇一分为二。北侧为古城，传统上称为府城，是一座铺着鹅卵石街道的有趣的迷宫；而新城位于南岸，俗称卫城。河水蜿蜒，以"S"形穿城而过；远观颇似太极图，故镇远又被称为八卦古镇。

The Zhenyuan Ancient Town has a long history. In 277 B. C., King Zhao of Qin made Zhenyuan the county. From the Yuan to Qing dynasties, the town remained as the seat of government for more than 700 years as either the "Dao"(an administrative district larger than a prefecture) or "Fu"(a prefecture). The city-walls of the Zhenyuan Ancient Town are located at the peaks of the Shiping Hills, north of the center of Zhenyuan County. The walls span several peaks of the Shiping Hills and extend westward along the undulating terrain. The walls were built in the early Ming Dynasty. After more than 600 years of wind and rain erosion, the walls become different in shape and color from the surrounding stones. According to the words from the old man in the town, the average height of the former city walls used to be 9 meters.

镇远历史悠久，秦昭王于公元前277年将镇远设为县。从元代到清代，镇远为道、府所在地，时间长达700多年。镇远府城垣，位于镇远县城北石屏山山顶上，府城垣跨石屏山顶几个山头，顺山势起伏延伸向西。城垣建于明代初期，经历600多年的风雨侵蚀，与城垣周围石质各异。镇远的老人说，以前的城垣平均高度为9米。

An Ancient Lane in Zhenyuan Ancient Town

The ancient town is rich in cultural relics. Inside the town, there are more than 50 ancient buildings, 33 ancient residential houses, 12 ancient dock, 8 ancient lanes and 5 ancient post routes. Walking on the cobblestone streets, visitors will find that it is not so crowded and time seems to pass by slowly. Ancient alleys or lanes remain the same as before, with stone tiles and black bricks, and ancient buildings are scattered in every corner of the ancient town. At night, local houses along the river will be lit by lanterns. The pavilions and towers decorated with lights are reflected in the river, showing the beauty and the poetic illusion of the ancient town. In 1986, Zhenyuan Ancient Town was listed as a National Historical and Cultural City, and in March 2009 the town won the title of China's Top Ten Most Beautiful Ancient Cities.

镇远古镇人文古迹众多。古镇里遗存古建筑50余座、古民宅33座、古码头12个、古巷道8条、古驿道5条。走在鹅卵石街道上，游客会发现这里没有那么拥挤，时间似乎在慢慢流逝。古巷依旧，石瓦青砖，古建筑散落在古镇各个角落。到了夜晚，沿河两岸的人家会点亮灯笼。被灯光装饰的亭台楼阁，倒映于河水中，展现出古镇的美丽和诗情画意。1986年，镇远古镇被列为国家历史文化名城，2009年3月荣获"中国最美的十大古城"称号。

Of course, the most famous site in the town is the Qinglong Caves, where the ancient architectural complex deserves attention. This complex is large in scale and exquisitely constructed, featuring Confucianism, Taoism and Buddhism, and seems to have fused with the hillside behind over time. The Qinglong Cave complex is mainly composed of the Zhongyuan Cave, the Longevity Palace, the Pavilion of the Jade Emperor and others. There are 36 single buildings, which are divided into six parts, namely, the Zhusheng Bridge, the Zhongyuan Chan Monastery, the Ziyang Academy, the Pavilion of the Jade Emperor, the Longevity Palace and the Incense-Burning Rock. This group of the ancient buildings is exquisitely constructed, and various construction techniques are adopted on the cliffs, such as the "hanging", "borrowing", "clinging to rocks", "embedding", and "platform construction". All of these present a unique style: "the buildings are constructed in the caves", "the caves hide the buildings", "the ground floors are raised", and "the attic is suspended". The Qinglong Caves lie between steep cliffs and the stone gate is open by the water. A stone plaque on the gate is horizontally engraved with the seal inscription that read "Entering the first cave paradise in Guizhou". The Qinglong cave complex covers an area of 6,600 square meters. The architectures are backed by the green hills and faces clear water. Some of them are beside the caves and close to the cliffs, some cling to the cliffs, and some others hang in the air. For every five stone steps, there is a building. Within ten steps, a pavilion appears. The eaves are warped and overhanging; the beams and pillars are painted and carved; the tiles are green; the walls appear red; the corridors are winding; and courtyards remain quiet. Accordingly, the architectural area has both garden charm and temple style. Experts and scholars agree that this is a rare architectural complex, which artistically combines the architectural forms of the Central Plains with the stilted or pole-railing style buildings of the Miao and Dong villages in Guizhou. An architect said, "The Maiji Mount Grottoes are world-renowned, while the complex of the Qinglong Caves is built straight up to the top of the hills. In this respect, it can be comparable to the Maiji Mount Grottoes. The Hanging Monastery in Shanxi is famous both at home and abroad, but the Qinglong excels in exquisite architectural art." The Qinglong Caves are the closest to the city, compared with other ancient architectural grottoes or caves in the country. As a unique tourist attraction, the caves maintain the nature of landscape and gardens. On February 23, 1982, the People's Government of Guizhou Province listed the Qinglong Caves as a Provincial-Level Cultural Relics Protection Unit. On January 13, 1988, the State Council declared the caves as a National Key Cultural Relics Protection Unit.

当然，该镇最著名的景点为青龙洞，那里的建筑群值得关注。其建筑群以儒道佛三教合一为特色，规模大，构造精巧。随着时间的推移，建筑群似乎与后面的山坡融为一体。青龙洞由中元洞、万寿宫、玉皇阁等组成，单体建筑36座，分为祝圣桥、中元禅院、紫阳书院、玉皇阁、万寿宫和香炉岩六个部分。这些古建筑群构置精妙，在悬崖上采用"下吊""借用""附岩""嵌入""筑台"等多种建筑工艺，使其呈现出"洞中建楼""楼中藏洞""底层吊脚""阁楼悬空"的独特风格。青龙洞在悬崖峭壁间，石门在水边敞开，门上石匾横刻着"入黔第一洞天"的篆刻文字。青龙洞建筑群面积6600平方米，背靠青山，面朝清澈水面，有的建筑依洞傍崖，有的贴壁，有的临空，五步一楼，十步一阁，翘翼飞檐，雕梁画栋，青瓦红墙，曲径回廊，庭院幽静。这个建筑区既有园林韵味，又具寺院风格。专家学者们一致认为，这是一处不可多得的中原建筑形制，是巧妙结合了贵州苗村侗寨吊脚楼或干栏式建筑的建筑群。一位建筑学家说："麦积山洞窟群举世闻名，青龙洞依山而建，直上山顶。在这一点上，青龙洞可与之比高。山西悬空寺蜚声中外，青龙洞在建筑艺术的精湛上较之更胜一等。"在我国古建筑洞窟群落中，青龙洞是离城市最近的洞窟。作为独特的旅游景点，青龙洞保持着山水园林本色。1982年2月23日，贵州省人民政府将青龙洞列为省级文物保护单位。1988年1月13日，国务院公布青龙洞为全国重点文物保护单位。

Well, so much for the introduction to the Qinglong Caves. Today, our tour route goes like this: in the morning, we will go to the Qinglong Caves to observe the ancient Chinese architectures built on the cliffs and then take a walk in ancient alleys and lanes of the Ancient Town. In the afternoon, we go to the Wuyang River, which is a beautiful place packed with white limestone gorges, weirdly shaped rocks cut by waterfalls and topped with lush green vegetation. Temperatures between day and night vary greatly, so when climbing hills, you should bring warm jackets and rain gear, and wear hiking shoes.

Guizhou Province
贵州省

好了，镇远古镇的简介到此为止。今天，我们游览线路是：上午到青龙洞，观摩中国古代贴崖建筑，然后漫步镇远古巷。下午去舞阳河，这是一处风景秀丽的地方，四处是石灰岩峡谷，形状奇特的岩石被瀑布遮蔽，峡谷顶上绿色植被郁郁葱葱。请大家注意：早晚温差较大，宜带保暖夹克和雨具；登山时，穿上登山鞋。

Wanfeng Forest Scenic Area in Xingyi
兴义万峰林景区

Wanfeng Forest Scenic Area (Ten Thousand Peak Hills) in Xingyi City is located in the southeast of Xingyi City of Guizhou Province. It borders Guangxi on the south. To the west, it is linked to the Sanjiang estuary at the junction of Yunnan, Guangxi and Guizhou. In the north, it reaches the main peak of the Wumeng Mountain. The scenery is the largest and most typical karst forest, with a total area of 2,000 square kilometers. In 2008, Wanfeng Forest Scenic Area was listed as the national 4A-level tourist attraction. In addition, it has been crowned with such titles as the National Geographic Park and one of the Five Most Beautiful Peak Forests.

兴义万峰林景区位于贵州省兴义市东南部，南端与广西交界，西到滇、桂、黔三省（区）交界处的三江口，北接乌蒙山主峰，总面积2000平方公里，是国内最大、最典型的喀斯特峰林。2008年，万峰林景区被评选为"国家AAAA级旅游景区"。此外，万峰林景区还获得"国家地质公园""中国最美的五大峰林"的荣誉称号。

About 364 million years ago, Xingyi was still a vast ocean, part of the ancient sea of Yunnan and Guizhou, according to archaeological and geographic studies. About 280 million years ago, land began to form in the carboniferous period. Through many orogenic movements of Yanshan,

Indochina and Himalayas, the earth's crust kept rising and peaks appeared. Under the hot sun baking and rain erosion, and under the action of carbon dioxide and organic acid, here gradually formed wonderful spectacles, such as low-lying lands, rivers, karst caves, peak forests, underground rivers, sinkholes, funnels, canyons, rift valleys, earth fissures, sedimentary rocks, peaks, stalagmites, vauclusian springs, and lakes.

根据考古和地理研究，大约3.64亿年前，兴义还是一片汪洋大海，是滇黔古海的一部分。约2.8亿年前，石炭纪开始形成陆地，又经历燕山、印支、喜马拉雅山等多次造山运动，地壳不断上升，出现山峰。在烈日的烘烤和雨水侵蚀下以及在二氧化碳和有机酸的作用下，逐渐形成低洼地、河流、溶洞、峰林、地下河、天坑、漏斗、峡谷、裂谷、地缝、钟乳石、堆积岩、石峰、石笋、龙潭、湖泊等奇观。

According to the shape of the Wanfeng Forests, it can be divided into five types, such as the array-formation peak forest, the sword-shaped peak forest, the many-dragon-shaped peak forest, the arhat-shaped peak forest and the hat-pile-shaped peak forest. The Wanfeng Forest Scenery is a typical representative of the most mature cone-shaped peak forests in karst geology and landform in China. It looks like the ocean waves, which adorn the plateau with enchanting loveliness. More than 360 years ago, Xu Xiake, a famous traveler in the Ming Dynasty, visited the Wanfeng Forests. He praised the landscape by saying, "There are so many peaks in the world, but only peaks here gather into forests."

万峰林按形态可分为列阵峰林、宝剑峰林、群龙峰林、罗汉峰林、叠帽峰林五大类型，是中国喀斯特地质地貌中发育最成熟的锥状峰林典型代表，犹如海洋波涛似的万峰林大观，把高原装点得妖娆可爱。360多年前，明代著名旅行家徐霞客就曾到过万峰林，赞叹："天下山峰何其多，唯有此处峰成林"。

The Wanfeng forests can be divided into the eastern and western Wanfeng forests, with different landscapes. The Eastern Wanfeng Forest is characterized by the towering clusters of karst peak and surrounded by ridges and peaks, creating a magnificent three-dimensional picture. In the vast forests, karst sinkholes and low-lying land are scattered everywhere and gullies and ravines are undulating, making it mysterious and unfathomable. The Eastern Wanfeng Forest, on the other hand, is a beautiful mountain, blended with green fields, winding rivers, primitive villages and lush forests, as if it were a landscape painting of which "every peak has its valley, and every valley has its peak; the peak has fields, and the fields have peaks; under the peak there exists a village, and within the village there is a peak."

万峰林又可以分为东、西峰林，景观各异。东峰林以峥嵘巍峨的喀斯特峰丛为特征，峰峦簇拥，构成雄伟壮丽的立体画卷；茫茫林间，喀斯特漏洞洼地星罗棋布，沟壑高低起伏，神秘幽深莫测。而西峰林是一座奇美的山峦，与碧绿的田野、弯曲的河流、古朴的村寨、葱郁的树林融为一体，如同一幅"峰有谷，谷有峰；峰有田，田有峰；峰下有寨，寨里有峰"的山水画。

The Wanfeng Forest Scenic Area has a number of scenic spots, such as the Jiangjun Peak, the Zhongxing Pengyue Peaks, the Bronze-Drum Square, the Moon Village, the Field of the Eight Trigrams, the Nahui River and the Dashun Peak. Of course, the sinkholes are a must-see sight in the Wanfeng Forest Scenery. So far, there is no accurate data on how many sinkholes in the forests. According to incomplete statistics, in the Western Wanfeng Forest, there are more than 30 sinkholes of the different sizes, forming a funnel landscape. The most typical ones are Yugulu Sinkhole, Yangping Sinkhole, Diaojingba Sinkhole and Xiafali Sinkhole. Geological experts believe that the Yugulu Sinkhole is the first sinkhole among the sinkholes found in China. The sinkhole, 40 kilometers northeast of Xingyi urban area, is surrounded by a forest of strange peaks. It is in the shape of a trumpet flower. Its bottom is flat, and its height is 600 meters. Around the bottom of the sinkhole, the houses of 126 families, some production and living tools are all made of stone, including stone bases, stone walls, stone benches and stone roads. In the east of the sinkhole, there is a spring that not only satisfies the drinking water for the people and animals in the village, but also irrigates nearly 20 hectares of paddy fields. As for the Field of the Eight Trigrams, it is a saucer-shaped funnel, with an underground river at its bottom. The funnel is formed by the partial collapse of the underground river and the dissolution of the surface water. The villagers farm the fields around the funnel, which forms a concentric circle in the middle. They pile up the field ridges on the basis of the original terrain, making the curved ridges become rhythmic lines and forming wonderful circle patterns like the Eight Trigrams on the earth. Also, there is the Nahui River, which passes across the fields and then disappears into the fields. According to investigations, the river runs underground for 20 kilometers before it appears outside and then flow into the Pearl River.

万峰林景区有若干景点，如：将军峰、众星捧月、铜鼓广场、月亮寨、八卦田、纳灰河、大顺峰。当然，在万峰林景区里，天坑是必看的景点。峰林中到底有多少天坑，至今没有精确数据。据不完全统计，就西峰林景区大小天坑就有三十多个，组成了漏斗奇观。雨古鲁、洋坪、吊井坝、下发励等天坑最为典型。地质专家称雨古鲁天坑为华夏已发现的天坑之首。这座天坑距兴义城区东北40千米，周围奇峰林立，底部平坦，喇叭花形，高低差600米。居住在坑底周围的126户人家的房屋和一些生产生活工具都是石头制造的，如：石基、石墙、石凳、石路。天坑东边有一泉，泉水除满足坑寨人畜饮用外，还灌溉近20公顷水田。八卦田是一个碟状漏斗，其下部为一条地下暗河。这种漏斗是因地下暗河的局部坍塌和地表水的溶侵作用而形成的，村民们以中间的漏斗为同心圆耕种，并根据原来的地形垒起了田埂，使这些弯曲的田埂成了富有韵律的线条，在大地上形成了像八卦图那样的奇妙无比的图案。还有一条纳灰河，它从田中穿过，却又消失于田野中。据考察，此河在地下穿延，在二十多公里外才出现，然后汇入珠江。

In the Wanfeng Forest Scenic Area, we will take a sightseeing van. It will stop at the observation platforms, where you can get off to take photos and enjoy the scenery around. In addition, the distances among several observation platforms are very short enough for a walk. In the Wanfeng Forests, there are a number of Bouyei villages. At noon, we will go to a village for lunch. The best dishes to be served by the villagers are the "Big Eight Bowls". We will taste the Eight Bowls, drink the Bouyei rice wine and listen to the Bouyei ancient music. Well, so much for my introduction to the Wanfeng Forest Scenic Area. Now, we get ready to move!

在万峰林景区，我们将乘坐观光车，观光车到观景台会停下来，可以下来拍照、观景。此外，有几个观景台相距很近，适合步行。在万峰山林中坐落着一座座布依族村庄。中午，我们会到村寨用午餐。村民们招待客人的最好菜肴是"八大碗"。我们可以吃着"八大碗"，喝布依米酒，听布依古乐。好了，万峰林景区讲解到此结束。现在我们准备出发吧！

⓴ Yeyuhai Scenic Area
野玉海

Yeyuhai Scenic Area is located south of Shuicheng County, Liupanshui City in western Guizhou. The site is composed of three parts, namely the Outdoor Sports Base in Yejiping Sub-plateau Area, Yushe National Forest Park and Haiping Tourist Resort Town with the Characteristics of the Yi Nationality. With a total area of 67.77 square kilometers, the site is considered to be a national key tourist attraction, which integrates tourism, vacations, outdoor sports, camping and agricultural sightseeing.

野玉海景区位于贵州西部六盘水市水城县南部。该景区由三部分组成：野鸡坪亚高原户外运动基地、玉舍国家森林公园和海坪彝族特色旅游度假小镇。景区总面积约67.77平方公里，是集旅游、度假、户外运动、露营、农业观光于一体的国家重点风景名胜区。

The word "Ye" in the name of Yeyuhai Scenic Site refers to "Yeji Sub-plateau Area", which is the mountain sports zone, the green paradise and the sea of flowers. In the area of 4,000 *mu* (267 hectares) there grow more than ten kinds of flowers and plants, such as coreopsis, sunflower, zinnia, canna and others. As visitors walk amidst the sea of flowers, the freshness of grass and scent of flowers overwhelm them, making them irresistible to embrace nature and forget about their busy daily life in cities. Also, this area is a base for outdoor sports, such as mountain bike races and spectacular camping.

野玉海中的"野"指的是"野鸡坪"。这是山地运动区、绿的天堂、花的海洋。在4000亩（267公顷）的土地上，种植了波斯菊、向日葵、百日草、美人蕉等十多种花草。游客漫步在花海中，草的清新、花的芬芳让他们陶醉，让他们拥抱自然，忘却繁忙的城市生活。这里也是户外运动的基地，有山地自行车比赛，也有精彩的露营。

The word "Yu" in the name of Yeyuhai Scenic Site refers to Yushe National Forest Park, formerly known as Yushe Forest Farm. It is not only a 4A-level scenic site in Liupanshui City, but also the first ski experience zone in Guizhou Province. In the forest, waterfalls cascade, and streams are gurgling. In spring, azaleas bloom, forming a sea of flowers; in summer, the wind whistle in pines, and the sea of clouds floats for several miles; in late autumn, the entire mountain is covered with red leaves, which are pleasing to the eye; in midwinter, icicles or snow hang from tree branches, much like a silvery world. In addition, the park is rich in wildlife resources, and plant species amount up to more than 1,000 kinds.

野玉海中的"玉"指的是玉舍国家森林公园，前身为玉舍林场。此地不仅是六盘水市AAAA级景区，也是贵州首个滑雪运动体验区。森林里瀑布飞泻，溪水潺潺。春天，满山杜鹃盛开，形成一片花海；夏日，松林间松涛呼啸，云海飘动数里；深秋，红叶满山，赏心悦目；隆冬，树枝挂上冰柱或雪，一片银色世界。此外，公园的野生动物资源丰富，植物种类多达1000多种。

Yushe National Forest Park covers an area of 25 square kilometers, with walking trails built along the mountain. The trails are so narrow that only two people can walk abreast at the widest part and only one person can pass sideways at the narrowest part. Even on relatively gentle trails, there are some exposed rocks blocking the way, where visitors may have to climb up and down, or take a detour.

玉舍森林公园占地25平方公里，依山修建了步行道，且山路狭窄，最宽处只可两人并行，最窄处仅容一人侧身通过。即便是在相对平缓的步行道上，也会出现一些挡道的裸露岩石，游客可能需要攀上爬下，或绕道而行。

The word "Hai" in the name of Yeyuhai Scenic Site refers to Haiping Tourist Resort Town with the Characteristics of the Yi Nationality. The town, located in the territory of Haiping Village, is composed of the Square of Yi Culture, the Streets of Yi Customs, the Tusi Manor, the Solar-Calendar Square, Jiuzhong Palace, the Yi Village of One Thousand Households, etc. In the small town, the buildings are mostly earthen houses with thatched roofs and earthen red walls to show their architectural features.

野玉海中的"海"指的是海坪彝族特色旅游度假小镇。该镇位于海坪村境内，由彝族文化广场、彝族风情街、土司庄园、太阳历广场、九重宫、千户彝寨等组成。小镇的建筑多为茅草屋顶、红墙的土掌房，以彰显其建特征。

This small town constantly showcases the rich and colorful culture of the Yi people through cultural exhibitions, films and theatrical performances. The Torch Festival, the Ancestor Worship Ceremony, the New Year of the Yi Calendar or other Yi folk activities will be held here when the Yi nationality festival comes. In this small town, the beautiful environment, warm hospitality and profound Yi culture make it a good place to take a vacation and experience folk culture.

小镇不断通过文化展览、电影、戏剧等方式，展示丰富多彩的彝族文化。每逢彝族节庆活动到来之时，这里都会举行火把节、祭祖大典、彝历新年等彝族民间活动。优美的环境、热情的款待和底蕴深厚的彝族文化，使这座小镇成为度假和体验民俗文化的好去处。

Well, so much for my brief introduction to Yeyuhai Scenic Area. The highlights of the site include skiing, hot springs in the forest, summer camping, outdoor rock climbing, outdoor tent camping, bonfire parties, folk performances, the sightseeing of the Yi village, etc. Today, the time schedule for our visit is arranged for two hours in Haiping, one hour in the forest park, one hour in Yejiping, and three hours in Haiping and the Yi Village. Wish you all a pleasant sightseeing!

好了,野玉海景区简介到此结束。景区游玩亮点有滑雪、森林温泉、夏令营、户外攀岩、户外帐篷露营、篝火晚会、民俗表演、彝寨观光等。游览的时间安排如下:海坪两小时、森林公园一小时、野鸡坪一小时、海坪+彝寨三小时。祝大家游览愉快!

Guizhou Third Line Construction Museum
贵州三线建设博物馆

Guizhou Third Line Construction Museum, located in Liupanshui City, Guizhou Province, is China's only museum with the theme of the "Third Line Construction". The museum covers an area of 40 *mu* (2.7 hectares) and is divided into two parts—the indoor exhibition halls and the outdoor cultural square.

贵州三线建设博物馆位于贵州省六盘水市,是国内唯一一座以"三线建设"为主题的博物馆。全馆占地40亩(2.7公顷),分室内场馆和室外文化广场两个区域。

The so-called "third line" refers to a strategic concept of my country in the 1960s. Chairman Mao Zedong divided the country into the front line, the central zone and the rear area, namely the first, second and third lines. The Third Line Construction began in 1964. This large-scale infrastructure construction was carried out across 13 provinces and autonomous regions in the central and western China. It was guided by the concept of the combat readiness and involved national defense, science and technology, industries, transportation and others. During the 17 years of the large-scale Third Line Construction, millions of construction workers worked hard together and made great achievements. Thanks to their joint efforts and hard work, the construction of China's strategic rear bases had been preliminarily completed, and the Third Line Construction had also contributed greatly to the industrialization of the central and western regions.

所谓的"三线",指的是我国20世纪60年代一个战略构想。毛泽东主席将全国划分为：前线、中间地带和后方,即：一线、二线和三线。三线建设始于1964年,这种大规模基础设施建设活动在中国中西部13个省、自治区进行,它以战备为指导,涉及国防、科技、工业、交通等方面。在历时17年的大三线建设中,数百万建设者齐心协力、艰苦奋斗,取得了巨大成就,初步建成我国的战略后方基地。三线建设也为中国中西部地区工业化做出了极大贡献。

Liupanshui City was the main battlefield for the Third Line Construction in Southwest China. In the 1960s, the trains transported the experts and equipment to the mountainous areas of Guizhou from important factories in the large cities in eastern China. Important coal bases and iron and steel bases were born in the Third Line Construction. In addition, more than 100,000 cadres, intellectuals, rural labor forces, and the PLA officers and soldiers from all over the country entered this mountainous town to support the construction, which rapidly developed Liupanshui from a small closed agricultural town into a new industrial city.

六盘水市是西南地区"三线建设"的主战场。20世纪60年代,火车把中国东部大城市里的重要工厂的专家与装备拉进了贵州山区,重要的煤炭基地、钢铁基地在"三线建设"中诞生。此外,10多万名来自全国各地的干部、知识分子、民工、解放军官兵走进这座深山中的城镇,支援建设,使六盘水从封闭的农业小城镇迅速发展成为一座新兴的工业城市。

The Third Line Construction Museum was formed on the basis of the transformation of the former third line factories. The old houses and old things include the office buildings, workshops, dining halls, auditoriums, post offices, Xinhua bookstores, supply and marketing stores, the construction headquarter, play grounds and the steam locomotives. All of them are basically what they looked alike in those days and a throwback to the distant past.

三线建设博物馆是在原三线工厂的基础上改建而成的。旧房旧物，如：办公楼、车间、食堂、礼堂、邮电局、新华书店、供销社、建设指挥部、操场、蒸汽机车，基本上是当年的原貌，再现了遥远的过去。

So far, the completed buildings include the Main Building of the Museum, the Restoration Hall and the City-Condition Hall, as well as the Third Line Square, the Industrial Sculpture Square and the Siyuan Square. The exhibition area in the Main Building of the Museum is divided into three zones: the Preface Hall, the People's Auditorium and the Main Exhibition Area. Among them, the Main Exhibition Area is divided into seven exhibition halls, which are respectively called the Strategic Decision-Making, the Joint Decisive Battles by Outstanding Workers, the Arduous Entrepreneurship, the Tremendous Journey, the Brilliant Achievements, the Cordial Concerns and the Grand Planning. At present, the museum has a collection of 9,502 cultural relics and documents. 1,128 pictures, 1,380 physical objects and more than 200 archive materials are on display. The audio-visual materials last about 1,080 minutes. In the museum, thousands of objects range from a pair of rain boots to as large as a lathe. Most of them were collected from the third line enterprises or the homes of the veteran third line workers. When some veteran workers learned that the museum was collecting the objects from the Third Line period, they also sent to the museum washbasins, wicker-suitcases and other objects. Dozens of collectors in Liupanshui City donated to the museum more than 10 pieces of their collections, such as the Food Vouchers for the Canteen of the Shuicheng Mining Bureau. Kitchen utensils, hammers for construction, coal trucks and product-manufacturing lathes are historical objects that accurately reflect the history and reality in those days. The outdoor exhibition area mainly display large material objects, such as steam locomotives, Dongfeng trucks, double housing planers, steel ladles and other precious cultural relics. In particular, the trucks from the period of the Third Line Construction tend to attract visitors' attention. Its historical particularity lies in that, with the sudden emergence of such vehicles, China has finally ended its history of not being able to make automobiles on its own.

现已建成了博物馆主楼、还原馆、市情馆，以及三线广场、工业雕塑广场、思源广场。博物馆主楼展区分为序厅、人民礼堂、主楼展厅。其中，主楼展区又分为七个展厅：战略决策、群英会战、艰苦创业、磅礴征程、辉煌成果、亲切关怀、宏图大展。现馆藏文物文献资料9502件，已展出图片1128张，实物1380件，档案资料200余份，音像资料时长1080分钟。博物馆里成千上万的实物，小到一双雨鞋，大到一架车床，大都是工作人员从三线企业，或从老三线建设者家中收集的。还有的老建设者得知博物馆在收藏三线时期的实物时，也主动把家中的脸盆、藤条箱等物件送到博物馆。六盘水市数十名收藏家曾将收藏的"水城矿务局机关食堂粮票"等十余件藏品捐献给博物馆。做饭的炊具、施工的铁锤、运输煤炭的汽车、制造产品的车床，都是历史文物，准确地反映了当时的历史和实情。室外展区主要展出大型实物，有蒸汽机车、东风牌卡车、龙门刨床、钢水包等珍贵文物。尤其是三线建设时期的卡车更易时常吸引游客的目光。其历史特殊性在于，随着该类车型的横空出世，我国终于结束了不能自主制造汽车的历史。

The Third Line Construction Museum was opened on August 17, 2013. The establishment of the museum has played an active educational role in promoting the Third Line Construction Spirit of the "Hard Work,

Entrepreneurship and Innovation, Selfless Dedication, and Unity and Cooperation". The Third Line Construction Museum has gradually become an important cultural landscape and a red tourism attraction in Liupanshui City. In addition, it has been listed as the one of China's Eight Most Worthwhile Museums to Visit. It also remains as Liupanshui's cultural landmark and urban name card. In addition, the museum reminds people to remember this period of history. In particularly, it is of great practical significance to let the current young generations know about this period of history.

三线建设博物馆于2013年8月17日开馆，博物馆的建立对弘扬"艰苦创业、勇于创新、无私奉献、团结协作"的三线精神发挥了积极的教育作用。三线建设博物馆逐渐成为六盘水市重要的人文景观和红色旅游观光点，也入选为国内最值得去的八大博物馆。它是六盘水市城市文化地标和城市名片。博物馆同时提醒着人们记住这段历史；特别是让当前年轻一代了解这段历史，具有十分重要的现实意义。

Well, so much for the introduction to Guizhou Third Line Construction Museum. Now please come with me to visit the museum. Here, entry to most exhibition halls and sightseeing areas around are free. The places where the museum tour guides offer interpretations include the seven exhibition halls in the main building, the Third Line Square, the Industrial Sculpture Square and the Siyuan Square. At noon, we will have dinner in an ancient town connected to the Third Line Construction Museum. We'll have the Guizhou snacks, such as the baked food in a pan and steamed cakes. Enjoy it please.

好啦，贵州三线建设博物馆简介到此结束，现在随我参观吧！大部分展览馆和周边游览区域不用门票。讲解员讲解范围在主楼的七个陈列展厅、三线广场、工业雕塑和思源广场。中午，我们在与三线建设博物馆相连的古镇就餐，品尝贵州小吃，如：烙锅和蒸蒸糕。希望你们喜欢。

22

Ancient Ginkgo Scenic Area in Tuole Village
妥乐古银杏

Tuole Ancient Ginkgo Scenic Spot is located in Tuole Village, Shiqiao Town, Panzhou City, Guizhou Province. It has been listed as a national 4A-level tourist attraction, known as "the hometown of ancient ginkgo trees in the world".

妥乐古银杏景区位于贵州省盘州市石桥镇妥乐村境内,是国家AAAA级景区,被誉为"世界古银杏之乡"。

Ginkgo is an ancient tree species left over from the ice age. It is a second-class rare plant and is called "living fossil". This scenic spot is the world's largest concentrated place of ancient ginkgo trees, which grow in high density and are best preserved.

银杏是冰川时期遗留下来的古老树种,属二类珍稀植物,被称为"活化石"。这个景区是世界上古银杏最集中之地,生长密度高、保存也最完整。

Specifically, in an area of less than three square kilometers there grow more than 1,150 ancient ginkgo trees. Here, the trees grow into patches, and Tuole village stays in harmony with them. The village is also known as "the Village on the Roots of Trees". There are nearly 100 families living in the forest of ancient ginkgo. Seen from a distance, the ginkgo trees are entwined with each other and branches are stagged. On the road in the village, the roots can be seen twisted on the ground, connecting to every household. In addition, children usually play on the roots, which are closely connected with each other. Also, under the trees are the houses, at the foot of these houses are the roots, and the whole Tuole Village seems to be supported by the roots of the ginkgo trees. It is reported that there are more than a thousand of ancient ginkgo trees in Tuole Village, where the youngest trees are more than 300 years old, and the oldest ones are more than 1,500 years old. Experts believe that ancient ginkgo trees are so concentrated and integrated with the village, it is unique in the world.

确切地说，在不到三平方公里的范围内，就生长着1150多株古银杏树。在这里，古银杏成片生长，妥乐村与之和谐相处。该村又称为"树根上的村庄"，有近百户人家，皆居住在古银杏树林里。从远处看，银杏树相互缠绕，树枝交错。在村里的路上，只见树根盘绕在地，一直连接到家家户户。此外，孩子常常在树根上玩耍，树根相依相偎，与树木紧密相连。再者，银杏树下是房屋，房屋墙脚边是树根，妥乐全村就像是由银杏树根托起的村庄。据了解，妥乐村的古银杏树上千株，最小的有300多年的树龄，最长的有1500多年的树龄。专家认为，古银杏如此集中，且与村寨融为一体，世上罕见。

In Tuole Village, ginkgo trees appear in different shapes, so the locals have given them popular and affectionate names. For example, "the Tree of Husband and Wife" has three trunks, two of which huddle together, just like an inseparable couple. "The Deer-Head Tree" is more than 700 years old, and its branches extend outward like the antlers of a sika deer, hence its name. One tree is called "Many Children and Diligent Mother". Its lower part is about to crack open, but the upper part has five branches, much like an elderly mother bringing up her five children. Unexpectedly, out of more than 1,000 ginkgo trees, there are only five "male" trees, which are located either around or in the middle of the scenic site, presumably to facilitate pollination of the "female" trees. "Ginkgo King", known as "the Sacred Tree", is considered to be the oldest and largest ginkgo tree in Tuole Village. According to experts' research, this tree is more than 1,500 years old, and thus it is affectionately referred to by the villagers as "the Aged Ancestor".

妥乐村的银杏树形态各异，当地人给予银杏树既通俗又传情的名称。如："夫妻树"有三株树干，其中的两株树干依偎在一起，如同形影不离的一对夫妻。"鹿首树"已经有700多年的树龄了，其枝干像梅花鹿的犄角一样向外伸展，由此得名。有一株树，取名"儿多母苦树"，树的下半部分即将裂开，而上半部分却生长出五根枝干，很像年迈的母亲在抚育五个孩子。令人想不到的是，在一千多株树中，只有五株"雄树"。这五株树要么在景区周围，要么位于景区中间，大概是为了便于给"雌树"授粉吧。"银杏王"被誉为"神树"，是妥乐最老、最大的银杏树。据专家考证，这株树已有1500多年的树龄，当地村民亲切地称之为"老祖公"。

In Tuole Village, the ancient ginkgo trees symbolize the blessing longevity and family prosperity. Therefore, according to the regulations of the village, those who destroy trees will be punished. "For a minor case, the punishment will be kneeling; if a case is serious, the violator will be beaten with a club." On the New Year's Day or other traditional festivals, the villagers usually hold grand ceremonies to offer sacrifices to the ginkgo trees. At the same time, other activities will be held, such as memorial recitations, folk song singing, stool dances and so on. Under the good care of the villagers, the ginkgo trees thrive and present a spectacular landscape.

在妥乐村，古银杏树象征着长寿和家庭繁荣的美好祝福。因此，寨里规定，毁树者将受到惩罚，"轻则罚跪，重则棒捶"。在元旦或其他传统节日，村民们通常举行隆重的祭树仪式，以及其他活动，如念祭文、唱山歌、跳板凳舞等。在村民们的精心照料下，银杏树茁壮生长，呈现出一派壮观的景观。

In the Ancient Ginkgo Scenic Spot, there are some other scenic attractions, such as the beautiful Mirror Lake, the well-preserved Ancient Post Route, and the waterfalls interlaced with ginkgo roots. In addition, the locals will offer a good opportunity for visitors to taste ginkgo tea, drink ginkgo wine and pick ginkgo nuts. Usually, the regular route is from the Ticket Office to the Golden Home Hotel via Xianma Lake, the Ginkgo Avenue, the Mirror Lake, the Tree of Husband and Wife, the Deer-Head Tree, the Tree of Many Children and Diligent Mother, the Tree of the Ginkgo King, and the Ancient Post Route. The whole trip lasts three hours.

在妥乐古银杏景区，还有其他景点，如：美丽的镜湖、保存较完好的古驿道、被银杏树根交织的瀑布。此外，当地人还会让游客尝银杏茶，喝银杏酒，体验摘银杏果的趣味。通常，游览路线是，由售票处到金色家园酒店，途经仙马湖—银杏大道—镜湖—夫妻树—鹿首树—儿多母苦树—树王—古驿道。观光时间为3小时。

㉓
Qianling Mountain Park
黔灵山公园

Qianling Mountain Park, located about 1.5 kilometers northwest of Guiyang City, consists of the Xiangwangling (Ridge of the Elephant King), the Tanshan (Tan Hill), the Baixiangshan (Hill of the White Elephant) and the Daluoling (Daluo Ridge). The park is named after the Qianling Mountain, which is known as the "first mountain in Qiannan".

黔灵山公园，位于贵阳市西北约 1.5 公里处，由象王岭、檀山、白象山、大罗岭等群山组成。公园以"黔南第一山"之称的黔灵山而得名。

A Sign of the First Mountain in Qiannan

According to legend, once an old monk came to Guiyang, where he found that on a mountain there gathered the rich aura of heaven and earth. So the old monk went there and planted a pine tree with its roots exposed to the earth surface and the other part of the tree buried beneath the ground. Unexpectedly, the tree survived and grew with widely spreading branches and luxuriant foliage. So, the monk built a monastery named Hongfu Monastery, which means "the promotion of Buddhism and bringing benefits to the people under heaven". And the mountain was thus called Qianling Mountain (Aura Hill of Guizhou).

据传说，有一位老和尚来到贵阳，发现这座山上，汇聚了大量的天地灵气。于是，老和尚来到此地栽了一棵松树，树根露在地表，其余部分埋在地下。这棵松树居然存活了下来，而且枝繁叶茂。于是，老和尚在这里修建了一座寺庙，名为"弘福寺"，意为弘扬佛法，造福天下。由此，这座山被称为"黔灵山"。

Qianling Mountain Park is a comprehensive sightseeing park. With towering ancient trees and lush vegetation, the park is home to more than 1,500 species of plants and flowers, as well as over 1,000 rare medicinal herbs. Clear springs and fantastic rocks can be seen everywhere and groups of rhesus monkeys and birds are found there.

黔灵山公园是一座综合性的观光公园，园内古木参天，植被茂密，生长着1500余种树木花卉，还有1000多种珍稀药材。清泉怪石，随处可见，并有成群的罗猴和鸟类栖息于此。

In addition, the park also has key provincial cultural relics protection sites, such as Hongfu Monastery, the Unicorn Cave and the Clusters of Cliff Stone Carvings. On the top of the mountain, there is a pavilion called Hanzhuting, the Pavilion of the Bird's-Eye-View, where you can have a bird's view of Guiyang City. At the foot of the hill is the Qianling Lake where breezes ruffle the clear water, and the surface of the lake is as tranquil as a mirror. The park also has a zoo in its quiet valley, while on its hill there exist the remains dating back to the quaternary glacial period. In 2006, the park was listed as a national 4A-level tourist attraction. In May 2009, it was renamed Qianling Mountain Park. In addition, the park is an excellent base for students to conduct field practice due to its complex geological structure and a wide variety of plants.

此外，黔灵山公园还有省级重点文物保护单位，如：弘福寺、麒麟洞、摩崖石刻群。在山顶，有"瞰筑亭"，在那里可以看到贵阳市远景。山脚下是黔灵湖，碧波粼粼，湖面如镜。公园还在幽静的山谷里建有动物园，山上有第四纪冰川期遗迹。2006年，黔灵山公园被列为国家AAAA级旅游景区，2009年5月更名为"黔灵山公园"。此外，由于公园地质构造复杂，植物种类繁多，也是教学实习的良好基地。

Among the park's many attractions, the Nine-Bend Path is particularly impressive. This is a stone path that winds uphill, leading to Hongfu Monastery. According to legend, this zigzag path was built by the old monk who planted the pine tree upside down. In the Qinglong 54th year of the Qing Dynasty (1789), Guizhou provincial administrative commissioner Chen Dawen advocated the reconstruction of the path. In the Xianfeng fifth year of the Qing Dynasty (1855), Abbot Wu Zheng collected alms for its restoration work. After the founding of the People's Republic of China, the local people's government allocated funds to widen and reinforce this path. In the park, the Nine-Bend Path winds up the hill from the entrance of the park with a total of 382 stone steps. It is said that "for every ten stone steps, there is a bend; within a few dozen steps, a curve appears." If hiking along the path seems like hard work, a cable car can take you straight to the top.

The path is hidden in the heavy shade of trees, and vegetation is everywhere. Many visitors prefer a walk along the path because the refreshing green shade makes them feel good at heart. On the Nine-Bend Path, visitors often stop to take a break. They may stand or sit on the rocks beside the path, while overlooking into the distance. What they see are a stretch of green hills. A breeze blows and the visitors feel relaxed and happy. Mr. Dong Biwu once came here for sightseeing. Seeing such a beautiful scenery, he joyfully wrote a poem to praise it. It says, "Unexpectedly, I am climbing up the first mountain in Qiannan; an old fellow like me still remains robust. Springs are clear, trees are age-old, and leaves are beginning to drop; and outside the monastery stand erect twin peaks, just like a passage-gate." Along the Nine-Bend Path there exist many natural attractions, including the Ancient-Buddha Cave, the Spiral-Shell-Blowing Wall, the Clink-Stone Cave, the Willow Well, the Alms-Bowl Washing Pool, as well as the Green Bamboo and Dragon Pond. In addition, there are numerous precious cliff carvings there, such as "Di Yi Shan"(the First Mountain) inscribed by Huang Zongyuan from the Qing Dynasty and "Hu"(the Tiger) written by Zhao Dechang, Guizhou Provincial General Military Commissioner in the Xianfeng 10th year of the Qing Dynasty (1860). Frequently, rhesus monkeys wander along the path side, begging food from visitors. Their behaviors add more fun to the hikers.

在黔灵山公园众多景点中，九曲径尤为值得一提。"九曲径"是一条蜿蜒而上的石阶小道，通往弘福寺。据传说，这条曲折小道是由把松树倒栽的老和尚修建的。清乾隆五十四年（1789年），贵州布政使陈大文倡导重修这条小径。清咸丰五年（1855年）主刹悟证为修复募化。中华人民共和国成立后，人民政府曾拨款拓宽加固这条小径。在公园里，九曲径从公园入口处蜿蜒上山，共有382级石阶。据称，"十数步一折，数十步一曲"。如果沿着小径登山很辛苦，也有缆车可直达山顶。小径四处绿荫如盖、植被遍地,许多游客喜欢沿着小径行走,清爽的绿荫让他们感觉格外愉快。在九曲径路上,游客常常驻步歇息,或站立,或坐在小径旁边的岩石上,眺望远方,只见山峦黛绿,延绵不断。微风吹过,游客顿觉心旷神怡。董必武先生曾到此游览,见如此美景,欣然吟诗赞曰:"竟上黔南第一山,老夫腰脚尚称顽。泉清树古叶微脱,寺外双峰峙若关"。九曲径沿途有不少自然奇观,如:"古佛洞""吹螺壁""响石洞""杨柳井""洗钵池""翠竹龙潭"。此外,这里还有众多珍贵的摩崖石刻,如:清代黄宗源题写的壁刻"第一山"和清咸丰十年(1860年)贵州总兵官赵德昌署名的"虎"字石刻。时常还有猕猴徘徊在路旁,向游客乞食,其举动给登山游客添加不少情趣。

Well, so much for my brief introduction to the Qianling Mountain Park. Today, the tour of the park will last two hours. You may take a cable car straight to the top of the hill, or walk to the Unicorn Cave to see pandas, peacocks, lions and tigers in the park zoo; you can also take a walk along the Nine-Bend Path towards Hongfu Monastery and then follow the trail down to the Qianling Lake. I will meet you at the entrance at four o'clock. By the way, please remember my cell-phone number in case you need assistance.

好了,黔灵山公园的介绍就到此结束。今天,游览黔灵山公园的时间为两小时。你们可以乘坐缆车直达山顶,或者步行到麒麟洞,在公园动物园看大熊猫、孔雀、狮子和老虎;你们还可以沿着"九曲径"向弘福寺方向走一走,然后顺着公园小路下山到黔灵湖畔。4点钟,我在公园门口等你们。记住我的手机电话,以便随时与我联系。

24

Jiaxiu Pavilion
甲秀楼

Jiaxiu Pavilion, located south of the Fuyu Bridge on the Nanming River, is the emblem and symbol of Guiyang City, like the Big Wild Goose Pagoda in Xi'an and the Yellow Crane Tower in Wuhan. In May 2006, Jiaxiu Pavilion was included in the list of National Key Cultural Relics Protection Units.

甲秀楼位于南明河浮玉桥的南面，是贵阳的市徽和标志，如西安的大雁塔、武汉的黄鹤楼。2006年05月，甲秀楼被列入全国重点文物保护单位名单。

Night Scene of Jiaxiu Pavilion

Jiaxiu Pavilion consists of three main parts, namely the Fuyu Bridge (Bridge of Floating Jade), the pavilion main building and the Cuiwei Garden (Garden of Greenness). The deck of the Fuyu Bridge is not straight and flat but undulating, like a jade belt floating on the river. At the entrance to the bridge stands a memorial arch architecture made of stone and wood. In the middle of the arch architecture are four Chinese characters "Cheng Nan Yi Ji"(Historical Remains of the Southern City). On the bridge lies a small pavilion called Hanbiting, the Pavilion of Deep Greenness. The Cuiwei Garden is a collection of several small buildings dating to the Ming and Qing dynasties, including the Gongnan Pavilion (Arched Southern Pavilion), the Cuiwei Pavilion (Pavilion of Deep Greenness) and the Dragon-Gate Academy of Classic Learning. The Gongnan Pavilion appears plain and lively, while the Cuiwei Pavilion looks dignified and beautiful. The Dragon-Gate Academy of Classic Learning is under the shade of dense trees, and the bamboo forest in the garden is dancing in the breeze. Therefore, the Cuiwei Garden is not only a must-see spot for non-local tourists, but also a good place for local citizens to relax, meet or make friends.

甲秀楼由三大部分组成，即浮玉桥、甲秀楼主体建筑和翠微园。浮玉桥桥面并不是平直的，而是轻微起伏，就像一条浮在水上的玉带。桥头矗立着一座石木牌坊，牌坊中央刻有"城南遗迹"四个大字，桥上建有"涵碧亭"。翠微园由几座明清古代建筑组成，包括拱南阁、翠微阁、龙门书院；拱南阁淳朴生动，翠微阁端庄美丽，龙门书院浓荫幽静，园内修竹婆娑；翠微园不仅是外地游客必游之地，也是当地市民休闲、聚会、交友的好地方。

Well, the main building is Jiaxiu Pavilion. It was built in 1598. Later, it was destroyed, rebuilt, then renamed as the Laifeng Pavilion (Pavilion of the Arrival of Phoenix). In the Qing Dynasty, the pavilion underwent several renovations, and restored to its original name. So far, the building has lasted for more than 400 years. Jiang Dongzhi, the then-governor of Guizhou, was believed to have first proposed the renovation of the pavilion. He used a huge boulder in the river as a foundation and had local people build a bridge to connect the river banks. At the same time, he built a pavilion for the purpose of nourishing *fengshui*(geomantic omen), hence the name "Jiaxiu Pavilion". The naming of the pavilion not only showed that the landscape in Guiyang was the best in Guizhou, but also encouraged the locals to study hard, so that a large number of outstanding people in Guiyang could stand out one after another. Well, the pavilion is made of wood. It is a quadrilateral building with three storeys, three-tier eaves and one tent-shaped attic. Its height is 22.9 meters from the bridge deck to the pavilion attic, topped with wooden spire. A number of ridges slope slightly downward with gently upturned ends and the four corners are decorated with the exquisite designs of rare birds and beasts. In addition, 12 stone pillars support the lowest eaves at the bottom of the pavilion, and the carved marble balustrades surround the base. The three Chinese characters "Jia Xiu Lou" are visibly inscribed on the top of the storey. When you ascend the pavilion to look far into the distance, the surrounding scenery is visible before the eyes. Fuyu Bridge looks like a white dragon lying on the waves, linking the two sides of the river. The Pavilion of Deep Greenness stands on the bridge, below which is the Pond of Deep Greenness, and the Water and Moon Platform. To the south of the bridge is the Cuiwei Garden. All these form a magnificent landscape. As early as in the Ming and Qing dynasties, Jiaxiu Pavilion remained as a regular gathering place for literati and poets to write poetry and calligraphy. Among these writings, the long antithetical couplet written by Liu Yushan from the Qing Dynasty is the most famous. The first line depicts the mountains, rivers and geographical scenery in Guizhou, while the other line recalls Guizhou's historical vicissitudes. It says at the beginning of the couplet, "For 500 years, Jiaxiu Pavilion has being standing firmly on the giant boulder, alone to prop up the heavens; it allows me to climb to a higher level, so my blurred vision will become clearer and more open."

当然，主体建筑是甲秀楼，始建于1598年，后楼毁重建，改名"来凤阁"。清代多次重修，并恢复原名，至今这座建筑已有400多年历史了。人们认为时任贵州巡抚江东知事最先倡导修建甲秀楼的。他以河中的一块巨石作为基础，并让当地人修建一座连接河岸的桥梁。与此同时，他为培育风水而建一楼，由此得名"甲秀楼"。最初的用意，不仅点明贵阳山水秀甲黔中，而且激励当地人努力学习，使贵阳人才脱颖而出。甲秀楼为木质结构，是四边形的建筑，三层三檐，攒尖顶阁楼。从桥面至楼顶高约22.9米，最上端为尖顶木柱；飞甍翘角；四个角上饰有珍禽走兽的精美图案。此外，底层还有12根石柱托檐，雕花大理石栏杆环绕基座，"甲秀楼"三字醒目地题记在顶层。登楼远眺，四周景致，历历在目。浮玉桥如白龙卧波，贯通两岸；桥上矗立着涵碧亭，桥下是涵碧潭、水月台，桥南有翠微阁；所有这些合成一组瑰丽的风景建筑群。早在明清时期，甲秀楼便是文人骚客常常聚集题咏之处。其中清朝的刘玉山所撰长联最为著名，上联书写贵州的山川地理胜景，下联追忆了贵州的历史变迁。开篇说道："五百年稳占鳌矶，独撑天宇，让我一层更上，茫茫眼界拓开。"

Well, so much for the introduction to Jiaxiu Pavilion. Today our tour route goes like this: we first take photos with the stone architecture and then cross the bridge into Jiaxiu Pavilion. After the tour of the pavilion, we go to the Cuiwei Garden. The whole trip takes about 1.5 hours.

好了，甲秀楼的介绍到此为止。今天我们的游览线路是，在石牌坊留影，然后过浮玉桥，进入甲秀楼；参观甲秀楼后，去翠微园。游览时间为一个半小时。

25
Sidonggou Scenic Area
四洞沟风景区

Sidonggou Scenic Area, an important part of the Chishui National Key Attractions, is located 15 kilometers away from urban area of Datong Town, Chishui City, Guizhou Province. Visitors from afar always ask whether the Sidonggou refers to the "valley with four karst caves". Actually, Chishui local people call the waterfall *dong*, so the Sidong means the "four waterfalls in the valley". Even the locals found evidence in *Orgin of Chinese Characters*, which reads, "*Dong*, is the rapid torrent."

四洞沟风景区是赤水国家级重点风景名胜区的重要组成部分，位于贵州省赤水市大同镇城区15公里之处。远道而来的客人总要问，四洞沟是不是指有四个溶洞的沟。实际上，赤水人称"瀑布"为"洞"，"四洞"就是峡谷里的四级瀑布。甚至赤水人在《说文解字》中还是找到了依据："洞者，疾流也。"

Sidonggou Scenic Area is mainly composed of the group of the Sidonggou Waterfalls and the other spots nearby, such as Tiansheng Bridge (Natural Bridge), Duxian Bridge(the Immortal-Crossing Bridge) and the Filial Piety Stone Memorial Archways of the Qing Dynasty. Among them, there is the Landscape Around the Liangcha River, the Huaping Waterfalls, the Dashuigou Waterfalls, the Rare Stones on the Mount Shiding, the

Datong Bamboo and Streams, the Datong Ancient Town and other scenic spots. Sidonggou Scenic Area was once called by the experts from the State Council's Tourism Resources Investigation Group as the Garden of Ten Thousand Bamboos, Xiaojia Biyu (the Small Pretty Jade) and the Flawless Scenic Site.

四洞沟风景区以大同四洞沟瀑布群及其附近的天生桥、渡仙桥、清代节孝石坊为主，其中包括两岔河秀色、华平瀑布、大水沟瀑布、石鼎山奇石、大同竹溪、大同古镇等景观。四洞沟风景区曾被国务院旅游资源考察团专家称为"万竹之园""小家碧玉""没有败笔的景区"。

When the Sidonggou Scenic Area was just discovered, many people came here to enjoy its wonders. Among them, the late calligraphy master Zhao Puchu, the leading figure in Chinese religious circles, also came for a visit. After his visit, he wrote the four Chinese characters "Si Dong Xian Jing", which mean "Four Waterfalls and Wonderland".

当四洞沟刚刚被发现时，就有许多人来此观看景点奇观。其中，已故的中国宗教界主要负责人、书法大师赵朴初先生，也前来游览。他游罢后，书题"四洞仙境"四个大字。

Sidonggou is hidden in lush greenery, with a total length of 4.5 kilometers. It is a deep valley, inlaid with four pretty and small waterfalls, such as the Water-Curtain-Cave Waterfall, the Moon-Lake Waterfall, the Flying-Frog-Cliff Waterfall and the White-Dragon-Lake Waterfall. Today, we will not only enjoy the spectacular waterfalls, but also see many spinulosa plants. These plants are giant woody ferns that grow to 10 meters long and have leaves as big as umbrellas. The ferns, which date back 200 million years to the Jurassic period, are known as "living fossils" or "food for dinosaurs".

四洞沟掩映在千姿百态的绿意之中，总长4.5公里。这是一条幽深峡谷，里面镶嵌着四级美丽的小瀑布，即：水帘洞、月亮潭、飞蛙崖、白龙潭。今天，我们不仅能欣赏壮观的瀑布，还可以看到许多棘齿植物。这些是巨大的木本蕨类植物，高达10米，长着伞状的大叶子，是2亿年前的侏罗纪时期植物，被称为"活化石"或"恐龙的食物"。

Of course, these four waterfalls are the focus of our trip. Trails on both sides of the valley lead to the waterfalls. We can walk up the trail on one side of the valley and then return via the trail on the other side. The first waterfall is the Water-Curtain-Cave Waterfall, which is about 37.5 meters wide and 31 meters high. Compared with the Shizhang Waterfalls, it can be regarded as the "Small Pretty Jade". The pool below the waterfall is known as the Green-Wave Pond that is equipped with bamboo rafts specially for tourists. There is a natural stone cave behind the waterfall. The waterfall is like a curtain over the stone cave, hence the name the Water-Curtain-Cave Waterfall. The cliff wall inside the cave is carved with three large characters "Shui Lian Dong"(Water Curtain Cave), making the waterfall look even more spectacular. Behind the waterfall, you can stroll along the stone path and watch the bonsai in the cave.

当然，四级瀑布是我们观摩的重点。山谷两边的小路一直通向瀑布，我们可以沿着山谷的一边小道上行，然后从另一边小道返回。第一洞为水帘洞瀑布。瀑布约宽37.5米，高31米，与十丈洞大瀑布相比，是"小家碧玉"。瀑布下方的水潭叫碧波潭，潭中有专门为游客准备的竹筏。瀑布后面有一条天然石穴，瀑布像帘子一样把石穴遮住，取名水帘洞。石穴内有"水帘洞"三个大字，刻于崖壁，更显瀑布壮观神奇。游人可漫步于瀑布后面的石径，观赏瀑布洞中盆景。

The Moon-Lake Waterfall is the second waterfall. It is 42 meters wide and 10 meters high. The waterfall cliff is like a gleaming half moon in the sky and the deep pool under the waterfall is like a full moon falling from the sky into the wide green bushes. There is a pagoda tree over there. According to folklore, the tree is "the deity who tries to bring two unmarried individuals together to promote marriage". As the story goes by, when local young men and women fall in love, they will come here to worship the pagoda tree, make wishes to the tree, hang the knots of true love and exchange gifts to each other.

第二洞为月亮潭瀑布。瀑布宽42米,高10米。那瀑布石崖,像天边银光闪闪的半边月,而瀑布下的深潭,又像一轮满月,从天上落在这万绿丛中。在那里,有棵槐荫树,民间传说是"月老大人"。据说,当地青年男女谈情说爱,都要双双邀约来这里拜月老,向槐树许愿,挂"同心结",互赠信物。

The Flying-Frog-Cliff Waterfall is the third waterfall. It is 43 meters wide, 26 meters high and about one kilometer away from the Moon-Lake Waterfall. The rock above the waterfall looks like a frog, so the waterfall gets its name. In the stream, three kinds of animal stones are placed in sequence. The Flying Frog is in front, the Giant Snake is behind, and the Image Stone Statue is on the tail of the snake. Legend has it that the Jade Toad once dreamed of the beauty of the mortal world. She secretly came to the Sidonggou to see the spectacular scenery. Unexpectedly, Chang'e came to look for her, so the Jade Toad hurried back to the palace, but left her shell behind. Nourished by the sun and the moon, the shell of the Jade Toad gradually turned red. The red shell caused a snake to attack, but it was discovered by Chang'e. She nailed the snake tail with an image statue and turned the snake into stone, so locals called it Flying Frog Rock.

第三洞为飞蛙崖瀑布。瀑布宽43米,高26米,距月亮潭瀑布约1公里,因瀑布上方大石酷似青蛙而得名。在溪流中,依次排列着三种动物。

"飞蛙"在前,"巨蛇"在后,蛇尾上有头"石像"。传说玉蟾梦想人间美景,偷偷来到四洞沟游览胜景。没想到,嫦娥寻来了,玉蟾便慌忙回宫,但却将躯壳遗落。玉蟾躯壳经日月精华滋养,渐渐变成红色。红色玉蟾壳引起蛇的偷袭,但被嫦娥发现了,她用石像镇住蛇尾,将蛇化为石头,于是当地人就将这叫作"飞蛙岩"。

The White-Dragon-Lake Waterfall is the fourth waterfall, which is 60 meters high, 23 meters wide and about 1.1 kilometers away from the Flying-Frog Rock Waterfall. It is the highest and most spectacular waterfall among the Minxi waterfalls. Here, the ecological environment is good. There are large ferns, the bamboo sea, strange stones and unusual trees. The waterfall powerfully falls straight down to the bottom of the valley. It is like silvery streams falling from the sky, like the white dragon coming out of the mountain, like the brocade falling from the clouds. The water strikes on the rock and splashes high, forming countless crystal drops.

第四洞为白龙潭瀑布,距飞蛙岩瀑布约1.1公里。瀑布高60米,宽23米,是闵溪瀑布中最高、最壮观的。这里生态环境良好,有桫椤、竹海、奇石、异树。瀑布直落沟底,气势宏伟,如银白色溪水从天而降,如白龙出山,云中落锦,冲击在岩石上,飞珠吐玉,形成无数晶莹的水滴。

Well, so much for the introduction to Sidonggou Scenic Area. Today, we will cover most of the valley in four hours. After the tour of the Moon-Lake Waterfall, it will be time for lunch. Our lunch will include the "Three Treasures of the Peasant Families" in Chishui Town, including the Tofu Pudding, Bamboo Shoots and Boiled Vegetables. In addition, there will be a series of dishes of the bamboo shoots. These are local green and healthy food. A final word of advice. Please wear sturdy hiking shoes or sneakers to ensure that the shoes are suitable for walking on steep stone slopes.

好了，四洞沟风景区讲解到此结束。今天，我们将在4小时内游完山谷大部分地方。游览月亮潭瀑布后，就到午餐时间。午餐有赤水乡的"农家三宝"，即：豆花、竹笋和白水菜，还有竹笋系列菜肴，这些都是当地绿色保健菜。最后，还有一个建议。请穿上结实的登山鞋或运动鞋，确保能在陡峭的石坡上行走。

㉖ Tianlong Tunpu Old Town
天龙屯堡

Tianlong Tunpu Old Town is located in Pingba, Anshun City, Guizhou Province, 72 kilometers away from Guiyang. The old town is actually a village with 1,200 households. As early as in the Yuan Dynasty, the old town was an important post named Fanlongyi(Fanlong Post). In the early Ming Dynasty, Emperor Zhu Yuanzhang stationed a large number of military soldiers there due to its important military geographic position and its location of the western strategic passage to Yunnan. These soldiers were all from the Han nationality in Jiangshu and Zhejiang. During the Kangxi's reign of the Qing Dynasty (1662–1722), the local military families transferred their status and became ordinary people, so the village was renamed Fanlongpu(Fanlong Town). At the early 20th century, a local Confucian scholar renamed it Tianlong Tunpu (Tianlong Tunpu Old Town).

天龙屯堡位于贵州省安顺市平坝区，距贵阳市72公里。屯堡实际上是一个村寨，有1200户人家。早在元代，屯堡就是一个重要驿站，名"饭笼驿"。由于其重要的军事地理位置和地处通往云南的西部战略要道，明朝初期，皇帝朱元璋在那里大量屯兵，这些兵士皆是来自江浙的汉族人士。清朝康熙年间（1662—1722），当地人由军户转变为普通百姓，屯堡更名为"饭笼铺"。20世纪初，当地一位儒士将其改名为"天龙屯堡"。

As we known, more than 600 years ago, Emperor Zhu Yuanzhang stationed more than 300,000 troops in Southwest China, where they settled down on the Yunnan-Guizhou Plateau and built numerous walled villages or towns. In the historic vicissitudes, many old military villages and towns have gradually disappeared along with their features. Only the Tianlong Tunpu Old Town still retains southern China's culture and customs, which existed 600 years ago in the Ming Dynasty.

众所周知，六百多年前，皇帝朱元璋在西南驻扎了30多万大军。这些人在云贵高原定居下来，建起了一个个屯和堡。在历史变迁中，许多古屯堡和其特征逐渐消失了，只有天龙屯堡仍保留着600年前明朝江南文化风俗。

Such culture is relatively isolated. It differs from other existing Han culture, nor from the culture of local ethnic nationalities. Its features are often seen in its language, clothing, residential architecture and religion. As for its language, it contains retroflex and is pronounced quickly. It sounds like the mandarin of the Ming Dynasty. Linguists call it the "Tunpu dialect in Anshun".

屯堡文化相对封闭，不同于其他现存的汉族文化，也不同于当地的少数民族文化。其特点表现在语言、服饰、住宅建筑、宗教信仰等方面。在语言方面，有卷舌音，发音快，听起来像明代的官话。语言学家称之为"安顺屯堡方言"。

As for its clothing, women of the town still wear dark blue long dresses with long sleeves. Their exquisite lace reflects the charm of embroidery in the Southern Yangtze. Their shoe soles are made of cloth. Shoe uppers are crescent-shaped, and shoe-tops are embroidered with patterns of flowers or birds. As early as in the Ming Dynasty, this dressing style prevailed among

Han women in the Southern Yangtze. Accordingly, women's clothing in the town has become a living material for studying the costumes of the Ming Dynasty.

在服饰方面，屯堡妇女依旧穿着宝蓝色的大袖长衣；精致的花边，体现了江南刺绣的神韵；她们的鞋底是布做的，鞋帮呈月牙形，鞋尖饰有花鸟图案。早在明朝，这种服饰风格就在江南汉族妇女中盛行。因此，屯堡妇女的服饰成为研究明代服饰的活资料。

As for the Tianlong residential buildings, they are particularly impressive. These buildings are the first landmark you will see as you approach the town. Most houses are not easily found elsewhere because they follow the architectural style of the Ming-dynasty stone villages or towns in the lower reaches of the Southern Yangtze. The town is actually a stone castle with stone tiles, stone houses, stone alleys and stone walls. Stone alleys crisscross, interconnecting the entire old town. The two huge pillars of the main entrance are made of huge stones that support the finely-carved upper part of the gate. The alley connecting the gate rises step by step. Some alleys are so narrow that even two people can't pass side by side easily. On the either side of the alleys are stone walls, often with small windows. Near these windows are doors, which are no more than 1.5 meters in height. Behind the door is a small courtyard, where window lattice and wooden frames on doors are carved into elaborate decorative patterns. Some of the patterns look like the Chinese character – Ren (人 , human being), some look like Wan (万 , ten thousand) and some others look like Shou (寿 , longevity). The details of the carving, showing fine workmanship and profound cultural deposits, could only be found in the Ming-dynasty villages or towns along the lower reaches of the Southern Yangtze. All these facts show that the culture of the Tianlong Tunpu Old Town has its own style, and people of the old town still follow their cherished images of the Ming-dynasty social life, which existed in their hometown of the Southern Yangtze.

而屯堡民居建筑，尤其引人注目。这些建筑是你走近屯堡看到的首个地标。大多数房屋在别处难以看到，因为这些建筑沿袭了江南下游石头村落的建筑风格。古镇实际上是一座石头城堡，石头的瓦盖、石头的房、石头的街道、石头的墙。古镇的石巷纵横交错，将整个古镇连在一起。大门的两根巨柱是用巨石勾垒的，支撑着精雕的门头；连接大门的小巷逐渐升高；有的小巷太窄，两人并排而过并非易事；小巷两边是石墙，通常上有小窗，窗旁有门，高度不超过1.5米。门后是小院，窗楣门楣有雕刻精致的装饰图案；有的图案像"人"字，有的像"万"字，还有的像"寿"字。雕刻的细枝末节显示出精湛的工艺和深厚的文化底蕴，也只有在明朝江南村镇中才看得见。所有这些说明了屯堡文化自成一体，而"屯堡人"仍然在梦中延续江南故乡的明代社会生活。

Well, so much for the introduction to the Tianlong Tunpu Old Town. Now let's walk into the old town, where we will see the stone houses and watch the Dixi Opera. The sightseeing time is 1.5 hours. Please follow the stone signs so that you won't get lost. The old neighborhoods, alleys and interesting attractions will be pleasant places for a leisurely stroll.

好了，天龙屯堡的介绍到此为止，现在让我们步行游览古镇吧。我们在那里观屯堡民居，看"地戏"表演，游览时间为一个半小时。请按石刻的指示牌行走，这样就不会迷路了。旧街坊、小巷、有趣的景点将是悠闲漫步的好去处。

Culture of Miao Ethnic Minority
苗族文化

The Miao is an ancient ethnic group that originated more than 5,000 years ago. It is one of the large populated ethnic nationalities in China. The Miao people mainly reside in Guizhou, Hunan, Yunnan, Sichuan, Guangxi, Hubei, Hainan and other regions. The stories about the ancestors of the Miao have long been recorded in ancient Chinese books and archives. These ancestors, known as the "Southern barbarian" clans and tribes, lived in the areas from the basin of the Yellow River to the south of the middle reaches of the Yangtze River. Guizhou is the most populous province of the Miao Ethnic Minority. The Miao people in Guizhou are mainly distributed across Qiandongnan Miao-Dong Autonomous Prefecture, Qiannan Bouyei Miao Autonomous Prefecture, and Qianxinan Bouyei-Miao Autonomous Prefecture.

苗族是一个古老的民族，起源于五千多年前，是我国人口较多的民族之一，主要分布在贵州、湖南、云南、四川、广西、湖北、海南等地。有关苗族的先民，在中国古代典籍中早有记载，是被称为"南蛮"的氏族和部落，生活在从黄河流域到长江中游以南的地区。贵州是苗族人口最多的省份，当地苗族主要集中在黔东南苗族侗族自治州、黔南布依族苗族自治州、黔西南布依族苗族自治州。

The Miao speak their own language, but with no written script. It is divided into three major dialects, seven sub-dialects and eighteen kinds of local vernaculars. All of them fall into the Miao Branch of the Miao-Yao Language Family. The Miao areas are dominated by agriculture and supplemented by hunting. The Miao are well known at home and abroad for their cross-stitch work, embroidery, tapestry, batik, paper-cutting. Among them, the Miao's batik workmanship has lasted for thousands of years.

苗族人有自己的语言，但没有文字，分为三大方言、七个次方言、18种土语，都同属苗瑶语族苗语支。苗族地区以农业为主，以狩猎为辅。苗族以挑花、刺绣、织锦、蜡染、剪纸而驰名中外。其中，苗族的蜡染工艺已有上千年的历史。

The Miao culture has a long history. The Miao clothing, food, living, transportation, singing and dancing, as well as weddings and funerals, reflect a kind of cultural charm. For instance, the Miao people use a variety of costumes and personal adornments to display their cultural symbols. There are 173 kinds of the Miao costumes and personal adornments listed by *The Costume Records of China's Miao Ethnic Nationality*. The Miao attach importance to etiquette. When guests arrive for a visit, the Miao people will surely slaughter chickens or ducks and prepare rich meals for guests. As a rule, if guests come from afar, they will first invite the guests to drink the wine in an ox-horn container. For the Miao New Year, every family of the Miao should prepare rich festival foods. They particularly care about the "Appearance of Seven-Color Foods" and the "Integrity of All Five Flavors". Meanwhile, they make "New Year cakes" with high-quality glutinous rice. For the Miao houses, they are usually three-storey wooden structures, with tile, fir-bark or thatched roofs, a type of the architecture originated from the southern style of pole-supported residential dwellings, which can be traced back to a distant time. The Miao opt for Monogamy. Both young men and women of the Miao ethnic nationality have their own traditional social activities before marriage, such as "Hui Gu Niang"(Meeting the Girls), which indicates that the Miao young people have the freedom to choose their spouses. Miao songs and dances are colorful. During the festival, young men and women wear their best clothes, gather together to sing songs to each other and dance with reed instruments.

苗族文化源远流长，从苗家服饰、饮食、住行、歌舞娱乐、婚丧嫁娶，一切无不折射出一种文化魅力。如：苗族以多种服饰来展示其文化符号，《中国苗族服饰图志》列有苗族服饰共173种。苗族注重礼仪。客人来访，一定会杀鸡宰鸭，为客人准备丰盛的食物；一般来讲，客远道而来，会先请客人饮牛角酒。苗年各家各户都要备丰盛的年食，讲究"七色皆备""五味俱全"，并用最好的糯米做"年粑"。而苗族的房屋，通常为三层木楼，以瓦、杉树皮或茅草盖顶，这种建筑源于远古南方干栏式的民居建筑。苗族实行一夫一妻制，苗族男女青年婚前都有自己的传统社交活动，如"会姑娘"，就是苗族青年自由恋爱的方式。苗族歌舞丰富多彩。节日期间，男女青年身着节日盛装，欢聚对歌，跳芦笙舞。

Of course, the most noteworthy is the celebration of the Miao festivals. Among many traditional Miao festivals, the Drum Sacrifice Festival is regarded as the largest sacrificial activity. Such a festival is usually held once every seven years and the largest one takes every 13 years. On this day, a young bull is slaughtered, the dance is performed with reed instruments, and ancestors are worshiped. Every year on the fifth day of the first lunar month of the lunar calendar, it is the Flowery Mountain Festival, also known as the Excursion to the Flowery Mountains. During this festival, local Miao people get together to play reed instruments and dance in a light and graceful way. They also carry out competition activities, such as the crossbow shooting, horse racing, hemp twisting, needle threading, and clothes and skirts wearing. Of course, the Miao New Year celebration is considered the biggest festival. It is usually held after the autumn harvest. A few days before the Miao New Year, every family will clean their houses and prepare the New Year goods, such as brewing rice wine, making bean sprouts, and making bean-curd and glutinous rice cakes. In addition, people also slaughter pigs or buy pork. Some families also make sausages and blood-curd. On the eve of the Miao New Year, the whole family stay at home to have the Miao-New-Year's eve dinner and stay up late into midnight before opening the door and setting off firecrackers. At dawn, the ancestor worship is held in each family. After breakfast, young and middle-aged men walk into the community and exchange New Year wishes with their neighbors. In the first two days of the Miao New Year, there are some taboos at home, such as not going out to fetch water; not chopping firewood on the mountain; not cleaning floors; not doing needlework. In some areas, women don't cook and men prepare food instead. In the Miao communities, weddings are usually held on the days of the Miao New Year. From the fourth day, some old people will visit their friends and relatives with wine, meat and glutinous-rice cakes. Some other old people are busy entertaining guests at home. Some young men and women stay in their villages to dance and play reed instruments, or perform the bronze-drum dance and bullfighting. Some other young men go to other villages, where young people sing to each other. The celebration activities of the Miao New Year usually last for about nine days.

当然，最值得一提的是苗族的节日庆典。在苗族众多的传统节日中，"祭鼓节"是最大的祭祀活动；这种仪式通常七年举行一次，十三年一大祭；届时要杀一头牯子牛，跳芦笙舞，祭祀先人。每年农历正月初五，是花山节，又名"踏跺花山"；每逢花山节，当地苗族人从四面八方聚在一起，吹奏芦笙，翩翩起舞；还开展射弩、骑马、绩麻、穿针、穿衣裙等竞赛活动。不过，苗年最为隆重，通常在秋后举行。快到苗年的那几天，家家户户都会打扫房子，积极准备年货，如：酿米酒、发豆芽、打豆腐、打糯米粑。此外，还要杀猪或买猪肉。有些人家还做香肠和血豆腐。在苗年三十的晚上，全家都要在家吃年饭，守岁到午夜，才打开大门放鞭炮。黎明时分，家家祭祖。早餐后，中青年男子走进社区，与邻居们相互祝贺新年快乐。在新年头两天里，家里有若干禁忌，如：不出外挑水；不上山砍柴；不扫地；妇女不做针线活；有的地区，妇女不做饭，由男人来做。苗乡的男婚女嫁，一般都选在过苗年的时间。从第四天开始，一些老年男女会带上酒、肉、糯米粑走亲访友，也有的老人在家忙着招待来客；一些年轻男女留在各自的村寨里跳舞吹笙，或表演铜鼓舞、斗牛；也有些小伙子去别的村子，在那里年轻的男女相互对歌。苗年的庆祝活动通常持续九天左右才结束。

In 2005, Leishan held Miao New-Year Culture Week. The culture week witnessed the opening ceremony of the China Nationalities Museum–Xijiang Thousand-Household Miao Village Hall. The hall illustrates the traditional culture of the local Miao people, involving their marriage customs, festivals, costumes, food and drinks, handicrafts and production activities.

2005年，雷山举办了苗年文化周。在此期间，"中国民族博物馆西江千户苗寨馆"举行了开馆仪式。该馆展示了当地苗族人民的传统文化，涉及其婚姻习俗、节庆、服饰、饮食、工艺、生产活动。

28

Culture of Dong Ethnic Minority
侗族文化

The Dong people live mainly in an extensive stretch of territory on the Hunan-Guizhou-Guangxi borders. More than half of the Dong people live in Guizhou Province, where the Dong is subdivided into the Northern Dong and Southern Dong. The Dong has their own language, which falls into the Tai-Kadai Language Family, with two separate southern and northern dialects. Before the founding of the People's Republic of China, the Dong people had their language, but with no written script. In 1958, the Dong writing system was established based on the Latin letters. Since then, textbooks, dictionaries, and reading materials have been printed out in accordance with the new writing system.

侗族主要分布在湖南省、贵州省及广西交会处，其中超过一半的侗族人在贵州。贵州侗族分为"北侗""南侗"两个部分。侗族有自己的语言，属壮侗语系，分南、北部两个方言。中华人民共和国成立前，侗族人民有语言，但无文字。1958年，设立了以拉丁字母为基础的侗文方案。从那以后，按照新的书写系统出版了课本、词典和读物。

The name of the Dong was originally called Yiling. The ancient name can be found in the documents of the Song Dynasty. During the Ming and Qing dynasties, some other names appeared, such as Dongman, Dongmiao,

Dongren, Dongjia and soon. After the founding of the People's Republic of China, the name of the Dong was generally called Dongzu (Dong Nationality), while Dongjia, another name for the Dong, is more commonly used among the local Dong people themselves.

侗族的名称，最早以"仡伶"，见于宋代文献。明清时期，曾出现别的名字，如："峒蛮""峒苗""峒人""洞家"等。中华人民共和国成立后，统称侗族，民间多称"侗家"。

The Dong culture has a long history, covering many aspects. For instance, the Drum Tower is the symbol of Dong villages. Most Dong villages have at least one drum tower. In the village, the tower is a high-rise building with up to 15 storeys. The Flower Bridge, also known as the wind and Rain Bridge, is antique bridge built by the Dong. The pavilions of the bridge can shelter people from wind and rain, and provide a place for people to get together, take a rest or enjoy the scenes around. Both the drum tower and bridge are decorated with painted carvings, usually made of patron saints or symbolic animals, such as dragons or phoenixes.

侗族文化源远流长，涵盖方方面面。如：侗族鼓楼是侗寨的标志，多数侗寨至少有一座鼓楼；在侗寨，鼓楼属高层建筑，可高达15层。花桥又叫风雨桥，是侗族人修建的独特桥梁。桥梁的亭楼可以遮风挡雨，是人们会面、休息和观景之处。鼓楼和桥梁都饰有彩绘雕刻，通常由守护神或具有象征意义的动物（龙和凤凰）组成。

The Dong costumes are fine in workmanship and rich in patterns. The Dong brocade, Dong cloth, cross-stitch work, embroidery and silver handicrafts fully reflect the features of colorful Dong culture. Dong men can be identified from their head gear and clothing. They often wear black, white or black and white turbans. The females wear pleated skirts over skin-tight indigo trousers and embroidered leggings, topped with embroidered jackets, buttoned to the right, and blue and white headscarves. Accessorized with exquisite neck rings, earrings and bracelets, their outfits appear dignified and graceful.

侗族服饰做工精细、图案丰富。侗锦、侗布、挑花、刺绣以及银饰工艺品等，都充分表现了侗族丰富多彩的文化特色。从头饰和衣装就可以辨认出侗族男子，他们常围着黑色、白色、或黑白色包头巾；女子下着百褶裙、贴身靛蓝色裤，裹绣花绑腿，上穿绣花右衽短衣，围蓝白相间的头巾，并配上精致的项圈、耳环、手镯，服装显得雍容华贵。

As for the Dong's diet, their culinary culture has their own style, which can be summarized in three aspects: various types (diet structure), sourness (taste preference), and joyousness (feast atmosphere). Sour dishes account for more than half of the Dong cuisine. As the saying goes, "There is no dish without pickled vegetables, and no dish without sour sauce." Liquor plays an important role in the Dong diet. During festivals, celebrations or social occasions with relatives and friends, the Dong people always take wine as a gift and enjoy wine.

侗族的饮食文化自成一体，大致可在三个方面加以概括："杂"（膳食结构）、"酸"（口味偏好）和"欢"（筵宴氛围）。在侗家菜中，带酸味的菜肴占半数以上，有"无菜不腌、无菜不酸"的说法。酒在侗族饮食中占重要的位置。在节日、庆典、亲友交往中，侗族人总以酒为礼，以酒为乐。

Many Dong villages have their own festivals every month. The main celebration activities include the Dong New Year Festival, the Primogenitor Worship Ceremony, the Singing Festival in Commemoration of Sha Su (an ancient heroine), the Bullfighting Festival, the New Harvest Festival and so on. The common feature of the Dong festival is that every festival has a big singing and dancing performance, as well as a large-scale show of folk customs.

许多侗寨月月有节，影响较大的有春节、祭萨节、踩歌堂、斗牛节、吃新节等。侗族节庆活动的共同特点就是每个节日都有歌舞艺术大表演和民俗大展示。

Of course, the most noteworthy is that Dong areas are always hailed as "the sea of songs". Everyone in Dong villages is good at singing. There, children learn songs, young people sing songs, and old folks teach songs. In view of their singing styl, there are too numerous to mention one by one. These include the monophonic "minor songs", the polyphonic "grand songs", the "accompaniment songs" for weddings, the "pipa songs" sung by young people while playing pipa stringed instruments, as well as the "blocking-the-way songs" by villagers when welcoming guests. The Dong grand song is a polyphonic and multi-voice chorus without a conductor and a music accompaniment. The grand song is not only an art of music, but also an important part of understanding the Dong's social structure, marriage relationships, cultural inheritance and spiritual life. The most unusual distinctive form, however, is the blocking-the-way songs, a special ceremony for welcoming guests into the village. Whenever a guest arrives, the host will come to the village entrance, where he barricades the way with benches, colorful ribbons, dustpans, tree branches and other objects. He blocks the guest and sings to the guest while toasting. Usually, the host starts singing blocking-the-way songs. In his song, he enumerates various reasons of his obstruction. In return, the guest sings path-breaking songs, refuting the host's excuses one by one. Their songs sound witty and funny, making everyone burst out laughing. After the joyful singing and drinking, the host removes the obstacles and conducts the guest courteously into the village. The host's blocking-way etiquette fully expresses the respect for the guest. At the same time, the "blocking-way" antiphonal singing and toasting activities can improve the understanding and communication between villagers and the guest.

当然，最值得一提的是，侗族地区一向被誉为"歌的海洋"。侗乡人人能歌善唱。在那里，小孩们学歌，年轻人唱歌，老年人教歌。他们的演唱风格，不胜枚举。有单声部的"小歌"、多声部的"大歌"、婚嫁时的"伴嫁歌"、青年人自弹自唱的"琵琶歌"、迎客时的"拦路歌"等。侗族大歌是一种无指挥、无伴奏、多声部的复调合唱。侗族大歌不仅仅是一门音乐艺术，也是人们了解侗族的社会结构、婚恋关系、文化传承和精神生活的重要组成部分。当然，最有特色的要数"拦路歌"，一种迎宾进寨的特殊仪式。每当客人到来，主人都会来到寨门口，用板凳、彩带、箕、树枝等物什把路拦起来。他把客人挡住，一边向他敬酒，一边对歌。通常，主人唱起拦路歌，歌中列举种种拦路的理由。客人唱起开路歌，逐一驳倒主人拦路的借口，他们唱的歌诙谐逗趣，令人捧腹。唱好了，喝好了，主人才拆除障碍物，恭迎客人进寨。主人拦路礼仪充分表达了对客人的尊敬；同时，通过"拦路"对歌、敬酒活动，增进寨民与客人之间的了解和交流。

Well, my introduction to the Dong Ethnic Nationality is over. However, the introduction is so brief that it is difficult to cover all the aspects of their culture. Therefore, I sincerely hope that you can take this opportunity to visit Dong villages, where you can further experience the Dong culture and understand the Dong people.

好了，我的讲解到此结束。讲解简短，难以涵盖侗族文化方方面面。对此，我殷切希望你们借此机会去参观侗族山寨，进一步感受侗族文化，了解侗族人民。

Culture of Bouyei Ethnic Minority
布依族文化

The Bouyei, one of the ethnic minorities in China, are native people from the southeastern Yunnan-Guizhou Plateau. According to textual researches, the Bouyei dates far back to the ancient Baiyue nationality. Prior to the Qin and Han dynasties, these people were called Puyue or Puyi. In the period between the Tang and Song dynasties, they were known as Fanman. From the Yuan Dynasty to the time prior to the founding of New China, they were named as Bafan, Zhongjia, Nongjia, Bulong or Yizu. However, the Bouyei people called themselves Puyue or Puyi. In 1953, Bouyei was adopted as the unified name for this ethnic nationality in accordance with the wishes from the people of the nationality and upon approval by the State Council.

布依族，中国少数民族之一，为云贵高原东南部的土著居民。据考证，布依族历史悠久，可以追溯到古"百越"。秦汉之前，布依族人被称为"濮越"或"濮夷"，唐宋时期称为"蕃蛮"，从元朝到中华人民共和国成立前称为"八蕃""仲家""侬家""布笼""夷族"等。然而，布依族人自称"濮越"或"濮夷"。1953年，根据本民族意愿并经国务院批准，统一使用"布依"为本民族名称。

Most of China's Bouyei people live in several Bouyei-Miao autonomous counties in Xingyi, Anshun prefectures and Qiannan Bouyei-

Miao Autonomous Prefecture in Guizhou Province. Others are distributed in counties in the Qiandongnan Miao-Dong Autonomous Prefecture or near Guiyang, the capital of Guizhou.

大部分布依族居住在贵州省兴义市和安顺市的几个布依族苗族自治县以及黔南布依族苗族自治州。其他分布于黔东南苗族侗族自治州或贵州省会贵阳附近的县。

The Bouyei language is of the Zhuang-Dai branch of the Zhuang-Dong group belonging to the Sino-Tibetan family of languages. In the past, the Bouyeis had no written language of their own, and used Han characters instead. After 1949, the government helped formulate a Bouyei writing system based on Latin letters.

布依语属于汉藏语系壮侗语族壮傣语支。过去布依族没有自己的文字，通用汉文。1949年后，政府帮助制定了以拉丁字母为基础的布依文书写体系。

The Bouyei culture has a long history. We can learn about their culture from the several aspects, such as dwelling environment, clothing, religion, festivals and marriage. The Bouyeis live mostly in villages, which are located in plain areas or near river valleys. Their houses are made of stones, and the roofs are covered with slates. In addition, Bouyei villages often have arched stone bridges. The Bouyeis have long been known for their home-made cotton cloth made by Bouyei peasant families. The Bouyeis like wearing cotton clothes in blue, green, black or white. Also, both men and women wear white or blue check scarves on their heads. The Bouyeis believe in polytheism and worship Nature. Every year there are many memorial days, offering sacrifices to the deities of mountains, the deities of trees, as well as the deities of rivers, lakes or ponds. In addition, on the New

Year's Day or other festivals, every Bouyei family will worship the ancestors whose tablets are enshrined in the family's main room. The traditional Bouyei festivals include the Spring Festival, the Dragon-Boat Festival and the Mid-Autumn Festival. Some other festivals, which have typical Bouyei characteristics are er yue er (the second day of the second lunar month), san yue san (the third day of the third lunar month), liu yue liu (the sixth day the six lunar month) and the Ox King Festival.

布依族文化源远流长。我们可以从居住环境、服饰、宗教、节日、婚姻几个方面了解其文化。布依族多居住在平坝或靠近河谷的村寨里，房屋由石块砌成，屋顶盖有石板，村寨常有拱形石桥。布依族农家纺织的布依土布久负盛名。布依人喜欢穿蓝、青、黑、白色布服装，男女用白色或蓝格头巾包头。布依族信仰多神，崇拜自然，每年都有许多祭祀日，如祭祀山神、树神、水神等。此外，逢年过节，布依族每户家庭都要祭拜供奉在堂屋中的祖先牌位。布依族传统节日有大年、端午节、中秋节，还有"二月二""三月三""六月六""牛王节"等富有本民族特色的节日。

The etiquette of the Bouyei marriage is impressive. In early history, Bouyei men or women had the freedom to choose their spouses. In modern times, the Bouyei marriage generally underwent the following stages. First, young people themselves may locate their prospective spouses through social activities, or families of unmarried boys or girls may invite a matchmaker to help their children find a prospective spouse. Typically, the matchmaker go back and forth several times between the two families before the marriage proposal is accepted. Then it is time for the marriage engagement. The boy's family chooses a good time to visit the girl's family, where the engagement ceremony, known as the "Drinking Engagement Wine", is to be held. For the ceremony, the boy's family may invite several friends and relatives to bring gifts and go with them. In some places, the boy's family will deliver bride dowry and gifts as they go to the ceremony. Meanwhile, the girl's family will feast guests at home, formally announcing their daughter's engagement. Finally, it was the consultation of the horoscope and the wedding ceremony. Prior to the marriage, the boy's family will prepare a table of dishes and drinks, a pair of a rooster and a hen, as well as gifts and firecrackers and invite some of their friends and relatives to deliver those items to the girl's family. In addition, the boy's family will present the *Luanshu* Letter indicating the date and the time of the boy's birth. The girl's family will slaughter chickens, hold a banquet and worship their ancestors. Meanwhile, the family will invite a fortuneteller to determine the date of the wedding based on the dates and the time of birth of the boy and girl. On the wedding day, the groom's family will invite a group of young men and women to go to the bride's house to escort the bride back to the wedding. Meanwhile, the bride's family will invite some women and girls to accompany the bride to the groom's house. In most areas, the bride will walk to the groom's house, and the bridal sedan chair is not often used. On the second or third day after the wedding, the newly-married couple will return to the bride's home. On this occasion, the bride's parents will give them a special treatment, along with a big lunch and wine.

布依族婚姻的礼仪值得一提。历史上布依族先是男女自由择偶。近代，布依族婚姻一般经历以下几个阶段：首先，年轻人自己可以通过社交活动自由恋爱，或者未婚男女的父母可能会请媒说合。通常情况下，媒人要往返数次，求婚才能决定下来。其次是订婚时间，男方家选择某个好日子到女方家举行订婚仪式，称为"吃定亲酒"。为此，男方家可能会邀请二三亲友，携礼物前往。有的地方，男方家参加订婚仪式时，会将聘金和礼品一起带去交清。与此同时，女方家在家里大宴宾客，表示女儿已订终身。最后是"要八字"和结婚。结婚前，男方家备酒肴一桌、公母鸡一对，以及礼物、鞭炮，并邀亲友数人把这些东西送到女方家。同时，男方家还送上新郎生辰八字"鸾书"。女方家杀鸡设酒席祭祖，请人根据双方男孩和女孩的八字，排定结婚日期。结婚时，新郎家会请青年男女数人到新娘家接亲，护送新娘来到婚礼现场；新娘家会请几位妇女和姑娘陪伴新娘去新郎家。在大多数地区，新娘是步行到新郎家的，用花轿迎新娘的并不多。婚后的第二或第三天，新婚夫妻要回门娘家，届时会受到娘家隆重接待，并备有丰盛的午餐和酒。

Well, my introduction is over. I sincerely hope that you can take this opportunity to visit Bouyei villages, where you can further experience the Bouyei culture and understand the Bouyei people.

好了，我的讲解到此结束。我殷切希望你们借此机会参观布依族山寨，进一步感受布依族文化，了解布依族人民。

Sichuan Province
四川省

四川省《导游服务能力》考试大纲

01. Sanxingdui Museum
    三星堆博物馆 /245
02. Jiuzhaigou National Park
    九寨沟国家公园 /251
03. Chengdu Research Base of Giant Panda Breeding
    成都大熊猫繁育研究基地 /257
04. Mt. Emei
    峨眉山景区 /261
05. Dujiangyan Irrigation System
    都江堰景区 /267
06. Daocheng Yading Nature Reserve
    稻城亚丁自然保护区 /272
07. Mount Guangwu Scenic Area
    光雾山风景区 /277
08. Bifengxia Scenic Area
    雅安碧峰峡 /283
09. Leshan Giant Buddha
    乐山大佛景区 /288
10. Mt. Qingcheng
    青城山 /294
11. Chengdu Wuhou Shrine
    成都武侯祠景区 /300
12. Du Fu's Thatched Cottage
    杜甫草堂景区 /306
13. Southern Sichuan Bamboo Sea
    蜀南竹海 /312
14. Wangjiang Tower Park
    望江楼公园 /317
15. Meishan San Su Shrine Museum
    眉山三苏祠博物馆 /322

（注：根据2024年全国导游资格考试大纲，四川省外语类考生景点讲解范围包括01、02、03、04、05、06、07、15共计8个景点，其余为补充内容。）

① Sanxingdui Museum
三星堆博物馆

Sanxingdui Museum is 40 kilometers south of Chengdu. It is located northeast of the Sanxingdui Ruins, by the Yazi River in Guanghan. The museum started its construction in August 1992 and officially opened to the public in October 1997. Currently, the museum is one of the five top tourist attractions in Sichuan Province. In addition, it was admitted into the first group of the National 4A-level Tourist Attractions and listed as one of China's 50 Most Desirable Places for Overseas Tourists to Visit.

三星堆博物馆位于成都以南40公里处，地处三星堆遗址东北角，广汉鸭子河畔，博物馆于1992年8月奠基，1997年10月正式开放。目前，博物馆是四川省对外重点推出的五大旅游景区之一；此外，三星堆博物馆为首批国家AAAA级旅游景区、中国最值得外国人去的50个地方之一。

The Sanxingdui Ruins cover an area of 12 square kilometers and can be traced back to the period between 3,000 and 5,000 years ago. So far, the ruins are believed to be the largest, best-preserved and earliest Shu cultural site discovered in southwest China. It is also one of the greatest archaeological discoveries in the 20th century. The excavated sites show rich cultural information closely related to the ancient city, ancient kingdom and ancient Shu culture. For the first time, it proves that the origin of Chinese civilization is diverse. Like the Yangtze River and Yellow River basins, the Sichuan Basin is the matrix of Chinese civilization and known as "the source of the Yangtze River Civilization".

三星堆古遗址占地面积12平方公里，距今已有3000至5000年历史。迄今为止，该遗址是在西南地区发现的范围最大、保存最完整、延续时间最长的古蜀文化遗址，也是20世纪最伟大的考古发现之一。挖掘的遗址展示了与古城、古国、古蜀文化密切相关丰富的文化信息，第一次昭示了中华文明有着多样化的起源，四川盆地与长江流域、黄河流域一样，同属中华文明的母体，被誉为"长江文明之源"。

You may wonder how and when the ruins were discovered. It happened in the spring of 1929 when a farmer and his family dug an irrigation ditch in Nanxing Town. There, they stumbled upon 400 pieces of jade articles typical of ancient Shu. The discovery attracted the attention of archaeologists at home and abroad. Since the 1930s, several generations of archaeologists have been exploring this area. From July to September 1986, two large sacrificial pits of the Shang Dynasty were excavated successively, and thousands of exquisite cultural relics were unearthed. Since then, the Sanxingdui Ruins in Guanghan have been well known all over the world.

或许，你想知道遗址是如何被发现，是什么时候发现的。事情发生在1929年的春天，当时一位农民和他的家人在南兴镇挖水沟，偶然发现了400余件具有古蜀特色的玉石器。这一发现引起了中外考古学家的重视。自20世纪30年代以来，几代考古学人便在此发幽探微。1986年7月至9月，古学工作人员先后发掘了商代两个大型祭祀坑，出土了数千件精美文物。从此，广汉三星堆名扬天下。

Later, Sanxingdui Museum was built in the northeast corner of the ruins. At present, the museum consists of two halls. The first hall is called the Comprehensive Hall. It contains six units. Unit 1 summerizes the history of ancient Shu over two thousand years. Unit 2 displays the development of agriculture and commerce in ancient Shu. Unit 3 shows the achievements in the local pottery technology. Unit 4 contains various jade wares unearthed from the ruins. Unit 5 shows a number of bronze ritual vessels, which display ancient Shu smelting technology. Unit 6 exhibits the bronze sacred tree, a symbol of the wisdom and spirit of ancient Shu people. The second hall is named as the Special Hall of Bronze Relics, consisting of six exhibition sections. Their names are as follows: the Strange and Secret Masks, the Images of a Group of Sorcerers, the Grand Sacrificial Rites, the Superiors of the Groups of Sorcerers, the Rare Artifacts of Ancestral Temples, and the Archaeological Records of the Sanxingdui Ruins.

后来，在遗址东北角建起了三星堆博物馆。目前，博物馆设有两个展馆。第一馆为综合馆，共有六个单元。第一单元勾勒了古蜀2000年历史；第二单元介绍了古蜀的农业与商贸；第三单元反映了当地制陶工艺的成就；第四单元展示从遗址出土的各种玉器；第五单元展示部分青铜礼器，以反映古蜀国的冶金工艺；第六单元展示通天神树——古蜀人智慧与精神的象征。第二馆为青铜专馆，设有六个展厅，分别是：奇密面具、神巫群像、祭祀大典、群巫之长、奇绝的宗庙神器和三星堆考古录。

Of course, there are many precious sacrificial objects on display in the halls. Among them, the golden scepter and the bronze sacred tree are worth mentioning. The scepter is 1.43 meters long, 2.3 centimeters in diameter and 463 grams in weight. Archaeologists found some carbonized wooden remains in the golden scepter, so they inferred that the golden scepter was made of a golden bar. It was first hammered into a thin sheath, and then a wooden scepter was encased in the thin sheath. One end of the scepter, engraved with 46-centimeter long pattern, consists of three units. The first unit, closest to the end, has two human heads of similar size and shape. The two men smile, wear the same five-pronged crowns and have triangular earlobes. The other two units have the same patterns, above which are two birds with their heads opposite to each other, and below are two fishes with their backs also opposite to each other. In addition, there is something like an arrow overlying the necks of the birds and the heads of the fishes. Some people believe that the unearthed golden scepter is a symbol of political and religious power. Others argue that the scepter, like the bronze sacred tree, is an ideological product worshiped by ancient Shu people. None of these explanations are convincing, however, and the patterns remain a mystery to this day.

当然，在馆内陈列着许多珍贵的祭祀物品。其中，金杖和通天神树值得一提。金杖长143厘米，直径2.3厘米，重463克。考古专家发现，在金杖里有些碳化的木渣，由此推断出金杖是用金条做的，是把金条捶打成金皮后，再包卷在木杖上的。金杖一端，刻有长46厘米的图案，共分为三组。第一组靠近端头，有两个类似大小和形状的人头像；这两人面带微笑，头戴五齿高冠，耳垂三角形耳坠。其他两组图案相同，其上方是两只头部相对的鸟，下方是两条背对着的鱼，还有鸟的颈部和鱼头上各叠压着一根似箭翎的图案。有人认为出土的金杖是代表政治与宗教权力的权杖；还有一种观点认为，金杖与神树一样，是古蜀人崇拜思想的产物。然而，这些解释难以令人信服，至今仍然是个谜。

The bronze sacred trees were unearthed from the Sanxingdui Ruins in 1986. There are eight trees in total, all made of bronze. Two of them are large, one being called No.1 Bronze Tree, and the other No. 2 Bronze Tree. No. 1 Bronze Tree is 3.96 meters tall, and its incomplete trunk is 3.84 meters long. The tree is made of two parts—the trunk and the base of the tree. The tree base is slightly conical with the patterns of cloud lines. There are three layers of branches on the trunk, with three branches on each layer, one on the left, one on the right and one in the middle. The left and right branches each have a fruit bud. One bud faces upward, and the other downward. A bird stands on each fruit bud and faces upwards. A dragon is embedded in the lower part of the tree, with its head downward and tail upside. Only the lower part of the No. 2 Bronze Tree remains, so the overall pattern of it is not obvious. At its bottom is a disk-shaped base on which stand three diagonal braces like roots, and between them a man is kneeling with his hands stretching forward as if he had held something before. Its restored trunk, which has three branches per layer, is basically the same as No. 1 Bronze Tree. However, the main parts of the branch are stretched outward and upturned, while the birds rest on the buds. The bronze sacred trees vividly present birds, dragons, trees and other natural things, express the religious moral of totem worship, and reflect ancient Shu people's sincere worship to the sun deity.

这些青铜神树是1986年在三星堆遗址出土的，共8棵，通身用青铜制造；其中大型神树两件，称为一号铜树和二号铜树。一号铜树高达3.96米，树干残长3.84米，由树干和树座两部分组成。树座略呈圆锥状，上面饰有云气纹。树干上有三层树枝，每层为三枝丫，位于左、右、中间；左、右边的树枝各有一个果芽，或上翘，或下垂，每个果芽上站着一只仰面朝天的小鸟；神树的下部悬着一条龙，龙的头朝下，尾在上。二号铜树仅保留着下半段，整体形态不明显。在其底部是一个圆盘形的底座，底座上立着三条象征树根的斜撑，在斜撑之间各跪一人，人像的双手前伸，似乎原先拿着什么东西。复原的树干每层都有三根树枝，与一号铜树基本相同；但枝条的主体外张并且上翘，鸟儿歇息在花蕾的叶片上。青铜神树形象地表现了鸟、龙、树等自然之物，表达了图腾崇拜的宗教寓意，体现了古蜀人对太阳神的真诚敬拜。

Well, so much for my brief introduction to the Sanxingdui Museum. The tour of the museum takes two hours. Be sure to remember the parking place, departure time and my phone number. Don't hesitate to contact me whenever you need assistance. If you need an English tour guide service in the museum, please go to the guide desk for relevant procedures.

好了,三星堆博物馆简短介绍到此结束了,参观博物馆共需两小时。注意,大家要记住停车地点、发车时间,以及我的手机电话。如果需要帮助,请随时与我联系。如需要馆内英文导游服务,请到导览台办理相关手续。

02
Jiuzhaigou National Park
九寨沟景区

Jiuzhaigou National Park or Jiuzhai Valley is located in Jiuzhaigou County under the Aba Tibetan and Qiang Autonomous Prefecture of Sichuan Province. Jiuzhaigou obtained its name from nine Tibetan villages in the scenic valley. These villages include He Ye Village, Shu Zheng Village, Ze Cha Wa Village, Hei Jiao Village, Pan Ya Village, Ya La Village, Jian Pan Village, Re Xi Village, and Guo Du Village.

九寨沟位于四川省阿坝藏族羌族自治州九寨沟县。九寨沟得名于景区内有九个藏族村寨,即:荷叶寨、树正寨、则查洼寨、黑角寨、盘亚寨、亚拉寨、尖盘寨、热西寨、郭都寨。

According to legend, there is a folk story about the formation of Jiuzhai Valley. A long time ago, God Dage fell in love with Goddess Wonuo Semo. One day, Dage presented a precious mirror to his beloved female deity. Surprisingly, a devil named Shemozha, also fell in love with Wonuo Semo. So he waged a war to try to get Dage out so he could marry the female deity. In the battle between Shemozha and Dage, the devil snatched away Wonuo Semo, who was so scared that she accidentally dropped the precious mirror that Dage gave to her. The mirror broke into hundreds of pieces, which immediately became more than a hundred green lakes, like gems inlaid in valleys and forests.

传说，民间流传着九寨沟形成的故事。很久以前，一个名叫达戈的男神，他爱上了美丽的女神沃诺色嫫。一天，达戈向他心爱的女神献上一面宝镜。不料，一个叫蛇魔扎的恶魔也爱上了沃诺色嫫。于是，魔鬼发起了战争，试图赶走达戈，以便与女神成婚。在同达戈打斗时，魔鬼抓走了沃诺色嫫。女神非常害怕，不慎把达戈送她的宝镜掉到地上。宝镜碎成上百块的碎片，而碎片立刻又变成了百余个翠海，像宝石一样镶嵌在山谷丛林之中。

Jiuzhai Valley belongs to the landform of carbonate barrier lakes. Its scenery covers a space of 62 square kilometers. It is Y-shaped and consists of 108 lakes, 47 cliffside springs, 17 splashing waterfalls, 12 turbulent streams, 5 karst shoals and 3 Tibetan villages. These attractions create unique landscapes that attract tourists from China and around the world. When spring arrives, snow begins to melt, mountain flowers blossom, and streams begin to rise. In summer, Jiuzhai Valley is bathed in verdant green; Chinese pines and dragon spruces grow in layers. In autumn, colorful plants meet the eye on all sides; the sky in the distance is clear, blue and bright; colorful leaves and forests are reflected in the surrounding lakes. In winter, snow covers the mountains and woods; as the temperature changes, the ice of the lakes constantly varies fantastic ice veins.

九寨沟属碳酸盐岩堰塞湖地形，景区占地面积62平方公里，呈现Y字形，有108个海子、47条飞泉、17座飞溅瀑布、12道湍急溪流、5处钙华流滩，以及3个藏族村落。所有这些景点构成了奇异的自然风光，吸引着国内外游客。春天来到，冰雪消融，山花盛开，溪水上涨。夏日，九寨沟碧绿浸染，油松、云杉层峦叠翠。秋至，彩林满目，悠远的天空晴朗、蔚蓝、明亮，五颜六色的树叶和森林倒映在周围的湖面。冬临，山峦与树林银装素裹，湖面的冰层随着温度变化不断变幻着奇妙的冰纹。

In 1982, Jiuzhai Valley was admitted into the first batch of the National Key Scenic Sites. In 1990, it was listed as one of the 40 Best Scenic Spots in China. In 1992, it was listed as the World Natural Heritage Site. Jiuzhai Valley has been also crowned with several other titles, such as the World Bio-Biosphere Reserve, the Green Globe 21 and the National 5A-level Tourist Attraction.

九寨沟于1982年成为第一批国家重点风景名胜区,1990年被评为中国风景名胜40佳,1992年被列入世界自然遗产。九寨沟还获得了其他殊荣,如,被纳入世界人与生物圈保护区、获得"绿色环球21"认证、被批准为国家AAAAA级旅游景区。

For those who plan to visit the Jiuzhai Valley, the most popular route is to start from the main gate to the Zha Ru Valley through the Shu Zheng Valley, the Ri Ze Valley and the Ze Cha Wa Valley. The Shu Zheng Valley is a main tourist route. It has at least 20 attractions, including the Bonsai Shoal, the Reed Lake, the Lying Dragon Lake, the Shu Zheng Lakes, the Shu Zheng Waterfall, and the Rhinoceros Lake.

对于想要游览九寨沟的人来说,最常选用的游览景区路线是从九寨沟正门出发,经树正沟、日则沟、则查洼沟,到达扎如沟。树正沟是一条主要旅游路线,景区至少有20处景点,包括盆景滩、芦苇海、卧龙海、树正群海、树正瀑布、犀牛海。

In the Ri Ze Valley, the scenery stretches for about 18 kilometers from the Nuo Ri Lang Waterfall to the Virgin Forests. Its attractions include the Pearl Shoals, the Five Flower Lake and others. The Ze Cha Wa Scenery stretches for 18 kilometers southeast from Nuo Ri Lang to the Long Lake. Its attractions include the Lower Seasonal Lake, the Upper Seasonal Lake, the Five Colored Pond and the Long Lake. The trip ends after the sightseeing of the Za Ru Valley, where you can see the Tibetan beautiful countryside and appreciate the charm of the Tibetan folk culture.

日则沟风景线是从诺日朗瀑布到原始森林，全长18公里；景区有珍珠滩、五花海，等等。则查洼沟景区从诺日朗往东南方向延伸到长海，全长18公里，景区有下季节海、上季节海、五彩池、长海。游览了扎如沟后，游览就结束了。在扎如沟人们可以看到藏家的田园风光，领略藏族的民俗文化。

Here, I'd like to highlight two of the attractions. Hope you like them.
在此，我想重点介绍其中两处景点，希望你们喜欢。

Nuo Ri Lang Waterfall

The Nuo Ri Lang Waterfall is located at the junction of Nuo Ri Lang and the Shu Zheng Valley. Nuo Ri Lang literally means "magnificence". Being 30 meters in height and 270 meters in width, the waterfall is one of the largest calcified waterfalls in China. During the rainy season, the waterfall cascades and produces a tremendous noise that vibrates constantly in the valley. As the water hits the valley floor, it immediately splashes high up into the air in the form of countless tiny fine drops. The drops are tossed, blown or projected, forming a spectacular water curtain. Even at a far distance, the amazing waterfall can be seen; their thundering noise can be heard; and water mist and colorful rainbows form a wide and splendid water screen in the sky. In autumn when the water level drops, the waterfall takes another miracle, and the hanging cliff looks like colorful silk that matches the surrounding colorful bushes. In midwinter, the cliffs are dressed with icicles and ice curtains, forming spectacular ice waterfalls of different shapes, as if they were placed in a world of ice sculptures.

诺日郎瀑布位于诺日郎和树正沟交界处。"诺日郎"意指"高大雄伟"。瀑布高30米,宽270米,是中国最大的钙化瀑布之一。在雨季,瀑布飞泻,不停地声震山谷。瀑布跌入谷底,水花立即四溅,飞入高空,形成无数晶莹的水滴,四处抛洒、吹散、投射,化成了一幕壮观的水帘。即使在距离瀑布较远之处,也能够看到惊人的瀑布,听到雷鸣般的声音;水雾和缤纷彩虹在空中形成了一个宽大、壮观的水帘。秋日,水位下降,瀑布呈现另一壮美景观,高悬峭壁看起来像是多彩的丝绸,与周围多彩丛林相得益彰。隆冬,崖壁挂满冰柱、冰帘,形成了蔚为壮观、千姿百态的冰瀑,仿佛是冰雕世界。

In Jiuzhai Valley, the Five Colored Pond is the smallest lake, which is located one kilometer away to the Long Lake. The water in the pond comes from the Long Lake. It doesn't seem to be increasing or diminishing. The pond is translucent and dark blue and the bed of the pond is visible. In winter, ice and snow cover everywhere, except for the Five Colored Pond that doesn't freeze. In the pond there grow rich sponges, algae, ferns, as well as reeds and bushes. When the sunlight hits the water, the underlying sediments present the clusters of multiple colors due to the action of algae and bryophyte plants. In the same pond, some water areas appear sky blue, some crooked streams look pale green, and some water comes out bright yellow. There are still some flowing springs that remain pale blue. Many tourists usually stop and sit by the pond, where the beauty of the pond seems to make them feel ease at heart. There, they may marvel at the multi-colored clusters, which look like inexhaustible treasures bestowed by the Master Creator of All Things.

五彩池是九寨沟最小的海子,坐落在距长海一公里的地方。池水来自长海,似乎无增无减,水碧蓝半透明,可见池底。冬季,四周冰天雪地,而五彩池却不结冰。池里生长着丰富的水绵、轮藻、小蕨,还有芦苇、灌木丛。阳光照在水面上,池底沉淀物在藻类和苔藓植物的作用下,呈现出多彩的植物群落。在同一海子里,有的水域蔚蓝,有的湾汊浅绿,有的水色嫩黄色,有的流泉粉蓝。许多游客常常驻足坐在海子边,海子的美似乎使他们安心自在,他们惊讶地看着多彩的植物群落,好像这些是万物之主赐予的不尽的宝藏。

Well, so much for my introduction to the Jiuzhaigou National Park. We will be at the park entrance in ten minutes. I'd like to remind that you'd better take a warm jacket; be sure to wear a sun hat and apply sunscream, as the sun and ultraviolet rays are strong in the scenic area. In addition, care for plants; no fire in open area.

好啦,九寨沟国家公园讲解到此结束。10分钟后,我们将到达公园入口处。请注意:带上保暖衣物;一定要戴上太阳帽,涂抹防晒霜,景区日照强,紫外线强;另外,爱护景区草木,严禁野外用火。

Sichuan Province
四川省

Chengdu Research Base of Giant Panda Breeding
成都大熊猫繁育研究基地景区

Chengdu Research Base of Giant Panda Breeding (hereinafter referred to as Panda Base) is located on the Futou Hill in the northern suburb of Chengdu. Its construction started in 1987 and went through three stages. Among the constructed buildings, the Giant Panda Museum is the world's only thematic museum dedicated to rare and endangered wildlife. The numbers of pandas in the enclosures of the center increased to 176 in 2017 from six in 1987. As a result, the center has the largest population of captive pandas in the world. Visitors can watch pandas at short range when these animals are in open-door enclosures. Besides, the center has a Swan Lake, where about 116 species of birds reside. These include black-neck cranes, white storks, white swans, etc. In July 2006, the center was officially listed as a World Cultural Heritage Site by UNESCO and classified as the National 4A-level Tourist Attraction by the National Tourism Administration.

成都大熊猫繁育研究基地（以下简称熊猫基地）位于成都北郊斧头山。基地建于1987年，共分三期建设。在建造的建筑中，大熊猫博物馆是世界上唯一为珍稀濒危野生动物建立的专题博物馆。圈养场的大熊猫，数量从1987年的6只增加到2017年的176只，从而使中心拥有世界上数量最多的圈养大熊猫。熊猫在圈养地外面时，游人可以近距离观看它们。熊猫基地还有天鹅湖，栖息有黑颈鹤、白鹳、白天鹅等116种鸟类。2006年

7月，熊猫基地被联合国教科文组织评为世界文化遗产，并被国家旅游局授予"国家AAAA级旅游景区"。

Giant pandas are known to have lived on earth for at least 8 million years. It is an animal of the late Pleistocene and is known as "living fossil" and "national treasure in China". Pandas usually live alone in dense forests or bamboo groves. They prefer to live in mountain forests at an altitude of 2,300 to 3,200 meters. In spring and winter when the mountains are covered by heavy snow, pandas go down to live in lower areas. In summer and autumn, as the valleys become warm, they return to higher altitudes. It is said that zoo pandas can live up to 35 years old. Scientists are not sure about the life span of pandas in the wild, although they know that pandas in zoos live longer than those in the wild. Pandas are carnivores, but they're too slow to catch animals. Therefore, they mainly live on a vegetarian diet of bamboo and sugar cane leaves. They also eat sugar cane, rice gruel, a special high-fiber biscuit, carrots, apples and sweet potatoes. A newborn panda cub weighs 90 to 130 grams. Its skin is pink. Within two weeks, the skin will turn gray. A month after birth, the baby panda has the same skin color as its mother. Pandas begin eating bamboo when they are five months old, and they become accustomed to foods other than breast milk when they are six months old.

众所周知，大熊猫已在地球上至少生存了800万年，是更新世晚期的动物，被誉为"活化石"和"中国国宝"。大熊猫通常独自生活在茂密的森林或竹林中，喜欢住在海拔2300米到3200米的山区森林地带。在春冬之时，大雪封山，熊猫会到较低处的地方生活。在夏秋之际，山谷变暖，它们又返回海拔更高的地方。据称，动物园的熊猫寿命可达35年。虽然科学家知道动物园里的熊猫比野外的要活得长，但是不确定野生熊猫的寿命期限有多久。熊猫是肉食者，但它们捕捉动物的速度太慢。所以，他们吃的东西大部分是素食，如：竹子和甘蔗叶。它们也吃甘蔗、白米粥、特殊高纤维饼干、胡萝卜、苹果、红薯。新出生的熊猫幼仔重90~130克。刚出生的熊猫幼仔皮肤是粉红色的。在两周内，皮肤变成灰色。出生1个月后，熊猫幼仔的肤色就和它们妈妈的一样了。5个月后，熊猫便开始吃竹子。6个月后，它们习惯了母乳以外的食物。

According to some ancient records, giant pandas lived in many areas in ancient China 2,000 years ago. Due to the continuous expansion of human production activities, the habitat of giant pandas gradually shrank. Currently, they only live in the southern slope of the Qingling Mountains, Minshan Mountains, and Qionglai Mountains, as well as Daxiang and Xiaoxiang Ridges and some areas of Liangshan Mountains. Recent data show that there are only about 1,500 wild giant pandas, 85 percent of which inhabit within the borders of Sichuan, and there are several haunts of pandas near Chengdu. In 1957, the Third National People's Congress decided to establish forest nature reserves. In 1963, in order to protect pandas and other rare animals, China established its first five nature reserves, four of which were in Sichuan. In June 1992, the Chinese Government launched a "Project to Protect Giant Pandas and Their Habitats". One of the main contents of the project was to strengthen scientific studies on the ecology, artificial feeding and reproduction of giant pandas. Currently, there are several options for the panda tour. You can go to the Panda Base, which is 10 kilometers away from the urban area. Or you can travel to the giant panda habitats, 200 kilometers from Chengdu. One habitat is the Wolong Nature Reserve in Wenchuan County of Aba Tibetan and Qiang Autonomous Prefecture, and the other is the Fengtongzhai Nature Reserve in Boxing County of Ya'an.

据一些古代记载，2000年前大熊猫生活在古代中国的许多地方。由于人类生产活动的不断扩大，大熊猫的栖息地便逐渐缩小。目前，它们只栖息在秦岭南坡、岷山、邛崃山、大小相岭和凉山部分地区。最近的数据显示，只有约1500只野生大熊猫，其中85%的熊猫分布在四川境内，在成都周边也常有多处熊猫出没地方。1957年，第三次全国人民代表大会决定建立森林自然保护区。1963年，中国建立了最初的5个保护大熊猫等珍稀动物的自然保护区，其中有4个在四川。1992年6月，中国政府启动了"保护大熊猫及其栖息地工程"。该项目的主要内容之一是：加强对大熊猫生态和人工饲养和繁育的科学研究。目前，大熊猫之旅有几种形式：可以到距市区10公里的成都大熊猫繁育研究基地参观，也可前往距成都市200公里远的大熊猫栖息地考察。一处栖息地是阿坝州汶川卧龙自然保护区，另一处是雅安市宝兴蜂桶寨自然保护区。

Well, so much for my introduction to the giant pandas and the Panda Base. Here we are at its entrance. Our tour route goes like this: we follow the path to the hillside, where we will visit the Giant Panda Museum, the enclosures of giant pandas and the panda delivery rooms. Then we will go down to the Swan Lake. The tour lasts for two hours. Be sure not to feed pandas when you watch pandas at close quarters.

好了，大熊猫和熊猫基地讲解到此结束。我们到达熊猫基地的入口处了。今天游览路线是：我们沿着小道走到半山坡，在那里参观大熊猫博物馆、成年大熊猫别墅、大熊猫产房。然后，我们去天鹅湖。全程共2小时。在近距离观看熊猫时，请不要喂食熊猫。

Mt. Emei
峨眉山景区

Mt. Emei is located in Emei City, Sichuan Province. It has scenic area of 154 square kilometers and its highest peak, the Ten Thousand Buddha Summit is 3,099 meters high above the sea level. Many titles have been bestowed on Mt. Emei, such as the National Key Cultural Relics Protection Unit, the National Key Scenic Attraction and the National 5A-level Tourist Attraction. In 1996, it was formally listed as the World Cultural Heritage Site by UNESCO.

峨眉山位于四川省峨眉山市境内,景区面积154平方公里,最高峰万佛顶海拔3099米。峨眉山获得许多殊荣,如:全国重点文物保护单位、国家重点风景名胜区、国家AAAAA旅游景区。1966年,峨眉山正式被联合国教科文组织列为世界文化遗产。

Mt. Emei is one of the Four Great Buddhist Holy Mountains in China. The other three are Mt. Putuo in Zhejiang, Mt. Wutai in Shanxi and Mt. Jiuhua in Anhui. According to legend, Buddhism was introduced to Mt. Emei in the first century A.D., from which Mt. Emei was honored as the "Paradise of Buddhism". However, we do not know exactly when Mt. Emei was first identified as the abode of Puxian Bodhisattva. But as early as 400 A.D., a monk named Huichi arrived at Mt. Emei and began to build a temple to enshrine Puxian. In the past nearly 2,000 years, the development of Buddhism has left Mt. Emei with a wealth of Buddhist cultural heritage and brought up numerous eminent monks, making the mountain gradually become a famous Buddhist holy land in China and even in the world. Today, there are nearly 30 monasteries on the mountain. Among these Buddhist architectures, the well-known ones are Baoguo Monastery, Fuhu Monastery, Qingyin Pavilion, Hongchunping Monastery, Xianfeng Monastery, Huazang Monastery, as well as Wannian Monastery.

峨眉山是我国四大佛教圣地之一，其他三座山分别为浙江的普陀山、山西的五台山和安徽的九华山。相传，佛教于公元1世纪传入峨眉山，由此峨眉山被誉为"佛国天堂"。然而，峨眉山何时成了普贤的道场，我们不得而知。早在公元400年，一位名叫慧持的和尚来到峨眉山，开始建庙供奉普贤。近2000年来，佛教的发展给峨眉山留下了丰富的佛教文化遗产，造就了许多高僧大德，使峨眉山逐渐成为中国乃至世界著名的佛教圣地。如今，山上有寺庙近30座，其中著名的有报国寺、伏虎寺、清音阁、洪椿坪、仙峰寺、华藏寺、万年寺。

Mt. Emei is characterized with its unique geological landforms, biological soil and climate. It remains evergreen all year around. Fir trees, pines and cedars cover the slopes, crags are lofty, and precipices soar into clouds. In spring, forests look luxuriantly green; in summer, the azalea flowers bloom; in autumn, colorful leaves appear on the mountain; in winter, snow covers the mountain, like a silvery world. As tourists climb the mountain, they usually see different landscapes, such as the Buddhist Temples in Clouds, the Seas of Azaleas, the Chinese Orchids at Stalagmite Valley, and the Beautiful Views of the Golden Summit. In the eyes of tourists, Mt. Emei usually has four main scenic sections, such as the Baoguo Monastery Scenic Section, the Scenic Section between the Qingyin Pavilion and Jiulao Cave (Nine Immortals Cave), the Wannian Monastery Scenic Section, as well as the Golden Summit Scenic Section.

峨眉山终年常绿,具有独特的地质地貌、生物土壤和气候特征。杉树、松树、雪松覆盖斜坡;峭壁万丈,悬崖高耸入云。春季,树林郁郁葱葱;夏季,杜鹃盛开;秋季,满山彩叶;冬季,山脉白雪皑皑,仿佛是一片银色的世界。游客登山时,常常会见到不同的景观,如:云中寺庙、杜鹃花海、石笋谷兰花、金顶美景。一般说来,在游客的眼里峨眉山有四大主要景区,即:报国寺景区、清音阁—九老洞景区、万年寺景区和金顶景区。

The Golden Summit

Among the scenic sections, the Golden Summit Scenic Section is the most worth mentioning. This section is 3,077 meters above the sea level. It includes the Xixiang Pool (Elephant Bathing Pool) and the Golden Summit. The Xixiang Pool is a stone basin, which is three meters in depth. According to legend, Puxian washed his elephant here every time when he passed by. Also, the Xixiang Pool is the best place to enjoy the moon. Under the moonlight and azure sky, when the breeze gently blows, visitors can see the majestic peaks in the distance. However, the highlight of this section is the Golden Summit. The Golden Summit towers over vertical cliffs, with its golden roofs reflecting glaring sunlight. Below is a sea of floating clouds, surging forward with great momentum. Occasionally, foliage-covered peaks protrude out of the clouds. On the Golden Summit, there are four spectacular wonders: the Sunrise, the Sea of Clouds, the Halo of Buddhism and the Sacred Lamp. The so-called sunrise starts out like wisps of white threads in the east, and then the rays of lights shoot out of the horizon. Gradually, colorful beams come out and spray into half of the sky. Little by little, the sun slowly jumps out, rising higher and higher, until the sky becomes brighter, and the top of the mountain is bathed in the brightness of the rising sun. To enjoy the view of the Sea of Clouds, visitors can sit all day, watching the rolling clouds. The clouds drift in and out of the sunlight, like real waves in the sea. They may rise slowly, filling the cloudless sky. They may crash into the cliffs or hide the mountains, making the peaks look like isolated islands. Later in the afternoon, the Halo of Buddhism may appear in the sky, like a ring of multicolored light, but this phenomenon is not common. The viewer's figure is reflected in the middle of the ring, and as the viewer moves, the ring follows. This ring is traditionally known as the Buddhist Halo or the Emei Glory. In fact, it is a rainbow halo. When water particles concentrate in low-density cumulus clouds below the summit, the refraction of water particles on the viewer will create his/her shadow in the halo. The phenomenon of the Sacred Lamp is extremely rare. It appears below the Sheshen Cliff at some midnight in which there is no moon in the sky, no rain falls, no breezes blow on the peaks and no clouds remain below the peaks. At this particular dark midnight, a shimmering light like a firefly may come out and flutter in the air. Then two and more similar drifting lights come into view. Gradually, countless lights flock together, just like innumerable lamps. In ancient times, people called these lights the Sacred Lamps and hailed them as the "Thousands of Lamps Worshiping Puxian".

在这些景区中，金顶景区最值得一提。该景区海拔3077米，有洗象池和金顶景点。洗象池为3米深的一块石盆。传说，普贤每逢路过此处，必先浴象。洗象池还是赏月的最佳之处。每当碧空万里，月朗中天，微风和煦，游客可以看到远处庄严的山峰。不过，景区的亮点在金顶。金顶屹立在陡峭绝壁之上，在阳光照耀下，金色屋顶闪烁耀眼。在脚下，飘浮的云海波澜壮阔；偶尔也能看见树叶覆盖的山峰伸出云端。金顶有四大奇观：日出、云海、佛光和圣灯。所谓日出，最初是丝丝白色在东边吐出，继而地平线上射出缕缕光线，渐渐地出现了五彩光束，散漫半边天。旭日缓慢地跳了出来，愈升愈高，直至天空变得愈加明亮，山顶沐浴在冉冉升起的朝阳光辉之中。为看云海景色，游客们可以整天坐着观看绵绵翻滚的云海。云从阳光里钻进漂出，如同真正的大海波涛。可能它们会缓慢升腾，接壤无云的天空；可能它们会撞击山崖或者淹没群山，让山峰看起来像孤立的岛屿。傍晚，佛光可能会显现在空中，像多彩的光环，但这种现象不常见。观者的人影映入光环之中，人移动，光环相随。这种光环通常被称为佛光或峨眉宝光。其实，这是一种彩虹光圈。当水微粒子聚集在山顶下的低密度积云中时，水微粒子绕射到观者就会在光圈中产生观者的影子。圣灯现象极为罕见。在无月、无雨、山顶无风、山下无云的午夜之时，圣灯偶尔会出现在摄身岩下。在这种特有的漆黑夜晚，可能会出现一个微弱亮点，像萤火虫一样在空中飘动。继而又冒出两个、数个类似的飘忽亮点。渐渐地，无数的亮点汇聚一团，像数不清的明灯。古时，人们称之"圣灯"，赞为"万盏明灯朝普贤"。

Well, so much for my introduction to Mt. Emei. Our trip takes two days. We take a tour bus up to the Jieyindian Bus Station. From there, we transfer to a cable car to the Golden Summit and stay there overnight. Early tomorrow morning after viewing the sunrise, we walk down the mountain, along the route of the Xixiang Pool, the Jiulao Cave, Hongchunping Monastery, until we reach Baoguo Monastery at the foot of the mountain. Be sure to get everything ready by wearing hiking shoes and taking raincoats and warm clothes. Also, be sure not to view scenery while walking, and not to walk while viewing scenery. By the way, please remember my phone number in case you need assistance.

好啦，峨眉山的介绍到此结束。此次旅行共两天。我们乘观光车到接引殿汽车站，从那里转乘缆车到金顶过夜。第二天清晨，我们观看日出，之后步行下山，沿途经过洗象池、九老洞穴、洪椿坪，一直走到山脚下的报国寺。请注意：做好所有准备，穿上登山鞋，带上雨衣和保暖的衣服；走路不看景，看景不走路；记住我的手机电话，请随时与我联系。

Dujiangyan Irrigation System
都江堰景区

The Dujiangyan Irrigation System is located west of Dujiangyan City in Sichuan Province. It is not only a world-famous ancient water conservancy project in China, but also a well-known scenic attraction. Around the attraction there are numerous cultural relics, such as Fulong Temple, the Two-Kings' Temple, the Anlan Cable Bridge, Yulei Pass, and Lidui Park.

都江堰位于四川省都江堰市城西,它不仅是举世闻名的中国古代水利工程,也是著名的风景名胜区,周围景色秀丽,文物古迹众多,有伏龙观、二王庙、安澜索桥、玉垒关、离堆公园。

The Dujiangyan Irrigation System is an important part of the Scenic Attractions of Mt. Qingcheng – Dujiangyan Irrigation System. In 1982, it was admitted into the first group of the National Key Scenic Attractions. In 2000, it was listed as the World Cultural Heritage Site by the 24th Conference of the UNESCO World Heritage Committee. In 2007, Mt. Qingcheng – Dujiangyan Irrigation System was listed as the National 5A-level Tourist Attraction by the National Tourism Administration.

都江堰是青城山—都江堰风景名胜区的重要组成部分,1982 年被列入第一批国家级风景名胜区。2000 年,在联合国教科文世界遗产委员会第 24

届大会上，都江堰被确定为世界文化遗产。2007年，青城山—都江堰旅游景区经国家旅游局批准为国家AAAAA级旅游景区。

The Dujiangyan Irrigation System is the ancient technological marvel. As you stand on the Observation Platform, you will enjoy a panoramic view of the Dujiangyan Irrigation System. More than 2,000 years ago, Li Bing was appointed governor of the Shu Prefecture and began his career in governing Shu. During his tenure, he had people construct the Dujiangyan irrigation system, a water diversion project with no dam. Its water conservancy headwork is composed of the three major parts: the Fish Mouth Water-Dividing Dike, the Sand-Flying Fence and the Bottle-Neck-Shaped Channel. The three parts constitutes a scientific water conservancy engineering system, diverting water into Chengdu Plain from the upper reaches of Minjiang River. As a result, the system fosters a vast expanse of fertile farmland, making it become the Land of Abundance, where "there is no famine due to controlling floods and droughts". So far, this system is believed to be the world's oldest and only existing grand water conservancy project with no dam. In the past 2,260 years and more, the system has been continuously used and constantly improve efficiency, using its gravity irrigation to irrigate the farmland of more than 10 million *mu* (666, 667 hectares) and benefiting more than 40 counties or cities.

都江堰是千古奇功。在观景台上，都江堰水利工程尽收眼底。2000多年前，李冰被任命为蜀郡守，开始了他的治蜀生涯。在任职期间，他创建了以无坝引水为特征的都江堰。渠首工程由鱼嘴、飞沙堰和宝瓶口三大主体工程组成。三者形成科学的治水工程系统，把岷江上游之水引入成都平原，滋养出沃野千里，使之成为"水旱从人，不知饥馑"的天府之国。目前，这一系统是世界上年代最久、唯一留存、以无坝引水为特征的宏大水利工程。2260多年来，都江堰一直连续使用，不断发挥效益，利用自流灌溉1000多万亩（666 667公顷）农田，惠及了40余县（市）。

Sichuan Province
四川省

A Panoramic View of Dujiangyan Irrigation System

Well, I'd like to talk more about the water conservancy head-work, which is composed of the Fish Mouth Water-Dividing Dike, the Sand-Flying Fence and the Bottle-Neck-Shaped Channel. The Fish Mouth Water-Dividing Dike is located in the middle of the river. Long ago, when Li Bing was here for an on-the-spot investigation, he decided to construct an artificial water-dividing dike in the middle of the river. The dike looks like a whale lying against the river current, while the front of the dike is cylindrical, like a fish mouth. The Minjiang River is divided into the outer and inner canals by the Fish Mouth. The inner canal is an irrigation channel along the Yulei Hill. The outer canal is the main current of the Minjiang River, with is mainly used for flood and sand discharge. The Sand-Flying Fence is located at the end of the Jin'gang Embankment and on the side of the Lidui Hill. It is a low dam connecting the inner and outer canals. When the flow of water in the inner canal becomes small, the fence will block water, allowing it to flow along the inner canal into the irrigation areas. As the water level rises, especially during the flood period, the fence is used to discharge excess water into the outer canal. At the same time, the vortex flow also throws sediments into the outer canal. In ancient times, the fence was constructed temporarily with huge bamboo cages filled with pebbles. At present, concrete has been cast instead. The Bottle-Neck-Shaped Channel lies at the foot of the Lidui Hill. What Li Bing dug in those days is a narrow opening in the shape of a bottleneck, which is 20 meters wide, 40 meters high and 80 meters long. During the flood season, the narrow Bottle-Neck-Shaped Channel serves as a check gate, preventing excess water from pouring into the inner canal. Over the centuries, these three main engineering parts have worked together harmoniously to form a complete irrigation and drainage network, which ensures the success of irrigation with water from the Minjiang River.

好了，我想多谈一谈由鱼嘴、飞沙堰和宝瓶口组成的渠首工程。鱼嘴位于江心。李冰当年在此考察，决定在江心修筑人工分水堤，水堤像一条鲸鱼逆江而卧，堤前部呈圆柱形，像鱼之嘴。鱼嘴把岷江分为内、外两江；内江是沿玉垒山灌溉渠；外江是岷江的正流，主要用于泄洪排沙。飞沙堰位于金刚堤末端，在离堆一侧，是一道连接内江和外江的低坝。当内江水量小时，飞沙堰就会挡住水，让其进入内江灌区。当水量增大之时，特别在洪水期，飞沙堰将多余的水排放到外江；同时，旋流也将泥沙抛掷到外江。古时飞沙堰，是用巨大竹笼装满卵石临时建造的，如今已改用混凝土浇筑。宝瓶口位于离堆脚下，是李冰当年开凿的一条宽20米、高40米、长80米的狭窄口子，形如瓶颈。在汛期，狭窄的宝瓶口充当了闸门，防止多余的流水不至于通过宝瓶口涌入内江。数个世纪以来，这三个主要工程协调运作，形成完整的灌溉和排水网，成功确保了岷江之水用于灌溉。

Well, so much for my introduction to the Dujiangyan Irrigation System. Now let's begin tour of this world-famous water conservancy project. Our route goes like this: we first take a look at the Nanqiao Bridge. After that, we enter the Dujiangyan scenic area from the Lidui Park. There, we will see the

Bottle-Neck-Shaped Channel, the Sand-Flying Fence and the Fish Mouth Water-Dividing Dike. Then we will cross the Anlan Cable Bridge to visit the Two-Kings' Temple and have a panoramic view of the irrigation system on the Observation Platform. Afterwards, we take a bus to Mt. Qingcheng. The whole tour takes three hours.

  好啦，都江堰的介绍到此结束。现在开始游览这座世界著名的水利工程。我们的线路是：先参观南桥，再从离堆公园进入都江堰风景区，游览宝瓶口、飞沙堰、鱼嘴；然后过安澜索桥，参观二王庙，在观景台上观看都江堰全景；最后乘车去青城山。全程游览共需3小时。

Daocheng Yading Nature Reserve
稻城亚丁

Daocheng Yading, located in Ganzi Tibetan Autonomous Prefecture of Sichuan Province, is about 800 kilometers away from Chengdu and hidden deep on the edge of the Qinghai-Tibet Plateau and the Himalayas.

稻城亚丁位于四川省甘孜藏族自治州，距离成都约800公里，地处青藏高原和喜马拉雅山脉之边缘。

A View of Yading

Yading is a national nature reserve, known as "the last pure land on the blue planet", and "the last true Shangri-La". With an alpine landforms, dense forests, vast grasslands, charming valleys and sparkling lakes, Yading is considered to be one of the best tourist destinations in Sichuan. In 2003, Daocheng Yading was included in Man and Biosphere Programme to protect its precious and rare natural landscape wealth.

亚丁是国家级自然保护区,被誉为"蓝色星球上最后一片净土""最后的香格里拉"。亚丁是四川最好的旅游目的地之一,拥有高山地貌、茂密的森林、广阔的草原、迷人的山谷、波光粼粼的湖泊。2003年,稻城亚丁被列入"人与生物圈计划",以保护其珍贵稀有的自然景观财富。

Actually, Daocheng is a county, and Yading is a nature reserve within Daocheng County, so in a narrow sense, Daocheng Yading refers to Yading Nature Reserve. The reserve has more than 10 peaks over 5,000 meters above the sea level, more than 30 peaks over 4,500 meters above the sea level, and 62 ancient glacial lakes at high elevation.

其实,稻城是一个县,而亚丁是稻城县境内的自然保护区。从狭义上说,稻城亚丁指的是"亚丁自然保护区"。保护区还拥有海拔5000米以上的高峰10余座,海拔4500米以上的高峰30余座,高海拔的古冰川湖泊62个。

Yading comprises three sacred peaks by the names of Xiannairi, Yangmaiyong and Xianuoduoji. These three mountains nurture clear rivers, forested valleys and pristine lakes; at the same time, the mountains provide an environment for wildlife. In addition, as one of the main Tibetan pilgrimage places, these mountains have long been regarded as the mountain guardians to protect local Tibetan people in Yading. As a result, the pilgrimage routes can be found all over the mountains. At least once a year, the locals have to circle Mount Xiannairi whose highest point is 6,032 meters above the sea level. Even for non-religious hikers, the 35-km hike around Mount Xiannairi can be a very rewarding experience. The name of Mount Xiannairi means the Bodhisattva of Mercy. Mount Yangmaiyong is 5,958 meters above the sea level, representing the Bodhisattva of Wisdom, and Mount Xianuoduoji is also 5,958 meters above the sea level, representing the Bodhisattva of Power.

亚丁有三座神山：仙乃日、央迈勇和夏诺多吉。这三座山孕育了清澈的河流、丛林密布的山谷和原始的湖泊，并为野生动物提供了生存环境。此外，这三座山是藏区主要的朝圣地之一，一直被视为保护亚丁藏民的守护山神，而朝拜之路由此遍及三山各处。当地人每年至少会绕着仙乃日山转山一次，此峰海拔6032米。对于非宗教徒步旅行者来说，绕着仙乃日山行走35公里，也是非常有益的经历。仙乃日的山名意思是"观世音菩萨"；央迈勇的山名意思是"文殊菩萨"，海拔5958米；夏诺多吉的山名意思是"金刚手菩萨"，海拔也是5958米。

There are a few other attractions worth mentioning here. Luorong Pasture is a high plateau at an altitude of 4,150 meters, offering a spectacular place to see these three sacred mountains. The Milk Lake is located at the foot of Mount Yangmaiyong. In fact, it is an ancient glacial lake that covers an area of 0.5 hectares and is surrounded by the snow-capped mountain. The Five Color Lake, located between Mount Xiannairi and Mount Yangmaiyong, covers an area of 0.7 hectares, where the water in the lake will give off five different colors when exposed to sunlight.

这里还有值得提及的几处景点。洛绒牛场海拔4150米，是观赏三座神山的最佳地点。牛奶湖位于央迈勇山脚下，是一座被雪山环绕的古老冰湖，占地0.5公顷。五色海位于仙乃日与央迈勇之间，占地面积0.7公顷；阳光照射之时，湖水会变换五种不同的颜色。

Yading came to be known after Joseph Rock (1884–1962), a botanist and explorer, discovered this pristine wonderland. More than 60 pages of writing and photographs about his travels in this region were published in July 1931 issue of the US magazine *National Geographic*, giving the world its first glimpse of the region's incredible beauty. It was during this period that Joseph Rock's writing inspired writer James Hilton to write his famous novel *the Lost Horizon*, in which he described this land as a paradise hidden in Southwest China, and a peaceful place inhabited Tibetan people. Later, *the Lost Horizon* was made into a film and released in 1937. Both the novel and film helped the world know more about Yading, making this place the "Soul of China's Shangri-La".

植物学家、探险家约瑟夫·洛克 (1884—1962) 发现了这片净土乐园。之后，亚丁才逐渐为人所知。1931年7月的美国《国家地理》杂志刊登了60多页关于约瑟夫·洛克在该地区旅行的文章和照片，第一次让世界看到了此地如此之美丽。也正是在这一时期，约瑟夫·洛克的文章激发了作家詹姆斯·希尔顿的创作灵感，写出了著名的小说《消失的地平线》。在詹姆斯·希尔顿笔下，一片土地被描绘成在中国西南的一处净土乐园，一处宁静祥和的藏族生息之地。后来，《消失的地平线》被拍成电影，并于1937年上映。小说和电影让世界更加认识了亚丁，使之成为"中国香格里拉之魂"。

Well, so much for my brief introduction to the Daocheng Yading Nature Reserve. Today, we will follow the short hiking trail of Chonggu Monastery, Meadow, Pearl Lake and Mount Xiannairi. When hiking, please follow a local tour guide, be sure to respect the local religion and customs, and abide by the regulations issued by the reserve. There is a large temperature difference between morning and night on the plateau, so warm clothes are necessary when hiking.

好了，稻城亚丁讲解到此结束。今天，我们短途徒步旅行的路线是：冲古寺—草甸—珍珠海—仙乃日山。旅行时，请跟随当地导游，务必尊重当地宗教和习俗，遵守保护区的规定。高原早晚温差大，登山时要穿保暖衣服。

Mount Guangwu Scenic Area
光雾山风景区

Mount Guangwu is located north of Nanjiang County in Northeast Sichuan. When introducing Mount Guangwu, local tour guides inevitably quote a popular saying, "Mount Guangwu, a piece of fascinating emerald, is the place where immortals reside; It has fairy-tale and jade-pool scenery."

光雾山位于四川东北部南江县以北。说到光雾山，当地导游无不引用流行的说法："光雾山，一块迷人的翡翠，神仙居住的地方；有童话般的美丽，有瑶池般的风光。"

Guangwu Scenic Area covers a space of more than 400 square kilometers, with its main peak at altitude of 2,500 meters. In 1993, it was listed as a key tourist attraction at provincial level in Sichuan Province. In January 2004, it was approved as a national key attraction by the State Council. In 2020, it was classified as a national 5A-level tourist attraction.

光雾山风景名胜区面积400多平方公里，主峰海拔2500米。1993年，光雾山被列为省级重点风景名胜区。2004年1月，国务院批准光雾山为国家重点风景名胜区。2020年，光雾山荣膺国家AAAAA级旅游景区。

Mount Guangwu has beautiful scenery and is rich in high-grade natural resources in the northeast of Sichuan Province. Its scenery features unique karst peaks, pristine ecological vegetation, waterfalls, lakes and canyons. The mountain's natural scenery is just like a landscape painting, giving people the enjoyment of beauty.

光雾山景区风景优美,具有丰富的川东北部高品位的自然资源,集喀斯特山峰、原始生态植被、瀑布、湖泊和峡谷为一体。其自然风光就像一幅山水画,给人以美的享受。

Here, the scenery of four seasons is different, and it seems to take on a new appearance with every change in light. In spring, flowers bloom, and winter jasmine and azaleas come in different shade of color; in summer, trees are luxuriantly green, waterfalls are splashing, and the mountains are covered with mist; in autumn, leaves drift down the rivers and streams, and the forests are covered with layers of red autumnal leaves; in winter, icicles are seen on tree branches and rocks, much like a silvery world.

在这里,四季景色各异,似乎随着光线的变化而呈现新的景色。春天,鲜花盛开、迎春花、杜鹃花显示出不同的色彩;夏天,树木葱郁,瀑布飞溅,山雾弥漫;秋天,树叶顺流而下,森林里覆盖着层层红色秋叶;冬天,树枝上、岩石上都挂上了冰柱,一派银色世界。

Sichuan Province
四川省

Autumn Scenery in Mount Guangwu

Up to the present, the scenic area contains more than 360 main scenic sites, which are located in five major scenic sections, such as Taoyuan Section, Shenmen Section, Wanzige Section, Putuo Village and Xiaowu Gorge. The following is a brief introduction of some of the important attractions.

迄今为止,光雾山风景区有主要景点360多处,分别位于桃园、神门、万字格、普陀村、小巫峡五大片区。以下是部分重要景点的简介。

Eighteen Moon Pools: In this scenic site, what you mainly see is the water, from which you can feel its spiritual essence. Along the scenic route, there exist 18 pools, numerous waterfalls and dense forests, so this area is called "Jiuzhaigou of Northeast Sichuan".

十八月潭景区:在这个风景区里主要是看水,感受水之灵性。沿途有18个月潭,瀑布众多,森林茂密,被称为"川东北的九寨"。

Taoyuan Section: In this scenic site, what you mainly see is the mountain, from which you can feel the mountain's spiritual nature. There are more than 70 main attractions, such as Mount Longjia, Taohua Mountain Villa, the Three Impregnable Passes and the South-Sky Gate.

桃园片区：在这个景区里主要是看山，感受山之灵气。主要景点70处，如：龙驾烟云、桃花山庄、三道关、南天门。

Mouyang Old Town: This is a picturesque area that used to be a military town called "Mou Yang Cheng". In this scenic site, what you mainly see are the red leaves, from which you can feel the leaves' magic. In October, when the frost falls in early autumn, the plants change colors overnight. The colorful leaves and forests seem to bring the viewers into a dreamlike world, where red leaves constantly take on a new look, mixing with other colors, such as blue, green, yellow or orange.

牟阳故城：这是一处风景如画的地方，曾经是一座叫牟阳城的军事重镇。在这个景区主要是看叶，感受红叶之灵幻。十月初，秋霜悄然降临。一夜之间，植物变了颜色。五彩缤纷的树叶与森林仿佛把观赏者带入了梦幻般的世界，红叶时时呈现出新的面貌，与蓝、绿、黄、橙色相融并存。

Among scenic sections in Mount Guangwu, the Xiaowu Gorge is especially impressive. Known as the "First Miraculous Gorge under Heaven", this site contains unique gorges, beautiful caves, majestic peaks, grotesque rocks, lakes, as well as a sea of clouds. The peaks are peculiar, and the cliffs are picturesque. The gorges remain deep and secluded, so deep that one can see the sky like a thread. Rare fowls and valuable animals, such as macaques and flying squirrels, are often seen climbing the cliffs. Moreover, jagged rocks are oddly shaped: some resemble heaps of hexagonal hives, some are similar to swirling whirlpools, some are like chrysanthemums or ink-slabs, and some others look like the images of a golden monkey looking at a high peak, or a lion climbing a green cliff, or a white elephant drinking from a pool.

在光雾山风景区里，尤为值得提及的是小巫峡。这座峡谷以"天下第一奇峡"而著称，有奇峡、秀洞、雄峰、怪石、湖泊、云海。景区山峰奇特，壁峭如画；峡谷幽深，天开一线；飞禽走兽，如猕猴飞鼠，常见飞攀其间。此外，景区怪石嶙峋，如蜂房水涡、菊花石砚；还有的像金猴望山，青狮爬崖，白象饮水。

In this section, there are several karst caves, such as Tongtian Cave and Chuanhua Cave. Tongtian Cave, also known as the Multicolored Cave, occupies an area of 120,000 square meters with a total length of more than 10,000 meters. Inside, there are two huge grottoes, three halls, four sub-caves, a five-layer labyrinth, six deep and green pools, as well as seven waterfalls. In addition, trails meander, and rivers flow underground.

在峡谷片区，还有若干溶洞，如：通天洞、穿花洞。通天洞又名五彩洞，占地12万平方米，全长1万余米。洞内有两大石窟、三大厅堂、四条支洞、五层迷宫、六泓碧潭、七道飞瀑。此外，洞里路径蜿蜒，暗河流淌。

Chuanhua Cave lies in the middle of the east side of the Xiaowu Gorge. It covers a visitable area of 300,000 square meters with a total length of more than 10,000 meters. Up to now, its scenic area covers a stretch of about 100,000 square meters and consists of seven halls, respectively located in wind sub-caves, dry sub-caves and water sub-caves. Some of these halls feature the images of all beasts presenting an auspicious scene, or fairies scattering flowers in the sky, some resemble weather-beaten ancient battlefields. Particularly, one of the halls, similar to a great performance stage between heaven and earth, is magnificent and can be called a unique spot in the cave. In addition, there are many other interconnected open caves nearby, allowing visitors to easily move back and forth among the caves. Inside these caves, the scenery is spectacular, forming a fine contrast to the view of the gorge outside. All these caves are known as the "Qin-Ba Treasure" and the unique karst resource pool in northern Sichuan.

穿花洞位于小巫峡中峡东岸。穿花洞可游面积30万平方米，全长1万余米。目前，穿花洞游览面积10万平方米，由七座大厅组成，分别位于风洞、旱洞和水洞。这些大厅有的像喜庆的百兽呈祥，或像仙女撒花，或像饱经风霜的古战场。尤以"天庭大舞台"景色为甚，其景观宏伟壮美，堪称溶洞一绝。此外，附近有许多明洞，且洞洞相通，可以在数洞之间轻松地穿来穿去。洞中景色壮观，与峡谷景色相映成趣。这些溶洞堪称"秦巴瑰宝"，是川北独特的岩溶资源库。

Well, so much for my brief introduction to Mount Guangwu. We have two days to visit the mountain, so we will try the route from Guangwu Town to Ganling Temple via Taohua Mountain Villa, the Three Impregnable Passes, the South-Sky Gate, Yanyan Rock Forest, the Cherry Valley, Jiexian Post Station and the Mouth of the Lianghe Rivers. The scenery in Mount Guangwu is spectacular, although the hiking is tiring. No matter whether you are ascending or descending, you may stop occasionally to get a longer view and enjoy the beautiful landscape.

好了，光雾山景区讲解到此结束。我们有两天的时间游山，行走的线路是：光雾山镇—桃花山庄—三道关—南天门—燕岩石林—樱桃河谷—截贤驿—两河口—感灵寺。虽然徒步行走很累，但光雾山景色很美。无论是上山，还是下山，偶尔也要驻足流连，欣赏美丽的景色。

08
Bifengxia Scenic Area
雅安碧峰峡

Bifengxia Scenic Area is located about 16 kilometers north of Yaan City and about 128 kilometers from Chengdu. The site includes an Ecological Canyon Scenic Site, a Wildlife Park, and the Base of China Conservation and Research Center for the Giant Panda. On December 28, 1999, the scenic area was officially open to the public. In December 2019, it was classified as national 5A-level tourist attraction.

碧峰峡风景区位于雅安市北部16公里处，距离成都约128公里。景区由生态峡谷风景区、野生动物园、中国大熊猫保护和研究中心基地组成。1999年12月28日，景区正式开园。2019年12月，景区荣膺国家AAAAA级旅游景区。

When tourists enter the Ecological Canyon Scenic Site from the Tourist Center, they are warmly greeted by "Nuwa's Hand", the largest hand in the world. Then, a 91.8-meter-high sightseeing elevator takes tourists down into a canyon, where steep cliffs, dense forests, clear water and cool breezes all overwhelm them, who immediately find themselves as if in a fairy kingdom amidst the towering cliffs and exotic flowers. In the scenic area, there are two V-shaped canyons, one being 7 kilometers long and the other 6 kilometers long. These canyons are about 30-70 meters wide, and the relative height of their cliffs ranges from 100 to 200 meters.

当游客从游客中心步入生态峡谷风景区的时候，迎面会受到世界上最大的手"女娲之手"的热情欢迎。然后，91.8米高的观光电梯将游客带进峡谷，那里悬崖陡峭，森林茂密，流水清澈，微风送爽，让游客立刻感到如同置身于童话王国之中，四周是参天的崖壁和珍奇的美花。景区内有两条"V"字形峡谷，一条长7公里，另一条长6公里，宽约30~70米，峭壁相对高度为100~200米。

What is more impressive in the canyons is the waterfalls, which has the most beautiful scenery and is also a cool place. Yuanyang Waterfalls, more than 30 meters high, cascade downward, and the rapid water is divided by high rocks into two sub-waterfalls; the sub-waterfalls on the left is called *yin*, because the flow is large; the flow on the right are so small that it is called *yang*, hence the name of Yuanyang or Mandarin Duck Waterfalls. The water at Bailongtan Waterfalls is inexhaustible all year round. The waterfalls are about 45 meters high, and the width of the water surface ranges from 3 to 5 meters. Legend has it that the waterfalls used to be the home where resided the white dragon from the Heavenly Palace. Qiancengya Waterfalls, which are about 100 meters high and 10 meters wide, plunge down the overhanging cliffs and splash onto the mountainside platform, and then the water flows slowly down the layers of rocks, forming countless silvery water threads. Besides the waterfalls, there are many other attractions, such as the Nvwa Pool, which is believed to be where Goddess Nuwa took her bath, Shenying Peak, which is said to be the guardian of Bifengxia, and Yanu Garden, where brooks are murmuring and flowers are blooming.

峡谷里最壮观的是瀑布群，有最美的景色，也是凉爽之地。鸳鸯瀑布，高30余米，飞泻直下，受高岩阻挡后，湍急的水流一分为二，为两座子瀑布；左边水流较大，为阴；右边水流较小，为阳，因此得名鸳鸯瀑布。

Sichuan Province
四川省

白龙潭瀑布终年不竭,瀑高约45米,水面宽3~5米不等,相传该瀑布为天宫白龙的住所。千层崖瀑布,高约100米,宽约10米;瀑水悬空飞泻,落入半腰台地上;然后瀑水顺着层层岩石缓缓流下,形成无数银色水丝。除了瀑布以外,还有若干景点,如:女神女娲曾在此沐浴的女娲池、碧峰峡的保护神神鹰峰,以及溪水潺潺、花儿盛开的雅女园。

Usually, tourists will spend three to four hours touring the Ecological Canyon Scenic Site before taking a sightseeing van to the Panda Breeding Base. Covering an area of 1,074 *mu* (71 hectares), the base has more than 20 laboratories and special sites, such as panda breeding farms, a panda nursery, a panda hospital and a panda research institute. The Panda Breeding Base started construction on October 18, 2002, with a total planning area of 6,000 *mu* (400 hectares). After Wenchuan Earthquake that occurred on May 12, 2008, the first-phase project was put into use, covering a space of 1047 *mu* (70 hectares). The space was divided into four functional sections, namely the panda breeding ground, the wildlife training area, the bamboo plantations, as well as the office and living section. In 1869, Armand David, a French biologist, discovered the world's first giant panda in Baoxing County of Yaan in Sichuan Province, and his discovery caused a worldwide sensation. Since the founding of the People's Republic of China in 1949, Yaan has presented 18 pandas as "the national gifts" to the USA, UK, Japan, Germany and other countries and regions. Although the Bifengxia Panda Breeding Base is a branch of Wolong China Protection and Research Center for the Giant Pandas, it is still the world's largest free-range panda ecological park, which attracts a growing number of tourists from home and abroad.

通常,游客在生态峡谷景区游览3~4小时后,才会乘观光车前往大熊猫繁育基地。基地占地1074亩(71公顷),有20多个实验室和场所,包括大熊猫繁殖场、大熊猫幼儿园、大熊猫医院和大熊猫科研所。碧峰峡大熊猫基地于 2002 年 10 月 18 日开工修建，总规划面积 6000 亩（400 公顷）。2008 年 5 月 12 日汶川地震后，首期项目投入使用，占地 1047 亩（70 公顷），分四大功能区，即：饲养繁殖区、野生训练区、竹类基地区、办公生活区。1869 年，法国生物学家阿尔芒·戴维在四川雅安宝兴县发现了世界上第一只大熊猫，引起了世界轰动。中华人民共和国成立以来，雅安先后作为"国礼"向美国、英国、日本、德国等国家和地区赠送了 18 只大熊猫。尽管碧峰峡熊猫基地是卧龙中国保护大熊猫研究中心的分支机构，但它目前是全球最大散养式大熊猫生态园，吸引着越来越多的国内外游客前来参观。

If tourists have enough time, they can also go to the Wildlife Park. That is China's largest ecological zoo, which covers an area of 25,000 square meters and houses about 11,000 wild animals. Of the 400 species, there are more than 30 species under first-class state protection and 50 species under second-class state protection. The zoo consists of three zones, namely the Wild Beast Zone, the Domestication Zone and the Night Zoo. Tourists can take a sightseeing bus to the Wild Beast Zone to watch tigers, lions and bears, or walk to the Domestication Zone to take a close look at docile animals. Of course, a night trip to the zoo is a must-see in itself. What could be more exciting, curious and mysterious than walking in the dark under moonlight and listening to the howling of wild animals?

如果时间充裕，游客还可以去野生动物园。这是一座国内最大的生态动物园，占地面积 2.5 万平方米，有野生动物约 1.1 万头（只、尾）。在 400 种动物中，国家一级保护动物三十余种，二级保护动物五十余种。动物园由三个区域组成，即：野兽区、驯养区、夜间动物园。游客可以乘坐观光车到野生动物区观看老虎、狮子、熊，或步行到驯养区近距离观察温顺的动物。当然，夜晚去动物园本身就是一大亮点。在月光下，走在黑暗中，听着野兽的嚎叫，还有什么比这更令人兴奋、好奇、神秘的呢？

Well, so much for my brief introduction to Bifengxia Scenic Area. Now please follow the local guide to visit the Ecological Scenic Site. We will follow the route from the elevator to the exit of the scenic site via Qiancengya Waterfalls, Bailongtan, Nuwa Pool, Nuwa Temple and Yanu Garden.

好啦，雅安碧峰峡简介到此结束了，现在请大家随导游参观生态峡谷风景区。行走线路是：电梯—千层崖瀑布—白龙潭—女娲池—女娲庙—雅女园—景区出口。

09

Leshan Giant Buddha
乐山大佛景区

Leshan Giant Buddha, also known as Lingyun Grand Buddha or Jiazhou Grand Buddha, has been chiseled on the cliff of the Qiluan peak at Mt. Lingyun, where the Buddha seats at the place bordering on the confluence of the "Three Rivers". The Buddha is not only the largest cliff stone statue of Maitrya in a sitting position in China, but also the largest religious stone

Giant Buddha

Sichuan Province
四川省

carving art treasure in the world. In 1982, it became a national key cultural relics protection unit. In 1996, Mt. Emei—Leshan Giant Buddha was officially listed as the World Natural and Cultural Heritage Site by UNESCO.

乐山大佛，又名凌云大佛、嘉州大佛，濒临"三江"汇流处，开凿在凌云山栖鸾峰的峭壁之上，既是中国最大的摩崖石刻弥勒坐像，也是世界首屈一指的宗教石刻艺术瑰宝。1982年，乐山大佛成为国家重点文物保护单位。1996年，峨眉山—乐山大佛被联合国教科文组织正式列为世界自然与文化遗产。

You may ask how big the Buddha is. This is almost the reaction of everyone who sees this majestic Buddha for the first time. "The hill is the Buddha, while the Buddha is the hill." It is 71 meters high. Its head is 14.7 meters in height and 10 meters in diameter. Its shoulder is 28 meters in width, and its ear is 6.72 meters in length. Its ear cavity can hold two persons, and his instep is large enough to seat over 100 people. An adult, who stand at the feet of the Buddha, is not as tall as the Buddha's instep.

人们会问大佛究竟有多大。这几乎是首次看到这座雄伟大佛的人之反应。"山是一尊佛，佛即一座山。"乐山大佛通高71米，头高14.7米，头宽10米，肩宽28米，耳长6.72米，耳朵空隙可容纳两人，脚背大到可以围坐100多人，一个成年人，站立大佛脚旁，也未能高出大佛脚面。

Wei Gao, the top envoy in charge of Jiannan West Sichuan in the Tang Dynasty, wrote an article *the Events of Maitreya Stone Statue of Lingyun Monastery in Jiazhou*. According to his article, the project took up 90 years and was completed in 803 A.D. Monk Haitong in Lingyun Monastery started the initial project design and raised funds for the construction. During his stay in Lingyun Monastery, he saw the three rivers rush rapidly, forming dangerous shoal. Haitong was therefore determined to cut down rocks off the cliff, which was 10,000 *ren* in height (very very high), hoping that the rocks would level up on the river base and slow down the swift flow of water. Unfortunately Haitong passed away before the completion of the Buddha statue, and the funding discontinued. Later, Zhangchou Jianqiong, the then top military commander in Jiannan areas, donated 200,000 *guans* (a *guan* equals 1000 coins), which enabled the construction to continue. Again, the construction stopped only because of the lack of funds. In 789 A.D., the Tang imperial government issued an edict to refurbish old or ruined Buddhist monasteries. Accordingly, Wei Gao donated 500,000 *guans* to fund the ongoing construction, which was eventually completed in 803 A.D. At that time, the statue of the Giant Buddha shone brightly with gilded and colorful paintings. In addition, a seven-storey pavilion with thirteen eaves was terraced up on the same ground, sheltering the Buddha statue. Later, the pavilion was destroyed in disastrous wars.

据唐剑南西川节度使韦高撰文《嘉州凌云寺大弥勒石像记》记载：工程耗时90年，于公元803年竣工。凌云寺海通禅师是最初规划、募集修造资金之人。他住持凌云寺期间，见三江水势激险，形成险滩，于是立志开凿大佛：削壁万仞，以石积平江河，以杀水势。不幸的是，大佛尚未完工，海通圆寂了，经费不继。后来，时任署理剑南节度使章仇兼琼捐俸钱20万贯以济不足，但又因缺少经费，仍未完工。公元789年，朝廷下诏，令各地重修旧佛寺。为此，剑南西川节度使韦高俸钱50万贯资助正在修造的大佛，终于在公元803年竣工。当时，大佛贴金彩绘，光艳夺目。在同一地面上，还依山造出一座七层十三重檐阁楼，用来遮蔽佛像。后来，阁楼毁于兵灾。

For more than 1,000 years, however, the Giant Buddha still remains intact, with a full and serene face. Why?

然而，经过1000多年，大佛仍能保持完好，面部饱满镇定。是什么原因呢？

Sichuan Province
四川省

The first fact is that the cliff where the Buddha statue seats has topographical advantages. It is situated on the south side of the hill, where verdant trees grow well enough to protect slopes and rocks from erosion. Although the Buddha statue seats at the confluence of the three rivers, it is carved in the cliff in the hill, which greatly reduces the erosion caused by wind and water. Another important fact is that the Buddha's drainage system covers its entire body. On the head of the statue are 18 layers of buns, of which the 4th, 9th and 18th layers each have a transverse drainage ditch and are decorated respectively with lime mortar, all of them are invisible from a distance. Also, there are ditches in the Buddha's robe collar and pleats. On the Buddha's chest is another ditch, which extends to the left until it joins another ditch on the back side of the Buddha's right arm. On the cliff behind the two ears of the Buddha, there are two caves, which open into each other. In addition, there are two caves in the back of the chest, one on the right and the other on the left. Those delicate ditches and caves form a scientific drainage and ventilation system that has effectively protected the Buddha from erosion and weathering for over a thousand years. Through centuries, the protection and maintenance of the Buddha has been going on. However, many repairs have been done by individuals on a small scale. After the foundation of New China, the local government usually arranged repairmen to clean up and repair the statue of the Buddha every ten years. One of the large-scale restoration works was carried out in March 2001. The workers first repaired the Buddha's head, shoulders, chest, and belly. Their work lasted for 36 days. During that period, they repaired the Buddha's coiled hair buns, washed the face, removed trashes and weeds from the body and mended the damaged parts with traditional materials. Another major restoration project started on November 7, 2001 and ended in August 2002. It included weatherproofing of the entire statue, improvements to the drainage system on the Buddha's body, and restoration of the statue's foot rest platform. Only by these painstaking restoration works can visitors get a good view of the statue of the Buddha located midst the lush, green landscape of Mt. Lingyun.

首先，佛像所居的悬崖峭壁，地形优势十分明显。它坐落在山的南面，周围翠绿的林木稠密，护坡保岩，使佛像免受侵蚀。大佛位于三江交汇处，但塑像凿在山体内的悬崖壁面上，大大减少风雨和江水对佛像的侵蚀和冲刷。另一重要原因是，大佛的排水系统遍布全身。在大佛头部共有18层螺髻，第4层、第9层和第18层各有一条横向排水沟，分别用石灰砂浆垒砌装饰而成，远望看不出端倪。大佛的衣领和衣纹皱褶也有排水沟，其正胸也有向左延伸的水沟，与右臂后背面水沟相连。大佛两耳背后靠山崖处，有两个彼此相通的洞穴。此外，胸部背侧有两个洞穴，一个在右，另一个在左。这些精妙的水沟和洞穴组成了科学的排水和通风系统，千百年来在保护大佛免受侵蚀性风化方面起到了重要的作用。数百年来，对大佛的保护和维护工作一直进行着，但大多维修范围小，而且都是个人行为。中华人民共和国成立后，当地政府每隔十年就对大佛进行清理和修缮。其中一项大型修复工程是在2001年3月进行的。工人们首先维修大佛的头、肩、胸和腹，工作一直持续了36天。在此期间，他们修复大佛的螺髻，清洗脸部，清除佛身垃圾杂草，并用传统材料修补破损部位。另一项大型修复工程于2001年11月7日开始，到2002年8月结束，工程包括加强塑像整体的抗风化性，改善佛体的排水系统，整修大佛歇脚的平台。通过这些辛勤的修复工作，游客才能欣赏到坐落在郁葱绿色的凌云山中的大佛塑像。

Well, so much for my introduction to the Leshan Giant Buddha. We will take our bus to the entrance to the scenic area of the Buddha. Then we go upwards to Lingyun Monastery, walk around the head of the Buddha and visit the Monk Haishi Cave. Afterwards, we descend a short zigzag stairway to the foot of the Buddha to get a close view of the Giant Buddha. After that, we go to the Mahao Cliff Tomb Museum and hike the Wuyou Hill. Be sure not to look at the scenery while walking, and not to walk while looking at the scenery. By the way, please remember my phone number in case you need assistance.

好啦,乐山大佛的介绍到此结束。我们将乘车到达大佛景区入口处,然后上到凌云寺,绕路走过大佛头部,去参观海师洞。接着,我们沿一条曲折阶梯小路,到大佛的脚下,近距离观摩大佛。然后,我们去麻浩悬墓博物馆,步行登乌尤山。请注意:走路不看景,看景不走路;记住我的电话,有需要请随时与我联系。

Mt. Qingcheng
青城山景区

Mt. Qingcheng is located southwest of Dujiangyan City, 68 kilometers away from downtown Chengdu. Laoxiaoding, its main peak, is as high as 1,600 meters above the sea level. The mountain is covered with forests and remains green all year round. Its green cliffs and multipeaks rise around like a city wall, so the mountain is called "Qingcheng", meaning the "green city". According to the ancient records, Mt. Qingcheng has "36 peaks", "8 huge caverns", "72 small caves" and "108 scenic attractions".

青城山位于都江堰西南，距成都市区68公里。主峰老霄顶海拔1600米。林木覆盖全山，四季常青，诸峰环峙，状若城郭，故名青城山。据古代文献记载，青城山有"三十六峰""八大洞""七十二小洞""一百八景"。

Mt. Qingcheng is an important part of the Scenic Attractions of Mt. Qingcheng – Dujiangyan Irrigation System. In 1982 it was admitted by the State Council into the first group of the National Key Scenic Attractions. In 2007, it was officially listed as the National 5A-level Tourist Attraction by the National Tourism Administration. In 2000, Mt. Qingcheng and the Dujiangyan Irrigation System were formally listed as the World Cultural Heritage Site by UNESCO.

青城山是青城山—都江堰风景名胜区的重要组成部分。1982年，青城山被国务院列入首批风景名胜区名单。2007年，青城山经国家旅游局正式批准为国家AAAAA级旅游景区。2000年，青城山—都江堰被联合国教科文组织列为世界文化遗产。

Mt. Qingcheng has been known for its unique *You* in the country. The implications of Chinese *You* are as follows: quietness, secluded woods, faintly fragrant flowers, silent and zigzag paths, delightful sounds of birds and leisurely flowing streams. In addition, towering old trees grow along mountain paths and thick foliage and brunches obscure the sky. A poem written by Wang Wei (701A.D.–761A.D.) of the Tang Dynasty depicts the scenes of the *You* in Mt. Qingcheng.

  Empty the hills, no man in sight,

  Yet voices echo here;

  Deep in the woods slanting sunlight

  Falls on the jade-green moss.

青城山以其独特之"幽"而闻名于世。"幽"的寓意如下：僻静、幽林、淡淡芳香的花、寂静曲折小道、鸟语欢声、悠悠流水。此外，山道旁古树参天，浓荫蔽日。唐朝王维（公元701—公元761）一首诗描绘了青城山的"幽"："空山不见人，但闻人语响。返景入深林，复照青苔上。"

Mt. Qingcheng is also one of the birthplaces of Taoism in China. It is known as the Taoist Fifth Cave. As early as the Eastern Han Dynasty, Zhang Daoling came to the mountain and founded the Five-Piculs-of-Rice Sect, or known as the Tianshi Tao Sect. Followers worshipped Lao Tzu as the founder of Taoism, and Mt. Qingcheng became a sacred place for Zhang to disseminate Taoism. In the following dynasties, Taoism gained in popularity on the mountain. In its heyday, there were more than 70 Taoist temples. So far, there are dozens of well-preserved temples, including Tianshi Temple, Jianfu Palace, Shangqing Palace, Zushi Palace, and Laojun Temple.

青城山也是中国道教发祥地之一，是道教第五洞天。早在东汉时期，张道陵来到山上，创立了"五斗米教"，又称天师道。该教奉老子为教主，青城山成了张陵传道的圣地。在之后的朝代里，道教在青城山日益发展，极盛时期全山道观多达70多座。至今有数十座道观保存完好，包括天师洞、建福宫、上清宫、祖师殿和老君阁。

Mt. Qingcheng consists of front mountain and back mountain. The front mountain mainly has key scenic attractions, with numerous cultural relics and historical sites. The back mountain covers an area of 100 square kilometers, with clear water, secluded forests and towering peaks. Among the numerous natural and cultural attractions, Tianshi Temple is worth a visit. It is the main site of Taoist temples, one key scenic attraction in the mountain and the place where Master Zhang Daoling built houses for the dissemination of Taoism. As you can see, the temple stands on a hill. In front of the hill is a valley like a cracked trench, about 70 meters long and 18 meters wide from the top of the cliff to the foot of the hill. The foreground disappears directly from our view and falls into the base of a cliff in the distance covered by thick trees, but the outline of the mountain makes people feel that the space has become vast. The original temple was destroyed in the early days and rebuilt in the Qing Dynasty. It is mainly composed of Sanqing Hall (Taoist Trinity Hall), Sanhuang Hall (Hall for Fuxi, Shennong and Huangdi) and Huangdi Hall (also known as Tianshi Hall in old times). Inside Tianshi Temple, the Sanqing Hall is worth seeing. It is the temple's main hall, a pavilion-style building with double eaves and a *xieshan* roof. A flight of stone steps leads to the hall portico, which is supported by six huge stone pillars. Each pillar stands on 1.2-meter-high stone base and is decorated with exquisite lions and other mythical animals. The entire hall, covering 580 square meters, is supported by 28 large stone pillars, 16 of which are engraved with couplets. One couplet says, "The Tao begets one; one begets two; two beget three; three beget the myriad creatures; the earth follows the way of Heaven; Heaven follows the Tao; the Tao follows nature." This couplet is all-embracing and reveals the profound connotation of Taoism. Again, the Sanqing Hall is a storied building with two floors. The upstairs space is called Wuji Hall (Hall of Infinite), where some precious cultural relics are stored, including eight pieces of the Ming-dynasty wooden-carved screen with hollow-cut lotus, peacocks and other patterns. Downstairs is the main hall, and in the middle of the hall hangs a horizontal plaque inscribed with the Chinese characters "Dan Tai Bi Dong (Red Table and Green Cave)" written by Qing Emperor Kangxi. Three supreme Taoist deities are enshrined in the hall: Yuanshi Supernatural Deity, who lives on Yuqing Celestial Land, has spiritual pearls in hand, symbolizing the Hongyuan or Flooding Era; Lingbao Supernatural Deity, who lives in Shangqing Celestial Land, carries the Taiji in the arms, symbolizing the Hunyuan or Chaotic Era; Daode Supernatural Deity, who lives in Taiqing Celestial Land, holds a feather fan in hand, symbolizing the Taichu or Remotest Era. According to Taoism, these three deities are no other than the Creators of All Things under Heaven. Well, in front of the hall, there are many figure carvings on the stone railings. These figures are happily tossing, wrestling or frolicking with bald heads and shoulders. In addition, they all wear open-seat pants. It is clear that they are images of babies. Taoist classics say that those who cultivate themselves up to a certain degree will return to their earliest nature, entering an original and pure state like babies of innocence and happiness.

青城山由前山和后山组成。前山是青城山风景名胜区的主体部分，文物古迹众多；后山面积100平方公里，水秀、林幽、山雄。在众多的自

English Tour Guide for Yunnan, Guizhou, Sichuan and Chongqing

云贵川渝英语导游讲解词

然和文化景观中,天师洞值得一游,它是道观的核心,是山上重要景点之一,也是张道陵天师结庐传道之地。如你所见,天师洞坐落在山上,洞前的山体像裂槽似的山谷,从崖顶到山脚,深约70米,宽约18米。眼前的景色在这里从人们视线中直接消失,远远地坠入被深色树林淹没的崖底,但山的轮廓却让人眼前一亮感到空间变得宽大广阔。天师洞原观早毁,清代重建,主要有三清殿、三皇殿和黄帝祠。在天师洞内,三清殿值得一看。它是天师洞的主殿,是一座重檐歇山顶楼阁式建筑。通廊前是几级石阶,通廊由六根大石圆柱支撑,分别立在1.2米高的柱基上,圆柱上雕刻着精致的石狮和其他神秘动物。全殿占地580平方米,由28根大石柱支撑着,其中16根柱子上刻有对联。有一副对联写道:"一生二,二生三,三生万物;地法天,天法道,道法自然"。这副对联包罗万象,揭示了道家深刻的寓意。三清殿一楼一底,楼上为无极殿,殿内保存着一些珍贵文物,有明代的木雕屏花八扇,上有镂空荷花、孔雀等图案。楼下为正殿,殿正中悬挂一匾额,上面刻有康熙皇帝手书的"丹台碧洞"。殿内供奉着道教至高无上的三位尊神:居于玉清仙境的元始天尊,手拈灵珠,象征洪元世纪;居于上清仙境的灵宝天尊,怀抱太极,象征混元世纪;居于太清仙境的道德天尊,手持羽扇,象征太初世纪。道教认为,这三位尊神正是天下万事万物的创造者。在殿前的石栏上,刻有许多人像,光头露肩,翻腾扑跌,嬉闹戏耍。他们都穿开裆裤。显然,他们是婴孩的形象。道教经义说,修道到一定程度,便达到返璞归真的状态,进入婴孩那种天真无邪、原始纯净的境界。

Well, so much for my introduction to Mt. Qingcheng. In half an hour, we will depart from the hotel and go for the sightseeing of the mountain. The temperature on the mountain varies greatly, so be sure to bring a warm jacket and waterproof coat. Also, I'd like to advise females not to wear high heels as most hill trails have stone steps. The trip takes three hours. Our route goes like this: we hike from the entrance up to Tianshi Temple, where we stay for an hour before following the same route back to the entrance. By the way, please remember my phone number in case you need assistance.

好啦,青城山的介绍到此结束,半小时后离开酒店前往青城山游览。山上温度变化很大,要随身带上保暖衣服和雨衣。此外,大多数路段都是石级山路,建议女性游客不要穿高跟鞋。此次游览共需3小时,我们行走的线路是:从入口处上山到天师洞,在那里停留一小时,然后原路返回入口处。顺便说一下,记住我的电话,请随时与我联系。

Chengdu Wuhou Shrine
成都武侯祠景区

Wuhou Shrine is located at Wuhouci Street in Chengdu. It was first built in 223 A.D. when the construction of Liu Bei's Hui Mausoleum was under way. The shrine is China's one and only ancestral hall complex shared by the emperor and his ministers. Meanwhile, it is also the most reputable memorial site devoted to Zhuge Liang, Liu Bei and other Shu Han heroes. In addition, the shrine is the most influential Relic Museum of the Three Kingdoms, compared with other similar museums in the country. In ancient times, men of letters highly praised Wuhou Shrine, Du Fu's Thatched Cottage and Xue Tao's Wangjiang Tower as the three major scenic attractions in Chengdu.

武侯祠位于成都武侯祠大街,始建于公元223年修建刘备惠陵之时,是中国唯一一座君臣合祀祠庙,也是最著名的诸葛亮、刘备及蜀汉英雄纪念地。此外,武侯祠也是全国影响最大的三国遗迹博物馆。在古代,文人们极力推崇武侯祠、少陵茅屋、薛涛望江楼,称其为成都三大名胜。

In late Ming and early Qing Dynasty, Wuhou Shrine and Xianzhu Temple (also known as Hanzhaolie Temple) were all destroyed in the war. In the eleventh year of Emperor Kangxi of Qing Dynasty(1672), the reconstruction was carried out. Afterwards, a few more repairs and expansion followed. All these efforts made the main buildings stand in five tiers, cypresses and bamboos grow luxuriantly, and pavilions and towers look magnificent. As a result, the shrine became a major scenic attraction in the south of Chengdu City. The newly constructed buildings consist of two main halls, namely the front hall and the rear hall where Liu Bei and Zhuge Liang are enshrined respectively. Such a layout forms a joint temple shared by the lord and his ministers. The front hall is named "Hanzhaolie Temple", and the rear one "Wuhou Shrine", but the locals in Chengdu collectively call these two halls "Wuhou Shrine". The shrine has 47 colorful clay figure statues made by folk artisans of the Qing Dynasty. All of these figures are known as the historical images of the Shu-Han Kingdom and are considered the largest figure group of the Three Kingdoms in the country. In addition, there are 53 stone tablets in the shrine. The most famous is the "Wuhou Shrine Tablet of Shu Prime Minister Zhuge". Its inscription was written by Pei Du, a former prime minister of the three emperors of the Tang Dynasty. His writing was copied by Liu Gongquan's brother Liu Gongchao and then carved onto the stone tablet by Lu Jian, a well-known sculptor. In history, this tablet is called the "Three Perfection Tablet".

明末清初，武侯祠和先主庙（又称昭烈庙）皆毁于战火。清康熙十一年（1672年）进行了重建，以后又多次修葺和扩建，使主体建筑达五重，松柏竹木茂盛，殿阁亭台壮丽，由此成为成都城南主要游赏之地。新建筑由两座大殿组成，分别是供奉刘备和诸葛亮的前殿与后殿，形成了君臣合庙的格局。前殿称为"汉昭烈庙"，后殿称为"武侯祠"，但成都人将其通称为武侯祠。祠内有清代民间艺人所塑的彩绘泥像47尊，均为蜀汉历史人物，是全国最多的三国人物塑像群。此外，该祠还有碑碣53块，最著名的是"蜀丞相诸葛武侯祠堂碑"，碑文由曾任三朝宰相的裴度撰文，柳公权之兄柳公绰书写，名工鲁建镌刻，世称"三绝碑"。

Liu Bei's Hall is located in the second gate courtyard. In the center of the hall is a gilden seated statue of Liu Bei. On the left is the statue of Liu Chen, one of Liu Bei's grandsons. To the right of the main hall is the statue of General Guan Yu, a red-faced man who is accompanied by the statues of his son and Zhou Cang. To the left is the statue of a black-faced man whose name is General Zhang Fei. He is accompanied by the statues of his son and grandchild. In the same courtyard, there are two terracotta galleries. On the right are the 14 statues of the generals of the Shu Han Kingdom, and on the left are the 14 statues of the civilian officials of the same kingdom. These figures have been loved by Chinese people, generation to generation.

刘备殿坐落在二门院内。大厅正中是刘备的贴金塑像，左侧陪祀的是他的孙子刘谌。大厅右边是红脸关羽塑像，旁边是他的儿子和周仓；大厅左边是黑脸张飞塑像，旁边是他的儿子和孙子。在同一院落里，有两座塑像廊房，右边塑有蜀汉武将14尊，左边是蜀汉文臣14尊，这些都是一代代中国人喜爱的人物。

The Entrance to Zhuge Liang's Hall

Of course, Zhuge Liang's Hall is the highlight of our visit to the shrine. The hall is a few steps lower than Liu Bei's Hall. It reflects the relationship between the feudal emperors and the ministers in those days, namely the emperors being superior and the ministers inferior. On the top of the entrance to the hall hangs a horizontal wooden plaque on which was written "Ming Chui Yu Zhou (Eternal Glory Remains in the Universe)". On the either side of the entrance hangs a couplet written by Zhao Fan of the Qing Dynasty. It says, "Attempts to carry out psychological attacks, and then revolts will automatically disappear. Even warlike elements, since ancient times, have not always resorted to wars. If he can't size up the situation correctly, leniency and harsh punishment won't succeed. The latecomers in charge of the State of Shu should think of it in depth." The statues of Zhuge Liang, his son and his grandson are enshrined in this hall. His seated statue is in the center, his son is on the right, and his grandson on the left. Zhuge Liang was dressed in a golden robe. With a feather fan in his hand, he looks as if he were lost in thought. In the Three Kingdoms period, heroes came forth in large numbers. Only chancellor Zhuge Liang alone shares the shrine with Zhaolie. It is simply because Zhuge is regarded as the embodiment of national wisdom. Meanwhile, Wuhou Shrine becomes the site of wisdom, which embodies impartialness, loyalty and dedication to the state. Zhuge Liang's brilliant wisdom in Shu administration, military matters, political affairs and daily life becomes an inexhaustible thought and nourishment for future generations. As the saying goes, "Two heads are better than one." It is clear that his wisdom is well-known, including women and children in the country. In Liu Bei's Hall hang wood carvings named *The Longzhong Plan* and *The Petition to the Throne Before a Military Expedition*. Zhuge Liang was not a litterateur, but his two writings to the throne, especially his first *Petition to the Throne Before a Military Expedition* became a famous ancient prose throughout the ages. Later generations have said that "Those who shed no tears while reading *The Petition to the Throne Before A Military Expedition* have no sense of filial piety." In his petition, the discourse "I'll do my utmost and serve with unwavering loyalty until death" is the most touching and can be hailed as the most famous quotations in ancient prose.

当然，诸葛亮殿是祠庙的主要参观点。诸葛亮殿比刘备殿低数节台阶，这反映了当时封建时代君臣之礼，即：君尊臣卑。诸葛亮殿门顶上悬"名垂宇宙"匾额，门两侧为清人赵藩撰书："能攻心则反侧自消，自古知兵非好战；不审势即宽严皆误，后来治蜀要深思。"大殿内供奉着诸葛亮和他的儿子、孙子的塑像，正中间是诸葛亮坐像，右侧是他的儿子，左有他的孙儿。诸葛亮身披金袍，手持羽扇，凝神沉思。三国时代，英雄辈出。唯诸葛武侯，独与昭烈同庙，实乃因孔明为民族智慧的化身。武侯祠为公忠体国的智星胜地，其高超的治蜀智慧、军事智慧、政治智慧和生活智慧，是后世取之不竭、用之不尽的思想养料。在民间有"三个臭皮匠，顶个诸葛亮"谚语。很明显，他的智慧妇孺皆知。在刘备殿里，悬挂着木刻《隆中对》和《出师表》。诸葛亮不是文学家，但他的两篇《出师表》，特别是《前出师表》却成为千古流传的古文名篇。后人有"读《出师表》不哭者不忠"的说法。文中"鞠躬尽瘁，死而后已"的话语最为感人，堪称古文名句中的名句。

In 1961, Wuhou Shrine became a national key cultural relics protection unit. In 2006, it was rated as the national 4A-level tourist attraction. In 2008, it was admitted into the first group of the National First-Grade Museums.

1961 年，成都武侯祠成为全国重点文物保护单位，2006 年被评为国家 AAAA 级旅游景区，2008 年被评为首批国家一级博物馆。

Well, so much for my introduction to Wuhou Shrine. Today our tour route goes like this: we enter the entrance of the shrine and watch the Three

Perfection Tablet. Then we walk into the second gate courtyard, where we visit Liu Bei's Hall, as well as the east and west galleries. Afterwards, we visit Zhuge Liang's Hall and go to a 'street' contained by red walls, which leads westward to Liu Bei's Mausoleum. The whole tour takes two hours. Well, I'd like to remind you not to smoke and litter in the halls.

好啦,武侯祠的讲解到此为止。我们今天的旅游路线如下:进入祠庙口后,先去看看三绝碑,然后进二门院落游览刘备殿和东西两廊,之后去诸葛亮殿,最后进入红墙夹道,西行到刘备墓。整个游览需两小时。温馨提示:请大家不要在馆内吸烟,不要乱丢果皮纸屑。

⑫ Du Fu's Thatched Cottage
杜甫草堂景区

Du Fu's Thatched Cottage, also known as the Museum of Du Fu's Thatched Cottage, is located at No.37 Qinghua Road, Qingyang District, Chengdu City. On both sides of the front gate hangs a couplet. It reads, "The cottage is on the west side of the Wanli Bridge, and to the north of the Baihuatan Park." The couplet indicates the cottage's original location.

杜甫草堂，又称杜甫草堂博物馆，位于成都市青羊区青华路37号。正门两侧挂着"万里桥西宅，百花潭北庄"的对联。这副对联点明了草堂原来的位置。

The Entrance to Du Fu's Thatched Cottage

Sichuan Province
四川省

Du Fu's Thatched Cottage was the former residence of Du Fu, a great realistic Tang-dynasty poet who lived here after he arrived in Chengdu. Du Fu, also known as Du Zimei, was born in Gongxian County (Gongyi City today), Henan in 712 A.D. He lived in the transition period from the prosperity to the decline of the Tang Dynasty. In 755 A.D., the An Lushan Rebellion broke out. In 759 A.D., Du Fu came to Chengdu with his family to escape the social upheaval caused by the rebellion. Near the Huanhua River, he built a thatched cottage as his residence. Apart from the temporary residence elsewhere to avoid chaos, Du Fu lived in the cottage for three years and nine months. This was a short but peaceful period that Du Fu had in troubled times. During his stay in Chengdu, Du Fu wrote more than 260 poems, collectively referred to as "Chengdu Poetry", many of which are quite popular. For instance, *The Pleasant Rain at Spring Nights*; *My Thatched Cottage is Ruined by Autumn-Wind*; *The Shu Prime Minister*; *Alone and Looking for Flowers on the River Bank* and others. Many famous lines are widely read, for instance:

"From my window the snow-crowned western hills are seen,
　Beyond the door the east-bound ships at anchor lie."
"And died before he saw the triumph of his troops,
　For him, generations of heroes shed tears."
"At dawn we shall see splashes of rain-washed red,
　Drenched, heavy blooms in the City of Brocade."
"Oh, for a great mansion with ten thousand rooms,
　Where all the poor on earth could find welcome shelter,
　Steady through every storm, secure as a mountain!"

杜甫草堂是唐代伟大现实主义诗人杜甫流寓成都时的故居。杜甫，又名杜子美，公元712年生于河南巩县（今巩义市）。杜甫生活在唐朝由盛至衰的转折时期。公元755年，爆发了安史之乱。公元759年，杜甫为避安史之乱携家来到成都，于浣花溪畔筑草堂卜居。除去避乱暂离之外，杜甫在浣花溪畔共住了3年零9个月。这是杜甫在乱世中的短暂安宁的一段日子。在成都期间，杜甫写诗260多首，被统称为"成都诗"，其中许多诗篇脍炙人口。如：《春夜喜雨》《茅屋为秋风所破歌》《蜀相》《江畔独步寻花七绝句》等。许多名句被人们广为传诵，如："窗含西岭千秋雪，门泊东吴万里船""出师未捷身先死，长使英雄泪满襟""晓看红湿处，花重锦官城""安得广厦千万间，大庇天下寒士俱欢颜，风雨不动安如山"等。

In 765 A.D., he left Chengdu for good. Later, his residence ceased to exist. In the Five Dynasties, Wei Zhuang (about 836 A.D.–910 A.D.), a poet of the Former Shu State, found the ruins of the thatched cottage and rebuilt it there. Later, in the Song, Yuan, Ming and Qing dynasties, the cottage had been repeatedly renovated. Two of the largest reconstructions, which took place in 1500 and 1811 respectively, basically laid the size and layout of the cottage courtyard. The thatched cottage also became the symbol of Chengdu, the mark of poetry, as well as the holy land of literature, attracting generations of people to come here for visit. At present, the cottage complex consists of six important parts, which are the Front Gate, the Lobby, the Hall of Historical Poetry, the Water Pavilion, the Gongbu Shrine and the Thatched Pavilion. These ancient-style buildings, pavilions and pagodas stand in the midst of age-old trees and green bamboos. In 1961, Du Fu's Thatched Cottage was listed as a national key cultural relics protection unit. In 1985, the Museum of Du Fu's Thatched Cottage was established. In 2006, it was rated as a national 4A-level tourist attraction.

公元765年，杜甫离开了成都。之后，草堂便不复存。五代前蜀诗人韦庄（约公元836—公元910）寻得草堂遗址，并在此重结茅屋，后又在宋、元、明、清时期多次修复。其中两次最大的重修是在1500年和1811年，基本上奠定了杜甫草堂的规模和布局，草堂也演变成为成都的标志、诗歌的象征、文学的圣地，同时吸引着一代又一代人前来瞻仰。目前，草堂由六大部分组成：正门、大廨、诗史堂、水槛、工部祠和茅屋。这些古代风格的建筑、亭台楼阁、宝塔掩映在古树绿竹之中。1961年，杜甫草堂被列入全国重点文物保护单位；1985年，杜甫草堂博物馆成立；2006年12月，杜甫草堂被评为国家AAAA级旅游景区。

Well, among the buildings of cottage complex, the Gongbu Shrine is the most worthy of mention. In China's feudal times, Gongbu was the name of the central government agency in charge of the construction projects. Du Fu was once appointed "associate department director of *Jian Jiao Gong Bu*", so he was called "Du Gongbu", and his shrine was thus named after that title. On the top of the front gate hangs a couplet, which reads, "The Jinjiang River and spring breeze Du Fu owns; on the Seventh Day for the Humans, did I come for a visit to his cottage." It was written by He Shaoji, a Qing scholar who served as Sichuan Provincial Education Commissioner in the Xianfeng years of the Qing Dynasty. Once, He Shaoji returned to Chengdu from Guozhou Prefecture (Nanchong today). On the way, he drew up this couplet. When he arrived in Chengdu, he deliberately stayed in the suburbs and waited until the Seventh Day for the Humans, and then he went into the cottage and wrote down his couplet draft. Soon after the couplet made its debut, it caused a shock in the literary world. Men of letters and poets followed suit. So, on the Seventh Day for the Humans each year, they would gather in Du Fu's Thatched Cottage, where they wrote or chanted poems to pay tribute to the saint of poetry. Well, in the center of the Gongbu Shrine is a statue of Du Fu, flanked by two other statues. One is Huang Tingjian, a poet of the Northern Song Dynasty and the other is Lu You, a poet of the Southern Song Dynasty. There are thousands of poets in the history of traditional Chinese literature. Why are

Huang Tingjian and Lu You chosen to accompany Du Fu in this shrine? The following three main facts may sound reasonable. Firstly, as later generations, Huang Tingjian and Lu You studied Du Fu's poetry and made great achievements in this respect. Secondy, like Du Fu, they were not native to Shu, but they had lived in Shu for a while and wrote many poems about the local scenery and customs. In addition, "even after they left Shu, they never forgot Shu." Therefore, local Shu people held them in high esteem. Thirdly, without companions, Du Fu's statue could feel lonely in the Gongbu Shrine. If three poets were in the same hall, they could discuss the art of poetry together, so they wouldn't feel lonely. In the hall there hangs a couplet. It says, "By the side of a neglected creek is built a cottage, with Du Fu who remains eternal; those who are placed in the hall are of different generations, with the two sages of the Song Dynasty." The couplet sums it up very well.

　　当然，在草堂的建筑群中，最值得提及的是工部祠。在中国封建时代，工部是中央官署名，为掌管营造工程的机关。杜甫曾被授"检校工部员外郎"之衔，由此人称他为"杜工部"，他的祠堂也就以此命名。在祠门前上方挂着一副对联，"锦水春风公占却，草堂人日我归来。"对联是由清代咸丰年间任四川学政的清代学者何少基撰写。一次，何少基从果州（今南充）返回成都。在途中，他拟好了这副对联。抵蓉后，他特意宿于郊外，等到初七"人日"这天，才进草堂题写。此联一出，在文坛引起震动，墨客骚人纷纷效仿。于是，他们在每年人日之时云集草堂，挥毫吟诗，凭吊诗圣。工部祠正中为杜甫雕像，两侧分别是北宋诗人黄庭坚和南宋诗人陆游的雕像。中国传统文学史上有成千上万的诗人，为什么在这座纪念祠里要选择黄、陆来配杜甫呢？其原因主要有三：一是黄庭坚、陆游均为后世学杜并获得极高成就；二是黄、陆与杜甫一样，不是蜀人，但都曾经居蜀地，写下不少吟咏蜀中风物的诗篇，而且又"去蜀而不忘蜀"，故深得蜀地百姓的敬重；三是殿内若只塑杜甫一人，未免过于孤单；若三位诗人同堂，则能共论诗艺，免除冷清。祠内有一副"荒江结屋公千古，异代升堂宋两贤"对联。这副对联对此做了很好的总结。

Well, so much for my introduction to Du Fu's Thatched Cottage. There are many attractions around the cottage. We will walk along the Lobby, the Water Pavilion, the Gongbu Shrine and the Thatched Pavilion. Of course, we will also visit the Hall of Historical Poetry. The sightseeing takes two hours. Be sure to remember the parking place, the departure time and my phone number. Don't hesitate to contact me whenever you need assistance.

好啦，杜甫草堂介绍到此结束。在草堂周围有许多景点，我们将去大廨、水槛、工部祠和茅屋。当然，我们还要参观诗史堂。在草堂参观共两小时。请注意，要记住停车地点、发车时间，以及我的手机号码。如果需要帮助，请随时与我联系。

13

Southern Sichuan Bamboo Sea
蜀南竹海

People often say, "Look at the ocean when you are in the southeast; see the forest when you are in the northeast; observe the sea of sand when you are in the northwest; and watch the bamboo sea when you are in the southwest." Southern Sichuan Bamboo Sea is known far and wide for its boundless bamboo sea. It lies about 430 kilometers north of Chengdu, at the junction of Changning and Jiang'an counties under the jurisdiction of Yibin City. In 1988, the Bamboo Sea was listed as the National Key Scenic Attraction by the State Council. Later, it was crowned with such titles as China's 40 Best Tourist Attractions", "the First Batch of the National 4A-level Tourist Attraction" and "China's Biosphere Reserve".

人们常说:"到了东南看大海,到了东北看林海,到了西北看沙海,到了西南看竹海。"蜀南竹海以万顷竹海著称,位于成都以北约430公里处,在宜宾市境内的长宁、江安两县交界之地。1988年,蜀南竹海被国务院确定为"中国国家风景名胜区"。之后,景区获得以下殊荣:"中国旅游胜地四十佳""国家首批AAAA级旅游景区""中国生物圈保护区"。

When did the Bamboo Sea take shape? There are many versions about its origin. In remote times, according to legend, the goddess Nuwa in Chinese mythology was engaged in the task of melting stones and repairing the sky with them. After completing the task, Nuwa piled up the remaining rubies here and soon after that, ten thousand hills and red ridges were formed. Later, a fairy named Yao Qing was banished down to the mortal world by the Jade Emperor for she violated the mandate of heaven. She came here and created a sea of bamboos.

竹海是何时形成的？说法很多。据传说，在太古时候，中国神话中的女娲娘娘炼石补天。女娲做完后，将剩下的红宝石堆放在此，随即形成了万山红岭。后来，仙女瑶菁因触犯天条被玉帝贬下凡间。她来到这里，营造了万顷竹海。

The Bamboo Sea, also known as Wanlingqing (Ten-Thousand Ridges with Clumps of Bamboo), covers an area of 120 square kilometers. The green bamboo spans 27 ridges and more than 500 peaks. The vegetation coverage rate of the mountain reaches 87%. As a story says, Huang Tingjian, a poet of the Northern Song Dynasty, once visited Tianhuang Temple in Jiang'an. Seeing the Bamboo Sea, Huang Tingjiang highly praised it, "What a spectacular view! The bamboo waves stretch for thousand miles like Mt. Emei, as if they were twin sisters!" Immediately, Huang Tingjiang wrote the three Chinese characters "Wan Ling Qing" on a yellow umbrella stone. In this world of bamboo forests, there grow 58 species of bamboo plants, such as Nanzhu (phyllostachys pubescenslong), Cizhu (sinocalamus affinis), Luohan bamboo (phyllostachys aurea), Qinsi bamboo (neosinocalamus affinis). In the bamboo sea there grow a small number of rare plants, such as Hongchun (a kind of ailanthus giraldii Dode), Nanmu (a kind of phoebebournei), Hongdoushan (taxus chinensis fir), camphor trees, ginkgo trees and camellias. Also, in this area there inhabit rare animals, such as Zhushu (bamboo rats), Zhuwa (bamboo frogs), Qingji(bamboo chicken), Qinwa (hylarana daunchina), egrets, and Xiangsiniao (red-billed leiothrix).

In addition, among the dense and almost inaccessible bamboo sea there exist numerous temple relics, which include Tianhuang Temple, Longyin Temple, Tianhou Temple and Shouchang Hall.

竹海又名万岭箐，面积120平方公里，翠竹贯穿27条峻岭、500多座峰峦，山地植被覆盖率达87%。据传，北宋诗人黄庭坚曾经到访江安天皇寺，他看到翠竹海洋，赞叹不已："壮哉，竹波万里，峨眉姐妹耳！"随即，黄庭坚在黄伞石上写下"万岭箐"三字。在这片翠竹世界里，生长着58种竹类植物，如：楠竹、紫竹、罗汉竹、琴丝竹。在竹海中有少量的珍稀植物，如：红椿、楠木、红豆杉、樟树、银杏和山茶花。此外，这个地方还栖息着一些珍稀动物，如：竹鼠、竹蛙、箐鸡、琴蛙、白鹭和相思鸟。在几乎人迹罕至的竹林深处，尚存众多的寺庙遗址，如：天皇寺、龙吟寺、天后宫和寿昌宫。

In the Bamboo Sea, the core scenic area covers 44 square kilometers. It consists of eight major scenic sections, including the Section of the Immortal-Abode Cavern, the Section of Tianhuang Temple, the Section of the Seven-Color Waterfalls, the Section of the Forgetting-Worries Valley, the Section of Qinglong Lake, the Section of Longyin Temple, the Section of the Windward Bay, as well as the Section of the Tiger and Dragon Ground. There are 63 main scenic spots in the scenic area, 10 of which are known as the "Top Ten Attractions in the Bamboo Sea". They are Tianhuang Temple, Tianbao Village, the Immortal-Abode Cavern, Qinglong Lake, the Seven-Color Waterfalls, the Ancient Battlefields, the Pavilion of Viewing Clouds, the Emerald Green Long Corridor, the Chahua Hill, as well as Huaxi 13 Bridges.

在蜀南竹海，核心景区面积44平方公里，共有8大景区：仙寓洞景区、天皇寺景区、七彩飞瀑景区、忘忧谷景区、青龙湖景区、龙吟寺景区、迎风湾景区和虎龙坪景区。景区有63处主要景点，其中10处被称为

"竹海十佳"：天皇寺、天宝寨、仙寓洞、青龙湖、七彩飞瀑、古战场、观云亭、翡翠长廊、茶化山和花溪十三桥。

Of course, among these attractions, the Emerald Green Long Corridor is commendable. The corridor, located deep in the Bamboo Sea, is the most unique landscape among the scenic spots. Walking through the corridor, you'll find that the old and new bamboo thickets stand like thick vertical green screens. The walkway is covered with local natural red sand stones that look like a red carpet. Along the walkway, the top of the bamboo forest becomes an arch, forming a canopy covered with branches and leaves. The green bamboo and walkway adds beauty to the corridor and delights visitors as they pass by. The corridor is a cool world, where the fresh air is filled with the pleasant scent of bamboo leaves, just like a poem in praise of the scenery. It says, "The red-sun glow blankets the walkway, while the green-jade columns stand as the frame of the corridor; the scotching sunshine is not hot when it is piercing, and the fierce wind becomes mild as it blows in." When the sky is clear, the sunshine drip through bamboo leaves, sprinkling on the ground with tiny spots of golden light, and dressing the corridor like a colorful world. On a snowy day, the snow blankets the ground like a silver brocade, turning leaves into evergreen flowers. Upon arrival at the corridor, visitors can't resist taking a stroll, have a rest or take pictures. The cool greenery soothes their eyes, the gentle breeze whispers in their ears, and the complete quietness refreshes their spirit.

当然，在这些景点中，翡翠长廊最值得称道。它位于竹海深处，与其他的景点相比，是最具特色的景观。人们穿过翡翠长廊时，会发现密集的老竹新篁像厚实直立的绿色屏风；路面是用当地的天然红色沙石铺成的，像红色地毯似的。沿着走道，竹林顶部变成拱形，形成枝叶掩映的遮篷。走道与绿竹给长廊平添了美的景色，游客凡经过此地，很是惬意。长廊是一处清凉之地，清新的空气弥漫着竹叶的清香。正如一首赞美它的诗所说："红霞铺垫，玉柱框廊；炎阳不炎，狂风不狂"。晴空万里之时，缕缕阳光透过竹叶，洒在地上，点缀着点点金光，把长廊打扮成色彩斑斓的世界。下雪天，雪像银锦似的铺在地上，树叶变成了常绿的琼花，别有情趣。游人到此，无不游憩，摄影留念。凉爽的绿色舒缓双目，温柔的微风在耳边低语，四下的幽静抚慰着心灵。

Well, so much for my introduction to the Bamboo Sea. Before we get off and check in, I'd like to let you know our tour route. After lunch, we depart from our hotel and go for sightseeing. We will visit the Museum of Bamboo Culture and have a sightseeing tour of the Forgetting-Worries Valley. Then we will hike the Bamboo-Sea hills and take photos in the Emerald Green Long Corridor. The trip takes about 2.5 hours.

好了，蜀南竹海就介绍到这里。在下车去住宿登记前，我想讲讲游览路线。午餐后，我们乘车前往景点，先去参观竹文化博物馆，游览忘忧谷；再上竹海，在翡翠长廊留影。全程大约两个半小时。

Wangjiang Tower Park
望江楼

Wangjiang Tower Park is located on the south bank of the Jinjiang River in Jinjiang District of Chengdu, covering an area of 120,000 square meters. Most of its land has been planted to bamboos in dense shade, so it is also called the "Bamboo Park" or the "Bamboo Garden in the City of Brocade". During the period of the Republic of China, it was referred as the Wangjiang Tower Park. In May 2006, it was listed into the sixth batch of the national key cultural relics protection units.

Xue Tao Well

望江楼公园位于成都锦江区南岸，占地 12 万平方米，大部分地面被竹林覆盖，故被称为"竹子公园"或"锦城竹园"，民国时期辟为望江楼公园。2006 年 5 月，公园被列入第六批全国重点文物保护单位名单。

In the Ming Dynasty, there was Yunujin near the Jiuyan Bridge across the Jinjiang River in Chengdu. Because it was located far outside the city, the seignior of Shu in the Ming Dynasty sent people there to fetch water to make Xue Tao writing paper. Therefore, the water source was later named Xue Tao Well. In the third year of Emperor Kangxi of the Qing Dynasty (1664), Chengdu Prefecture Governor Ji Yingxiong wrote down "Xue Tao Jing"(Xue Tao Well), which were engraved on a stele beside the well. Gradually, this place became a well-known site in commemoration of Xue Tao (about 768 A.D.–832 A.D.), a female poet of the Tang Dynasty.

在明代，成都锦江九眼桥畔有玉女津。此津远在城外，明蜀王命人在此汲水制作薛涛笺，水源地后被命名薛涛井。康熙三年（1664 年），成都知府冀应熊书立"薛涛井"石碑，此地逐渐成为纪念唐代女诗人薛涛（约公元 768—公元 832）的名胜之地。

In the late Qing Dynasty, a number of memorial buildings related to Xue Tao were built successively around this site, such as Huanjian Pavilion, Wuyun Fairy Pavilion, Quanxiang Pavilion on Terrace, Liubei Pool, Pipa Gate Lane, Yinshi Pavilion and Zhuojin Pavilion. In addition, the number of inscriptions, steles and plagues also increased gradually.

在清末，在井周围陆续建起了多座与薛涛相关的纪念建筑，如：浣笺亭、五云仙馆、泉香榭、流杯池、枇杷门巷、吟诗楼和濯锦楼。题咏碑刻、匾联也逐渐增多。

Sichuan Province
四川省

In the fifteenth year of Emperor Guangxu of the Qing Dynasty (1889), Chongli Tower was built next to Xue Tao Well. Its name comes from a line in *The Ode to the Capital of Shu* written by Zuo Si. The line goes like this: "The beauty (*li*) and loftiness (*chong*) really match the reputation and reality of Chengdu." Because of its location beside the Jinjiang River, it is also known as Wangjing Tower and has become the landmark of Chengdu City ever since then.

光绪十五年（1889年），在薛涛井旁建成崇丽阁，其名取左思《蜀都赋》中"既丽且崇，实号成都"之意。因楼身位于锦江边，故又名"望江楼"，从此成为成都市的标志性建筑。

Chongli Tower is one of the most attractive spots in the park. It is a four-storey wooden building with a height of 26 meters. The tower is gorgeously shaped and exquisite designed. The top of the tower is pyramidal and painted in gold, below the top are two octagonal storeys, and below the octagonal storeys are the other two square storeys with gently-upturned eaves. The bottom terrace of the tower is square, symbolizing that the universe is round in the sky and square on earth. Inside, the ceiling is painted with the patterns of "a phoenix playing among peony flowers" and "the dragons cuddling up together". There is a well-known long couplet, hanging on the wall of the lowest storey. It has a total of 212 Chinese characters written by Zhong Yunfang (1847–1911), a talented scholar of the late Qing Dynasty. Literally, part of the first line means: I climb the tower, where I can see a panorama of the nearby river and distant hills, which look like a landscape painting. As I face this beautiful landscape, I think of ancient poets, and a lot of feelings come to my mind. Both Li Deyu of the Tang Dynasty and Fan Dacheng of the Song Dynasty built the Choubian Tower in different periods, but where are the heroes? The precious mirror, which belonged to Huarui, the concubine of Emperor Meng Chang of the State of Later Shu, sank forever. Xue Tao's tomb was lonely there…Part of the second line means: for a thousand years, the situation of Shu changed constantly. In the history of Shu, there appeared in succession gallant heroes including Zhuge Liang who lived in seclusion in the Wolong Hill, Pang Tong who died on Luofeng Slope, Li Xiong who established Chenghan Regime and Gongsun Shu who had limited vison; sometimes they galloped on the backs of armored horses across battlefields with flashing spears; sometimes they were enchanted with songs and danced amid silver pipes and jade flutes; but all this seems to be as transient as a fleeting cloud...

崇丽阁是公园最有吸引力的景点之一，为四层全木建筑，高26米，造型宏伟，设计精巧。阁顶漆成金色攒尖，下面两层为八角形，再下面两层为四方飞檐，阁底石台为四方形，暗寓天圆地方之意。阁楼内天花板上绘有"凤凰戏牡丹"和"团龙"图案。崇丽阁有副全国闻名长联，悬挂在崇丽阁底层壁上，共212字，为清朝末年的才子钟云舫（1847—1911）撰写。部分上联大意说：登上高楼，通览远近河山，如山水画一般。对此大好河山，想起古代诗人感触颇多：唐代李德裕、宋代范成大修建筹边楼，可这些猛士在何处呢？后蜀孟昶的花蕊夫人的宝镜沉埋，薛涛香坟空留……部分下联大意说，千百年来，蜀中局势风云变幻。在蜀历史上英雄不断，有卧龙岗上的诸葛亮，死于落凤坡的庞统，成汉政权的李雄，井底之蛙的公孙述，一时铁马金戈驰骋疆场，一时银笙玉笛沉醉歌舞，都好似过眼云烟……

Why did the locals build Chongli Tower? There is an interesting story. It is said that a local scholar named Yang Sheng'an came out first in the final imperial examination and obtained the Title of Number One Scholar in the Ming Dynasty. Since then, no one in Shu had obtained such a title. This phenomenon has lasted for 300 years. Some local gentry believed that the outstanding spirit of literary talents in Shu might have drifted away along the Jinjiang River. Therefore, they donated money to build Chongli Tower to "control the river so as to help the surrounding terrain grow healthily". As the story goes by, when the setting sun bathed the tower after it was built, it cast its shadow right on the surface of the river, its shadow just traversed the river, thus preventing the superb literary spirit from floating away from Shu. As luck would have it, in the second year after the tower was completed, a man in a county near Chengdu successfully obtained the Title of Number One Scholar.

为什么要修建崇丽阁呢？有一个有趣的故事。据说，明朝期间当地学者杨升庵中了状元。从那时起，蜀中无人考中状元，而这种现象延续了300年。当地一些士绅认为，蜀地文风才气可能从锦江漂流而去。于是，他们捐资建造了崇丽阁，"压江流以扶地脉"。据说，崇丽阁建起后，落日照在阁楼上时，阁影投射在水上，其影恰好横截江面，由此挡住了蜀中文才外流。说来也巧，就在崇丽阁建成的第二年，成都附近县里就出了状元。

Well, so much for my introduction to Wanjiang Tower Park. Now we are approaching the park. Our tour route goes like this: we enter the north gate and walk along the path that leads to Xue Tao Well, Chongli Tower, Yinshi Pavilion and other scenic spots. I will meet you at the south gate. The tour of the park takes one hour. Be sure to remember the departure time and my phone number. Don't hesitate to contact me whenever you need assistance.

好了，望江楼公园的介绍到此为止。我们快到公园了。我们行走的线路是，从北大门进去，沿途参观薛涛井、崇丽阁、吟诗楼等景点。我在南门等你们，整个游览约一个小时。请大家记住离开时间和我的手机号。如果需要帮助，请随时与我联系。

Meishan San Su Shrine Museum
眉山三苏祠博物馆

San Su Shrine Museum, located in Shahuhang Street, Dongpo District, Meishan City, Sichuan Province, is the former residence of Su Xun, Su Shi, and Su Zhe, three famous literary scholars and also three generations in the Su Family in the Northern Song Dynasty (960-1127) . Originally the residence of the Su Family, this dwelling house was transformed into an ancestral hall in the Yuan Dynasty but was later destroyed in warfare in the late Ming Dynasty. In the fourth year during the reign of Emperor Kangxi of the Qing Dynasty (1665), it was rebuilt in situ into a hall for people to memorize scholars of the Su Family and a humanistic tourist attraction. The site now covers an area of 106 *mu* (6.67 hectares), with 16 ancient buildings and other historical sites, such as the ancient well, litchi tree, and ancient five-leaved chaste tree. It is now a national key protected cultural relic unit, a national 4A-level tourist attraction and a national first-class museum.

三苏祠位于四川眉山市东坡区纱縠行，是北宋著名文学家苏洵、苏轼、苏辙三父子的故居。南宋改宅为祠，明末毁于兵火，清康熙四年（1665）在原址上模拟重建，是历代名人雅士、文人墨客拜谒、凭吊三苏的文化圣地。现占地106亩，保存有16处古建筑及苏宅古井、苏宅丹荔、黄荆古树等遗迹。现为全国重点文物保护单位、国家AAAA级旅游景区、国家一级博物馆。

Sichuan Province
四川省

The South Gate of San Su Shrine

San Su Shrine is designed in the garden style of the Qing Dynasty. Its main buildings consist of the front hall, banquet hall, Qixian Hall, Laifeng Pavilion, as well as east and west wing rooms and corridors on both sides along the central axis.

三苏祠按照清代园林风格设计，主要建筑包括前厅、宴厅、启贤堂、来凤轩，还有中轴线两侧的东西厢房和走廊。

The main hall is constructed with three *jian* across its façade and a hard mountain tile roof, under which the seated statues of Su Xun, Su Shi and Su Zhe are enshrined on the altar. On the east side lies a group of landscape architecture surrounded by pond water, including the Oasis Pavilion, Baoyue Pavilion and Yunyu Tower. On the west side is a deep and wide pool crossed by a covered bridge, known as Baipo Pavilion. A view north from a cloak-like pavilion, known as the Pifeng Waterside Pavilion, reveals the Dongpo Pan Tuo Sitting Statue nestled within a bamboo forest.

正殿面阔三间，单檐硬山顶，下面供奉着苏洵、苏轼、苏辙坐像。东侧，池水环绕一组景观建筑，有绿洲亭、抱月亭、云屿楼。西侧，一泓池水，为"百坡亭"廊桥横断。从"披风榭"向北望去，可见竹林中的东坡盘陀坐像。

Dongpo Pan Tuo Sitting Statue

Of course, tourists who visit the San Su Shrine Museum can not only tour the local-style garden and appreciate the ancient architectural structures, but also expect to know the ancient culture related to the three Su scholars.

当然，游客来到三苏祠博物馆，不仅可以游览当地风格的园林，欣赏古代建筑，同时还希望了解与三苏有关的古代文化。

During the Ming and Qing dynasties, the San Su Shrine housed some cultural relics. Up to now, the museum houses nearly 10,000 cultural relics, including 4 first-class relics, 24 second-class relics, and 696 third-class relics. It also has about 10,000 items such as ancient books and manuscripts, ceramics, and calligraphy and paintings.

明清时期，三苏祠就收藏了一批文物。三苏祠博物馆馆藏文物近万件，其中一级文物4件、二级文物24件、三级文物696件，更有古籍善本、陶瓷、书画等约10 000件。

Apart from its collections, the museum also holds exhibitions throughout the year, such as "the Cultural Exhibition at the Former Residence Ancestral Hall of Three Scholars in the Su Family" and "the Achievement Exhibition of Three Su Scholars". "The Cultural Exhibition at the Former Residence Ancestral Hall of Three Scholars in the Su Family" is displayed in the places, including the front hall, the Worship Hall and the Sage Hall, the East and West Chambers, Mujiashan Hall, and Laifeng Pavilion. When visitors enter the exhibition spaces, they feel as if they have stepped into the Su's former residence in Meizhou Prefecture during the Northern Song Dynasty, as these stories are presented to them in the most genuine and intimate way of life.

除了文物藏品之外，博物馆还常年举办陈列展，如"三苏故居祠堂文化展""三苏生平成就展"等。"三苏故居祠堂文化展"位于前厅、飨殿、启贤堂、东西厢房、木假山堂和来凤轩。苏宅故事以最真实、最贴近生活的方式呈现在游客面前，游客走进展厅，仿佛步入了北宋眉州的苏宅故居。

The San Su Memorial Halls house "the Achievement Exhibition of

Three Su Scholars". The hall is comprised of two floors. The ground floor is an exhibition on the lives and achievements of Su Xun and Su Zhe, while the second floor is all about Su Shi's life and achievements. The exhibition is divided into four parts, including Life of Su Shi, Warmth to the World, Great Man of Literature, and Unique Taste. Four touchscreens are offered, namely "Dongpo Idioms" "Dongpo Witticism and Quotations" "Dongpo Clean Governance Quotes", and "Dongpo Food". From time to time, the museum also hosts special exhibitions, such as the Special Exhibition of Cultural Relics on the Subject of Su Shi and the Special Exhibition for Antique Catalog of the Complete Collection of Su Shi Calligraphy (45 volumes).

三苏纪念馆是"三苏生平及文学成就展"的场地，展馆分两层。一层展示了苏洵和苏辙的生平，以及他们的成就。二层为"苏轼生平及成就展"，主要分为四部分："苏轼生平""情暖天下""文坛巨擘"和"况味雅趣"。此外，二层还设有4个触摸屏，用来展示"东坡成语""东坡名言佳句""东坡廉政佳句"和"东坡美食"。博物馆还会不定期地举办专题展，如"苏轼题材文物特展""《苏轼书法全集》（四十五册本）图录特展"等。

The collections and exhibitions in the San Su Shrine Museum provide an effective means to popularize the outstanding traditional Chinese culture, facilitate the exploration of the connotation of the San Su culture, and better fulfil the functions of education and research of the museum.

三苏祠博物馆的藏品与展览，为普及优秀的中华传统文化提供了有效手段，有助于挖掘三苏文化的内涵，更好地履行博物馆教育和研究的功能。

Well, so much for my brief introduction to the San Su Shrine Museum. There are numerous attractions in the museum. Those interested in visiting the exhibitions can go to the San Su Memorial Halls and follow the route of the Multi-function Hall, the Preface Hall, Su Xun's Exhibition Hall, Su Shi's Exhibition Hall and Su Zhe's Exhibition Hall. The rest of you come with me and tour the Xiang Hall, the Qixian Hall, the ancient well of the former residence and other scenic spots. The entire tour takes 2 hour. Please refrain from smoking, throwing fruit peels, and spitting in the museum.

好了，三苏祠博物馆的讲解到此结束。博物馆里景点众多，凡是对陈列展感兴趣的游客，可以去三苏纪念馆，其线路是：多功能厅—序厅—苏洵展厅—苏轼展厅—苏辙展厅。其余的人随我参观游览飨殿、启贤堂、苏宅古井等其他景点。整个游览时间为2小时。请勿在馆内吸烟、乱扔果皮、随地吐痰。

Chongqing Municipality
重庆市

重庆市《导游服务能力》考试大纲

01. Three Gorges of the Yangtze River
长江三峡 /331

02. Dazu Rock Carvings
大足石刻 /336

03. An Urban City with Mountains and Rivers
山水都市 /342

04. Three Natural Bridges in Wulong County
武隆天生三桥 /346

05. The Capital of Hot Springs
温泉之都 /351

06. Hechuan Diaoyu Town
合川钓鱼城 /355

07. White Crane Ridge in Fuling County
涪陵白鹤梁 /360

08. The Heaven Pit and Ground Seam in Fengjie County
奉节天坑地缝 /365

(注：根据2024年全国导游资格考试大纲，重庆市外语类考生景点讲解范围包括01~05共计5个景点，其余为补充内容。)

Chongqing Municipality
重庆市

Three Gorges of the Yangtze River
长江三峡

The Yangtze River is the longest river in China and the third longest river in the world. Along the Yangtze River, the spectacular three gorges is one of the ten most famous scenic sites of China. With a full length of 191 kilometers, it is composed of Qutang Gorge, Wu Gorge and Xiling Gorge, starting from White Emperor City in Fengjie County, Chongqing Municipality and ending at Nanjin Pass in Yichang, Hubei Province.

长江是中国最长的河流，是世界第三长河。壮观的长江三峡是中国十大风景名胜之一。它全长191公里，由瞿塘峡、巫峡、西陵峡组成，起自重庆奉节县的白帝城，止于湖北宜昌市的南津关。

Sanxia(the Three Gorges)first appeared in *The Ode to the Three Cities*, written by Zuo Si (about 250 A.D.–305 A.D.) of the Jin Dynasty. One of his ode lines says, "Pass through the towering three gorges." Qutang Gorge is the shortest of the Three Gorges (only 8 kilometers). It stands between steep cliffs, which are very high and tilting forward. Along the gorge, some waterways are less than 100 meters at its narrowest, where the steep sides are so close together that the sky looks very small. And within a short distance between the two sides, a voice seems to be easily echoed. Wu Gorge is about 45 kilometers long. Its cliffs on either side are between 1,000 and 2,300 meters high, topped by spiky, jagged peaks on the northern side, including Shennv Feng (the Goddess Peak) and Jixian Feng (the Peak of the Immortals). Often, around the peaks there remains mist or clouds that change unpredictably. "As you pass by the Wu Gorge, you are attracted by the twelve peaks." Xiling Gorge is the longest of the three, a stretch of 66 kilometers. At an earlier time, it was known for hidden rocks, dangerous shoals and tortuous waterways.

"三峡"之名始见于晋代左思（约公元250—公元305）的《三都赋》。其中有句云："经三峡之峥嵘"。瞿塘峡是三峡中最短的一个（仅8公里），两岸悬崖绝壁，高耸前倾。在瞿塘峡，有些河道宽度不及百米，两岸峭壁相逼甚近，从此往上看天空显得格外小。而且在两岸近距离内，说话声都容易产生回音。巫峡绵延45公里，两岸山峰高为1000~2300米，北边山顶奇峰突兀，怪石嶙峋，有神女峰、集仙峰，山峰周围时常云雾缭绕，变幻莫测。"放舟下巫峡，心在十二峰。"西陵峡最长，绵延66公里，从前以暗礁、险滩、曲折水道而闻名。

There are many well-known verses composed by celebrities of the past dynasties when they passed by the Three Gorges. One of them was written by Li Bai (701 A.D.–762 A.D.), a poet of the Tang Dynasty. It says,

"In the morning I left the White Emperor City in colored clouds.

A thousand miles to Jiangling I returned in a day.

The monkeys on the cliffs, they cried without a stop,

While our little schooner slipped by ten thousand rangers."

历代名人经过三峡时，留下了著名诗句。其中一首是唐代诗人李白（公元701—公元762）所写："朝辞白帝彩云间，千里江陵一日还；两岸猿声啼不住，轻舟已过万重山。"

Chongqing Municipality
重庆市

Foreigners traveled these fabulous Three Gorges in the early 20th century. They stated that it took 20 to 60 days to traverse the stretch from Yichang to Chongqing. The first trip by power boat up the Yangtze River from Yichang to Chongqing took place in 1898. The following passage from a guidebook published in 1915 describes the danger and wild beauty of the river at that time.

20世纪初，外国人游历了这段神话般的三峡。他们叙述道，从宜昌峡口穿过三峡，到达重庆，需要20到60天的时间。第一次汽艇旅行就是从宜昌出发，沿长江而上，到达重庆，此事发生在1898年。以下文字取自1915年出版的一本手册，它描述了当时惊险的、野性美的江水。

"Leaving Yichang and going up for about 2 miles, we suddenly find the channel narrowing to about 60 yards. And the waters flowing in whirlpools and rapids, while on both banks rise lofty, precipitous, wall-sided mountains, almost shutting out the sunshine… The navigation is extremely difficult, on account of sudden bends in the channel and many projecting rocks on the both sides, which give rise to great irregularities in the course of whirlpools and eddies. A place called His-ling-shia (Xiling Gorge) is particularly famous on account of the wild grandeur of its section and the difficulty of navigation. Here, hundreds of trackers are often at work hauling a large junk (a dozen or more trackers are required even in the case of a small craft)– these men struggling over irregular boulders with their shoulder-hawsers 1,200 feet long and as thick as one's arm, all the time yelling, shouting, or chanting, their movements directed by the beating of a drum or gong – a veritable pandemonium in the midst of extreme danger." "The celebrated 12 peaks of Wushan which are all more than 1,000 feet high, making huge walls on the north side of the gorge. The channel here is not only very narrow, making it one of the most difficult passage, but so closed in by high mountains that it is impossible to see the sun except at noontime. And in the uppermost gorge, the river bed was filled with many huge boulders, which produce dangerous whirlpools when submerged during the summer flood, but which block the way when the river is low in winter, giving rise to many narrow, foaming, and dangerous rapids."

"离开宜昌，逆流而上，大约走了两英里，我们突然发现水道渐渐变得狭窄，宽度缩小约六十码。水在漩涡和急流中流动，这时两岸山脉高耸、险峻、陡峭，几乎遮住了阳光……航行尤其困难，因为江弯道急，两岸许多岩石凸出，导致漩涡、逆流此起彼伏。有个叫西陵峡的地方，以其地段荒凉、宏伟和航行困难而闻名遐迩。在此地，常常有数百个纤夫，忙着拖拽一艘大型帆船；即便是一条小船，也需要十几个纤夫拖拽。这些人在不平整的卵石上，在肩膀上使劲拽着长1200英尺、粗如手臂样的纤绳；他们不停地或喊、或叫、或唱，指挥他们的不是鼓，就是锣，场面确实喧嚣惊险。"著名的巫山十二山峰座座高达1000多英尺，在巫峡北侧形成巨大的山墙。这里，水道不仅非常狭窄，为最难通过的水路之一，而且与高山相距咫尺，不到中午难以看见太阳。在三峡最上端，河床巨石甚多；夏季洪水时期，巨石淹没于水中，产生危险漩涡；冬天水位下降，巨石又导致河水变成若干条狭窄、泡沫泛起的危险急流。"

Today, the terrifying hazards of the passage are gone. After the founding of New China in 1949, the workers struggled – by blasting, digging, and rechanneling – to eliminate more than 100 danger spots in the river. Moreover, thanks to the construction of the Gezhou Dam and the impoundment of the Three Gorges Reservoir, the river rises up and the water flows has become more gentle than ever before. Nevertheless, spectacular scenery and historical sites are still everywhere, and the journey along the Three Gorges is still unforgettable.

今天，令人恐惧的危险通道已经成为历史。1949年中华人民共和国成立后，工人们通过不懈努力、爆破、挖掘、改道，消除了河道里一百多个危险点。此外，随着葛洲坝工程的建成和三峡水库蓄水，水位上升，水流更为平缓。尽管如此，壮观景色和历史景点仍然比比皆是，三峡旅行依然令人难以忘怀。

Well, so much for my brief introduction to the Three Gorges. We will take a large cruise ship down the river from Chongqing to Wanzhou. Then we will pass the Qutang Gorge, the Wu Gorge, and the Xiling Gorge, until we reach Yichang. On the way, we will see natural scenery, cultural sites and the Three Gorges Project. The whole trip takes three days. I'd like to remind you that the climate along the Three Gorges is very changeable, so please bring your jackets and rain gear. In addition, please bring your own seasick pills in case you feel seasick on board. During the voyage, our cruise ship often stops at scenic sites and allows tourists to disembark for sightseeing. So wherever the cruise ship stops, listen carefully to the cruise broadcast to find out what time the cruise ship will set sail and the dock where the cruise ship will be waiting. Now please come aboard with me and join us for our three-day tour of the Three Gorges.

好了，三峡简介到此为止，我们将乘坐大型游轮从重庆顺江而下，经万州，过瞿塘峡、巫峡、西陵峡，至宜昌；一路上，我们将看到三峡的自然风光、人文景观、三峡工程。全程需要3天时间。请注意：三峡气候多变，请带上外套及雨具。此外，请自带晕船药，有备无患。在旅途中，游轮经常会停靠在旅游景点，允许游客下船观光。所以，每到一处，要仔细听船上的广播，记住游船启航的时间和游船停靠的码头。现在请大家随我一起上游轮，开始为期三天的长江三峡游。

02

Dazu Rock Carvings
大足石刻

Dazu Rock Carvings, located in Dazu District and 160 kilometers northwest of Chongqing, are the most important representative work of the Chinese late grotto arts. The rock carvings enjoy equal popularity along with Yungang Grottoes, Longmen Grottoes and Mogao Grottoes. The rock carvings were made in the first Yonghui year of the late Tang Dynasty (650 A.D.), continued in the Five Dynasties and thrived in the Southern Song Dynasty. Later, some more rock carvings were added during the Ming and Qing dynasties. So far, there are more than 50,000 existent carving statues, which are distributed in more than 40 places. Collectively, they are known as the Dazu Rock Carvings. The cliff carvings in Beishan Hill and Baoding Hill are the most famous with exquisite craftsmanship and rich connotation.

大足石刻位于重庆市西北160公里大足地区,是中国晚期石窟艺术最重要代表作品,与云冈石窟、龙门石窟、莫高窟齐名。石刻始建于唐末永徽元年(公元650年),历经五代,盛于南宋,余绪延至明、清两代。到目前为止,现存的雕刻造像5万多尊,分布在40多处地方,统称为大足石刻,尤以北山和宝顶山摩崖造像最为著名,其工艺精美,内涵丰富。

Chongqing Municipality
重庆市

Figurines Carved out of Stone Walls

The Dazu Rock Carvings are of religious nature and mainly Buddhist statues. However, the rock carvings humanize Buddhist statues and depict the scenes of daily life. Beishan Hill and Baoding Hill are the home of Buddhist carvings, while Nanshan Hill has Taoist carvings, and Shimen Hill has niches or caves shared with the statues of Confucian, Buddhist and Taoist figurines. Dazu Rock Carvings display the development and changes in the Chinese stone carving art and folk religious beliefs from the end of the 9th century to the middle of the 13th century. In ancient times, few scholars visited this place due to the inconvenience of transportation. Therefore, there is a lack of relevant historical records about Dazu Rock Carvings. However, for nearly one thousand years, due to Dazu's remote location, these carvings exist alone on the barren hills and have survived man-made destruction and wars. In 1961, the Dazu Rock Carvings was listed as the national key cultural relics protection unit. In 1999, it was officially listed as the World Cultural Heritage Site.

大足石刻具有宗教性质，以佛教造像为主。不过，石雕使佛教造像人性化，并有描述日常生活场面。北山、宝顶山主要以佛教雕刻为主，南山有道教雕刻，石门山则有佛教、道教、儒教三教合一龛窟造像。大足石刻展示了9世纪末到13世纪中叶中国石刻艺术风格和民间宗教信仰的发展和变化。在古代，由于交通不便，鲜有学者造访，也缺乏相关大足石刻史料记载。然而，在近千年里，由于大足石刻地处偏远，这些石刻独存在于荒山之中，幸免于人为破坏和战争浩劫。1961年，大足石刻被列为国家重点文物保护单位，1999年被正式列为世界文化遗产。

Well, the focus of our tour of the Dazu Rock Carvings is to see carvings on the Baoding Hill, which is 15 kilometers northeast of Dazu and the retreat of the Tantric Buddhism. On the hill, there are nearly 10,000 figurines, mainly distributed at Dafuwan and Xiaofuwan, where the figurines are carved out of stone walls, beams and pillars. Dafuwan is located at the lower left of Shengshou Monastery. It is a hilly, horseshoe-shaped valley with a total length of 500 meters. Its cliff face is 15 to 30 meters high, and the figurines are distributed on the east, south and north sides of the cliff. Totally, there are 31 huge figurines, which include the Group of the Figurines of the Dharma Protectors, the Picture of Transmigration in the Six Ways, the Pavilion of the Extensive Treasure, the Huayan Three Sages, the One-Thousand-Hand Guanyin in a seated position, the Sacred Symbol of the Sakyamuni Entering Nirvana, the Statue of the Nine Dragons Bathing the Prince, the Cave of the Peacock King, the Story of the Scripture on Parental Love, the Scripture on Mahopaya Buddha Requiting the Kindness of the Parents, the Eighteen-Layer Hell, the Picture of Cowherds and the Cave of Pratyeka Buddhas.

我们游览大足石刻，主要参观大足宝顶山石刻。宝顶山地处大足东北15公里，也是佛教密宗道场。山上有近万尊造像，主要分布在大佛湾和小佛湾，皆凿刻在石墙、石梁、石柱上。大佛湾位于圣寿寺左下方，是一座多坡的马蹄形山凹，全长约 500 米。悬崖面高 15～30 米，雕刻分布在东、南、北的崖壁上，共有 31 幅巨型雕像，包括护法神像、六道轮回图、广大宝楼阁、华严三圣、千手观音、释迦涅槃圣迹图、九龙浴太子、孔雀明王经变相、父母恩重经变相、大方便佛报恩经变相、地狱变相、牧牛图和圆觉洞。

Of course, the "Sacred Symbol of Sakyamuni Entering Nirvana" deserves to be mentioned. What is "Nirvana"? It refers to the supreme state and destination that Buddists want to achieve, that is, great awakening, firmness and eternity, which can enable people to achieve infinite enlightenment, floating off into immortal freedom and peace from life-and-death struggle. The "Sacred Symbol of Sakyamuni Entering Nirvana" is the giant statue of a reclining Buddha. It depicts the grand occasion as Sakyamuni enters Nirvana. In Dafuwan, the statue is the largest figurine, 31 meters long and 6.8 meters high. The Buddha reclines on his right side with his back facing east. He looks serene with his eyes half closed. His right shoulder is hidden under the ground, his left shoulder is among five-colored auspicious clouds, and his feet remain uncarved in the rock. The statue is well proportioned. It perfectly expresses the tranquility of Sakyamuni's Nirvana, implying that the Buddha reclines between the Heaven and the Earth. Its artistic conception is broad and full of vitality. In addition, coiling smoke comes out of incense burners in front of the reclining Buddha. About twenty busts of Bodhisattvas stand around respectfully. Some put their palms together on their chests, while some others hold flowers and fruits, showing the disciples' respect attachment to Sakyamuni. Meanwhile, the Buddha seems to close his eyes gradually, looking serene and free from pain. According to the Buddhist scriptures, as Sakyamuni was about to enter Nirvana, he said to Ananda, "Perhaps some of you think my teachings will end soon after I enter Nirvana. No, after my Nirvana, the Dharma I have taught and disciplines I have prescribed for you will be your teachers." So far, the Reclining Buddha Valley in Anyue, the Reclining Buddha Monastery in Beijing, the Thousand Buddha Cave in Dunhuang Grottoes and the Thousand Buddha Cliff in Hechuan, all have a full-body reclining Buddha Statues. Only on the Baoding Hill, the statue of the Reclining Buddha alone is a bust, with its lower part of the body hidden in the rock. So, there is a saying among Dazu folks. It says that the Buddha's body remains in Dazu County, his hands touch Baxian County, and his feet are in Luzhou.

当然,"释迦涅槃圣迹图"值得一提。什么是"涅槃"？它指的是佛教所要达到的最高境界和归宿,即大彻大悟,坚定永恒,能使人们获得无穷大觉,从生死的彼岸渡到不生不灭的境界。"释迦涅槃圣迹图"是一座巨大卧佛,造像描绘了释迦牟尼涅槃时的盛大场面。在大佛湾,这座造像为最大的一尊,长31米,高6.8米。卧佛右侧而卧,背朝东面,两眼半开半闭,安详平静；右肩隐于地表之下,左肩在五色祥云之中,双脚隐没于岩际。其造型比例恰当,而且还完美地表现出佛祖涅槃时的安详之态,寓意释迦牟尼横卧于天地之间,其意境博大而气魄。此外,放在卧佛前的香炉香烟袅袅,约二十尊半身菩萨雕像恭敬地站在四周,或合掌于胸,或手捧香花水果,表现出弟子对释迦牟尼崇敬厚爱和依依眷恋之情。卧佛似乎渐渐闭上双目,神色宁静而无痛苦迹象。据佛经记载,释迦牟尼在弥留之时,对阿难说："也许你们有些人会认为,我进入涅槃后不久世尊的教导就会终结。不,在我涅槃之后,我为你们大家宣说的教法和制订的戒律将成为你们的导师。"迄今为止,安岳的卧佛沟、北京的卧佛寺、敦煌千佛洞和合川千佛岩,都有全身卧佛像。唯有宝顶山的这尊卧佛是半身像,其下半身隐入石岩之中,故大足民间流传着一种说法：宝顶山卧佛身在大足,手摸巴县,脚踏泸州。

Well, my introduction to the Dazu Rock Carvings is over. Now please follow a local tour guide to tour the Baoding Hill. He will explain each statue in detail, and his explanation will be of great help to your tour of this site. Our trip takes about two hours.

好了，大足石刻的介绍到此为止。现在请跟随当地导游游览宝顶山，他会详细地讲解每尊造像，他的讲解对你们游览此地大有帮助。参观时间为两小时。

03

An Urban City with Mountains and Rivers
山水都市

Chongqing is a metropolis in Southwest China. It is located in the upper reaches of the Yangtze River and is known to the world as a "mountain city". It borders Daba Mountain to the north, Wushan Mountain to the east, Wuling Mountain to the southeast and Dalou Mountain to the south. The most prominent features of the city are the undulating topography and a strong three-dimensional sense. The landform is dominated by hills and mountains. There are many typical karst landforms within its border, such as stone forests, peak forests, limestone caves and canyons.

重庆是中国西南的一座大城市，位于长江上游，是举世闻名的"山城"。北与大巴山接壤，东与巫山为邻，东南有武陵山，南有大娄山。该城最突出的特点是：地形起伏，立体感强。地貌以丘陵、山地为主，境内多处有石林、峰林、灰岩溶洞、峡谷，呈现出典型的喀斯特地貌。

In addition to many mountains, Chongqing is endowed with a multitude of rivers, which crisscross its territory. The Yangtze River runs through Chongqing from west to east, stretching 665 kilometers. The Jialing River flows from northwest into the Chongqing section, the main channel of the Yangtze River. The other four major tributaries (Qujiang, Fujiang, Wujiang and Daning River) and hundreds of small rivers also converge in the Chongqing section of the Yangtze River. Besides, Chongqing has many lakes, such as the Changshou Lake, the Small South China Sea, and Qinglong Lake. Therefore, it can be said that Chongqing is a city on rivers and lakes.

重庆除了山多，就是水多。重庆境内江河纵横，长江自西向东横贯全境，全长665公里。嘉陵江自西北而来，汇入长江干流重庆段。另外四大支流（渠江、涪江、乌江、大宁河）以及上百条小河也汇入重庆段的长江。此外，重庆还有众多湖泊，如：长寿湖、小南海、青龙湖。可以说，重庆是一座河流湖泊之上的城市。

Most prominently, in the urban area of Chongqing, hills extend and rivers flow ups and downs, showing a strong sense of three-dimensional gradation. Its main urban districts are encircled with rivers on three sides, while the Yangtze River and Jialing River meander through the city and converge at Chaotianmen Dock before rolling eastward. The buildings are either constructed beside the rivers or on the hillsides. Inside the city, slopes are steep, streets are precipitous, and buildings are staggered on top of each other. "The city is amid the mountains, and the mountains embrace the city; the city is the mountain, and the mountain is the city as well." Accordingly, Chongqing is also known as the "City of Mountains". As a metropolis, Chongqing is the only one city, constructed entirely on mountains in China. The integration of architectural complex and natural surroundings makes Chongqing a landscape city with unique charms.

在重庆市区，最突出的特点是山水连绵、起伏有致，呈现出极强的立体层次感。主城区三面环水，长江、嘉陵江蜿蜒穿城而过，在朝天门汇合后滚滚东下。城市建筑或依山而建，或临江而筑，市内坡峭路陡；建筑物错落有致，高低叠置。"城在山中，山中有城；城即是山，山即是城"，故重庆也称为"山城"。作为大型城市，重庆是全国唯一一座完全建在山上的城市，建筑群和自然环境完美融合，使重庆成为具有独特魅力的山水园林城市。

Chongqing is built on the hillside and beside the rivers. Therefore, the night scene of Chongqing even largely reflects the charms of its urban landscape. As the popular saying goes, "A trip to Chongqing can really count for little without watching the local night scene." Its night scene was famous in ancient times. During the Qianlong period of the Qing Dynasty (1736–1796), the night scene was already listed as one of the "Bayu's Twelve Scenic Sights (Bayu referring to Chongqing in ancient times)". The beautiful night scene is impressive, just like a huge splash-ink landscape painting, showing a poetic illusion. The buildings, high and low in tiers, are well distributed on the hillside and by the river and boats are on the rivers, sailing to and fro in the evening. All these have created objective conditions for the beautiful night scene of the city. However, in ancient times, no matter how beautiful the night scene was, the light of oil lamps, candles and burning torches was faint and unstable, and it could hardly illuminate the entire city. Nowadays, because of the rapid pace of urban construction, new Chongqing is not only beautiful in the mountains and rivers, but also in every corner of the city. In the main urban district, high-rise buildings are densely blanketed with dazzling neon lights, illuminating the night sky. Along Binjiang Road, orange lights are linked up, just like fluttering colorful ribbons or dancing dragons. The surface of the river is sparkling, and countless flashing lights are reflected in the water, forming golden and silvery beams. Such colorful lights are closely intertwined, making Chongqing look like a floating palace on the water.

重庆都市依山而建，临江而筑。由于它的特点，重庆的夜景更彰显山水都市的魅力。常言道，"不看夜景，枉到重庆"。其夜景自古有名。清乾隆年间（1736—1796），夜景已被列为"巴渝十二景"之一。美丽的夜色让人难忘，就像一幅巨大的泼墨山水画，朦胧中透着诗的美景。高低叠置的建筑依山傍水，舟船夜里在江中穿行，为都市美丽的夜景创造了客观条件。然而，在古代，无论夜景多么美丽，油灯、蜡烛、火把也只能是微弱之光，星星点点，难以照亮整座城市。如今，城市建设日新月异，新重庆不仅美在山水岸边，而且美在市内各个角落。在主城区，高楼大厦布满了耀眼的霓虹灯，把夜空照得通亮；滨江路上，橘黄色的灯火连成一线，如飘逸的彩带，又像舞动的火龙；江面波光潋滟，无数闪烁的灯火倒映水中，形成无数条金银光柱。这些七色之光交织在一起，使重庆仿佛成了一座辉煌壮观的水上浮宫。

Well, so much for my introduction to the urban city with mountains and rivers. Tonight we will go by bus to enjoy the night scene. Our route goes like this: we will cross the Yangtze Multiple Track Bridge, overlook at Nanbin Road and then view Chaotianmen Dock. Afterwards, we will take the bus again up to the "One-Tree-Viewing Pavilion" on Nanshan Hill, overlooking the night scene of Chongqing. The whole trip takes two hours. By the way, please remember the parking place, the departure time and my phone number. Don't hesitate to contact me whenever you need assistance.

好了，重庆山水都市的讲解到此为止。今晚我们将乘车去观看重庆都市夜景。我们游览的线路是，经过长江复线桥，俯瞰南滨路，观朝天门；然后再乘车上南山一棵树观景阁，俯瞰重庆夜景。游览时间需要两小时。请记住停车地点、发车时间、我的手机号，你们可以随时与我联系。

04

Three Natural Bridges in Wulong County
武隆天生三桥

Three Natural Bridges are located 20 kilometers southeast of Wulong County, 160 kilometers away from the main urban area of Chongqing. The Three Natural Bridges consist of Tianlong Bridge (Heaven Dragon Bridge), Qinglong Bridge (Bluish Green Dragon Bridge) and Heilong Bridge (Black Dragon Bridge). These bridges, formed between 500,000 and 300 million years ago, were typical of karst landscape made of Triassic

A Sign of Three Natural Bridges

limestone. So far, they are considered the largest group of natural bridges in Asia.

天生三桥位于武隆县城东南20公里处，距重庆主城区160公里。天生三桥由天龙桥、青龙桥和黑龙桥组成，形成于距今50万年至3亿年间，属典型的三叠纪石灰岩构成的喀斯特地貌景观。迄今为止，天生三桥属亚洲最大的天生桥群。

The Three Natural Bridges are a unique eco-tourism area with unique geological wonders. Expedition specialists and geological experts enthusiastically call the area "an earth heritage site and the wonder of the world". In the scenic area, the natural stone bridges appear magnificent; woods remain thick and green; peaks and ridges are covered with greenness; spring water roll down from cliff-side; birds chirp and flowers give forth their sweet scents. Scenic spots can be seen everywhere, such as the Three Natural Bridges, Sheshen Cliff (the Cliff of Self-Sacrifice), Wangfeng Stone (the Looking-Over-Cliff Stone), Lvyin Pool (the Greenness Pool) and Xiannv Cave (the Fairies' Cave). The hills, streams, waterfalls, canyons and bridges constitute a perfect landscape painting, attracting numerous tourists who gradually indulge in nature and linger around the scenic spots, temporarily forgetting the hustle and bustle. In June 2007, the Three Natural Bridges, Furong Cave and Qingkou Skyhole Scenery in Houping were all listed as the World Natural Heritage Sites. In addition, the Three Natural Bridges is listed as the national 4A-level tourist attraction. Together with Furong Cave, it was awarded the title of the National Geological Park.

天生三桥是罕见的生态型旅游区，具有独特的地质奇观，探险专家和地质专家赞之为"地球遗产，世界奇观"。景区内，天生石桥气势磅礴，林森木秀，峰青岭翠，飞泉流水，鸟语花香。景点随处可见，有天生三桥、舍身崖、望峰石、绿茵塘和仙女洞。山、水、瀑、峡、桥构成一幅完美的山水画卷，吸引众多游客，让游人逐渐陶醉于自然之中，流连于景点之间，暂时忘却尘嚣。2007年6月，天生三桥与芙蓉洞、后坪箐口天坑景区一起被列为世界自然遗产。此外，天生三桥景区还被评为国家AAAA级旅游景区，同芙蓉洞一并被授予国家地质公园称号。

Of course, Wulong Three Natural Bridge Scenic Area is widely known mainly for the three bridges. Tianlong Bridge is tall and magnificent. It is the first bridge on Yangshui River Valley and also known as Toudao Bridge. The bridge is 235 meters in height and 150 meters in thickness, while the bridge deck is 147 meter in width. The average height of the arch is 96 meters, spanning 20 to 75 meters. Below Tianlong Bridge are two limestone caves, which have their own entrances and exits. There are some small caves inside the caves, making the two caves like a spectacular and magical maze. Qinglong Bridge is the second natural bridge on Yangshui River Valley. Usually, the rainwater falls off the bridge deck like waterfalls after the rain, forming cloudy vapor. When the sun shines upon the vapor, a rainbow appears, like a blue-green dragon, rising directly up into the sky. Accordingly, the second bridge is also known as Zhonglong Bridge (Central Dragon Bridge). Compared with the other two bridges, Qinglong Bridge is the highest. Its deck is 281 meters in height and 124 meters in width with an average arch height of 103 meters and a span of 13 to 58 meters. If you stand under the bridge and look up, you will find that the arches are tall and spacious, like thousand-*ren* (very high) vertical cliffs. In addition, the surface of the vault has gradually collapsed and exposed crevasses, which reveal the evolution of the natural bridge. Heilong Bridge is the third natural bridge located in the lower reaches of Yangshui River Valley. The bridge is widely known for its deep and dark arches, like a black dragon wriggling its way through the vault. The height of the bridge deck is 223 meters, while the average arch height is 116 meters, the highest among the arches of the three bridges. On the walls and top of the tunnel, various forms of corrosion and rill marks, such as cavities, dissolved holes and ceiling pockets, are widely distributed, reflecting the features of underground water flow millions of years ago. In addition, on the north sidewall there suspend four water springs of different shapes. They are the Foggy Spring, the Pearl Spring, the Thin Strip Spring and the Triple Lap Spring.

当然，武隆天生三桥景区主要以"三桥"而闻名。天龙桥高大宏伟，为羊水河峡谷上的第一桥，又名头道桥。桥高235米，厚150米，桥面宽147米，拱桥高度平均96米，拱孔跨度20～75米。天龙桥下有两个石灰岩洞穴，各有其出入口，洞中生洞，洞如迷宫，既壮观又神奇。青龙桥为羊水河峡谷上的第二座天生桥。通常，雨后飞瀑自桥面倾泻成雾，阳光照在水雾上，彩虹浮现，似青龙直冲云霄。由此，第二桥又名中龙桥。与其他两座桥梁相比，青龙桥最高；桥面高为281米，宽124米，拱孔高度平均103米，拱孔跨度13～58米。从桥下仰视，拱孔高旷，壁立千仞。此外，拱顶表面有逐渐塌陷暴露的裂缝，其断裂面揭示了天生桥演化过程。黑龙桥是位于羊水河峡谷下游的天生桥。这座桥因其拱洞幽深暗黑，似有一条黑龙蜿蜒于洞顶而得名。桥面高223米，平均拱孔高116米，为三桥中拱孔最高者。在洞道侧壁和顶部遍及流痕溶蚀形态，如：窝穴、溶孔、天锅等，所有这些反映了数百万年前伏流的水流特征。此外，洞壁北侧还有四处风格迥异的悬挂泉，分别是雾泉、珍珠泉、一线泉和三叠泉。

Well, so much for the introduction to the Three Natural Bridges. After breakfast in the hotel today, we'll take a bus to the front gate of the Three Natural Bridge Scenic Area. Then we take a 70-meters-high elevator to the bottom of the valley, where our tour route begins. We walk to Tianfu Official Post, part of the filming base for a movie *Curse of the Golden Flower*. Afterwards, we climb up the hill and walk through Tianlong Bridge,

Qinglong Bridge, Heilong Bridge, until we arrive at Xiaoxitan Pool. Finally, we return along the way we come from. The tour takes about two hours. The temperature in the valley is about 10℃ lower than that on the top of the hill, so be sure to bring warm jackets and waterproof coats. Also, I'd like to advise female tourists not to wear highheels, as most of hill trails have stone steps. Now let's get ready for our trip to the scenic area.

好了,天生三桥的介绍到此为止。今天,我们在酒店吃早饭,之后乘车去天生三桥景区入口处;接着乘坐70米高的电梯下到谷底,开始我们的行程:步行至天福官驿,那是电影《黄金甲》拍摄基地之一;然后登山,穿过天龙桥、青龙桥、黑龙桥,到达小溪潭,最后原路返回。游览时间约2小时。山谷里的温度比山顶低10℃左右,记住随身带件保暖衣和防水外套;景区内多是石阶路,女士出游最好不要穿高跟鞋。现在大家此次旅游做准备吧。

05
The Capital of Hot Springs
温泉之都

Chongqing, known as the "Capital of Hot Springs", has a long history of hot spring development. According to legend, Yellow Emperor Xuanyuan produced a "medicinal hot spring" in the current base of the Northern Hot Springs at the foot of Jinyun Hill. In 423 A.D., Master Ci Ying, a Buddhist Eminent Monk, mobilized the locals to build Hot Spring Temple. During the Wanli period of the Ming Dynasty (1573–1620), the resources of the Southern Hot Springs began to be exploited by locals. In the period of the Republic of China, the Western Hot Springs emerged. Successively in 1926, 1927 and 1935, the Southern Hot Springs, the Northern Hot Springs and the Western Hot Springs were further exploited and utilized. During the War of Resistance Against Japanese Aggression, Chongqing became a provisional war-time capital, where the Northern Hot Springs, the Southern Hot Springs and the Western Hot Springs were the gathering places for celebrities in military, political or cultural circles. Since then, hot springs in Chongqing have become famous at home and abroad.

重庆享有"温泉之都"的美誉,其温泉开发历史悠久。传说,轩辕黄帝曾在缙云山下的北温泉创造"温汤和药"。公元423年,佛教高僧慈应大师率众在缙云山创建了"温泉寺"。明朝万历年间(1573—1620),当地人开始开发利用南温泉。民国时期,又有了西温泉。1926年、1927年、

1935年人们先后对南温泉、北温泉和西温泉进行了进一步开发利用。在抗战陪都时期，北温泉、南温泉、西温泉是当时军政、文化界名人汇聚之所。从那以后，重庆温泉名扬海内外。

Hot springs in Chongqing not only have a long history of development, but also are rich in resources. Its local hot spring resources are found everywhere in Chongqing's territory. Characteristically, "every mountain has warm water; every valley has hot springs; their reserves are abundant and of good quality water." Within an area of 82,000 square kilometers alone, the proven hot spring distribution area is one million square kilometers, with about 100 hot springs. In addition, the hot springs typically have water temperatures of between 40 ℃ and 55 ℃ , with the highest temperature up to 60℃. Here, most of the local hot springs contain more than 30 minerals and micro elements, the water temperature is suitable, and acidity and alkali are moderate. Functionally, these hot springs can relax muscles and joints, relieve stress and fatigue, promote blood circulation, and accelerate the body's metabolism. Of course, the most famous hot springs should be the "Ten Springs on the Five Sides". On the east side are the Eastern Hot Springs and the Qiaokouba Hot Springs. The water temperature in the Eastern Hot Springs can reach up to 52°C. On the south side are the Southern Hot Springs and Baoli Hot Springs. The Southern Hot Springs is one of the best hot springs in China, mainly containing calcium sulphate, magnesium and calcium. On the west side are Tianci Hot Springs and Beidi Hot Springs. On the north side are the Northern Hot Springs, which are regarded as the earliest developed hot springs in China and even in the world. Tongjing Hot Springs is also located on the north side, known as "Wuling Wonderland" by the ancient literati. A number of hot springs have been opened in recent years in the central area, such as the Haitangxiaoyue Hot Springs and

Ronghui Hot Springs. In addition, there are Yisang Hot Springs and the Southern Hill Hot Springs. Nowadays, it can be said that the industry of Chongqing hot springs is in the heyday, with various kinds of hot springs springing up everywhere. In October 2012, the 65th General Assembly and International Scientific Congress of the World Federation of Hydrotherapy and Climatotherapy (FEMTEC) was held in Chongqing. At the conference, the FEMTEC awarded to Chongqing the title of the "Hot Spring Capital of the World".

重庆温泉不仅开发历史早，资源也很丰富。重庆温泉资源遍布各地，"山山有热水，峡峡有温泉，储丰质优"。在仅8.2万平方千米的范围内，现已探明的温泉分布区域为100万平方公里，温泉点约100处。此外，这些温泉的水温一般在40℃~55℃，最高可达60℃。在这里，当地大部分温泉含有30多种矿物质和微量元素，水温适宜，酸碱适中，具有松弛肌肉和关节，消除疲劳，促进血液循环，加速人体新陈代谢的功能。当然，最有名的当数"五方十泉"。东边有东温泉、桥口坝温泉；东温泉的水温最高可达52℃。南边有南温泉和保利小泉；南温泉是国内最好的热泉之一，主要含有硫酸钙、镁和钙。西边有天赐温泉、贝迪温泉。北边有北温泉，是中国乃至世界上最早开发的温泉；统景温泉也位于北边，被古代文人称之为"武陵仙境"。近年来，中部地区开发了若干温泉，如：海棠晓月温泉、融汇温泉。此外，还有颐尚温泉和南山温泉。如今，重庆的温泉产业可谓如日中天，各种温泉层出不穷。2012年10月，世界温泉及气候养生联合会第65届年会暨国际科学大会在重庆举办。在这次大会上，世界温泉及气候养生联合会授予重庆"世界温泉之都"称号。

Well, so much for my brief introduction to the Capital of Hot Springs. In five minutes, we will arrive at Tongjing Hot Springs. In this area, there are more than 100 hot spring pools, large or small, indoor or outdoor. These pools offer different options depending on the needs of the locals and tourists. If some of you want to take a bath in the hot springs here, I'd like to remind you of the following. Be sure to test the water temperature with your hand or foot before bathing in the pools. You can repeatedly soak in any of the regular hot spring pools, but no more than 15 minutes at a time. If you feel thirsty or chest tightness, please step out of the pool to take a rest and drink some water. We stay here for five hours. I will meet you at 4:30 p.m. at the entrance and then take the bus back to the hotel.

好了，温泉之都的简介到此为止。再过五分钟，我们就到达统景温泉了。在这个区域，有室内外大小温泉池共100余个，当地人和游客可以根据个人需要选择不同的水池。如果你们有人要泡温泉，得注意以下几点：先用手或脚探试池温，然后再下温泉池；可以在一般温泉池反复浸泡，但每次不能超过15分钟；如果感觉口干或胸闷，就走出水池歇一歇，喝些水。我们在此地逗留5个小时，四点半在统景温泉门口集合，然后乘车返回宾馆。

Chongqing Municipality
重庆市

06

Hechuan Diaoyu Town
合川钓鱼城

Hechuan Diaoyu Town is located on the Diaoyu Hill, five kilometers east of Hechuan, covering an area of 2.5 square kilometers. On the hill there is a huge rock with a smooth surface. According to legend, once on the rock there was a giant deity fished in Jialing River to relieve the famine of the local people. Since then, the hill has been called Diaoyu Hill, and the town is also known as Diaoyu Town.

合川钓鱼城位于合川城东五公里的钓鱼山上，占地2.5平方千米。山上有一块平整的巨石。传说，有一个巨神在石上钓嘉陵江中之鱼，以解一方百姓饥馑。从此以后，这座山就叫钓鱼山，城就被称为钓鱼城。

Diaoyu Town lies at the confluence of the three rivers—Qujiang River, Fujiang River and Jialing River. Due to its unique geographical location, it has numerous natural landscapes and cultural sites. In terms of the natural landscape, it has the well-known Eight Diaoyu Town Scenic Spots, such as the Flowing Spring in Ancient Caves, the Sound of Rain Drops on the Beach, the Soft Light on the Red Cliff, the Morning Rosy Clouds in the East Valley, the Sunset Glow Over the West Town, the Moon in Tianchi Lake at Night, the White Clouds Around the Peaks, as well as the Encircling Belts of Jialing River. Standing on Diaoyu Hill, visitors can overlook the confluence of the three rivers, where clouds and rains mingle with each other, and the Diaoyu Town is hidden in the misty rain.

钓鱼城位于渠江、涪江、嘉陵江三江交汇处，其地理位置独特，自然和人文景观不胜枚举。就自然景观而言，就有著名的鱼城八景：古洞流泉、沙滩响雨、赤壁文光、东谷晴霞、西市晚烟、天池夜月、顶峰白云、嘉陵萦带。站在钓鱼山上，俯瞰三江汇流，烟雨辉映，钓鱼城掩映于烟雨之中。

In ancient China, the Diaoyu Hill was always an ideal place where officials and literary men wrote poems or took walks for sightseeing. Also, in ancient times, a battle occurred here, namely, the Defense Battle of Hechuan Diaoyu Town Hechuan. In 1258, Mongke Khan, Kublai Khan and Senior General Uriyangqatai led the Mongolian army to attack the Southern Song Dynasty. Mongke Khan himself led the main troops to attack Sichuan. In February 1259, Mongke Khan and his army stood exactly in the doorway of the Diaoyu Town. Before they reached the town, the armoured cavalry troops led by Mongke Khan swept forward from victory to victory wherever they went. However, under the command of Chief Commander Wang Jian and Assistant Commander Zhang Yu, the town defending troops tenaciously resisted the Mongolian invasion, making it impossible to conquer the town. The fighting continued. In July, Mongke Khan was wounded by cannons from the town. He later died in the Hot Spring Temple, and the Mongolian army were thus defeated. Today, remnants of military constructions built during the Song and Yuan wars still exist, including the walls and gates of the town, Tianchi Lake, the Imperial Palace, the South Pier of the Water Forces and military barracks. In addition, in the town there are a large number of poetry, rhymed prose and inscriptions carved on relief and steles. These were all written by people of later generations when they visited the historical sites. For instance, Li Zuozhou, one of successful candidates in the highest imperial examinations of the Ming Dynasty, presented his four-character inscription "Du Diao Zhong Yuan (Fishing Alone in the Central Plains)". His inscription was engraved on the top of a stone memorial archway.

在古代中国，钓鱼山一直是士大夫、文人们吟诗和游玩的理想之地。也是在古代，这儿曾经发生过战争，即：合川钓鱼城保卫战。1258年，蒙哥可汗、忽必烈可汗、兀良合台率领蒙古军队进攻南宋。蒙哥可汗亲率主力攻打四川。次年2月，蒙哥可汗和他的军队兵临钓鱼城。蒙哥铁骑来合川前东征西讨，所向披靡。然而，在主将王坚与副将张钰的指挥下，城堡守军顽强抗击蒙军入侵，使其不能攻克城池。战斗在继续；7月，蒙哥可汗被城上火炮击伤，后逝于温泉寺，蒙哥军队由此战败。如今，此地依然还有宋蒙（元）战争期间所建的军事建筑的残留物，如：钓鱼城城垣及城门、天池、皇宫、南水军码头、步军营。此外，钓鱼城里还有大量的诗赋及浮雕碑刻，皆是后人凭吊历史的遗迹所做的，如：明代进士李作舟书写的"独钓中原"四个字，其题字就刻在一石制牌坊顶端。

The value of tourism of Diaoyu Town is not limited to the ancient war stories and related ruins of the military sites. There are other cultural attractions in the town, such as Huguo Temple, the Statue of the Suspension Reclining Buddha and the Thousand-Buddha Stone Cave. Among the cultural attractions, the Statue of the Suspension Reclining Buddha should be the most special one in Diaoyu Town. It is carved on the suspension cliff west of Diaoyu Platform. The statue of the Reclining Buddha is 11 meters long, 2.2 meters wide at the shoulder, 1.8 meters apart between the ears, and 1.2 meters wide between the feet. The Buddha leans his back against the rock and is faced with a steep cliff. A huge boulder protrudes from the rock, forming a natural shelter above the reclining statue. Under the shelter, the Buddha slightly closes his eyes, solemnly reclining on his side. The reclining Buddha is exquisitely carved, and its full face seems to show a dignified and peaceful smile. This sculpture was first built in the late Tang Dynasty. Although it has undergone almost a thousand years of historical vicissitudes, it is still well preserved. On the cliff, right above the Reclining Buddha's head, are engraved Chinese characters "Yi Wo Qian Gu (The Buddha Lying Through the Ages)" written by Wang Xiu, a man of letters in the Song Dynasty. These characters are magnificent, and the brushwork appear graceful. Also on the cliff, above the feet of the Reclining Buddha, are some other inscriptions. One of them reads, "Historical Sites on Diaoyu Hill" written by Liu Shikui, a magistrate of Hezhou in the Ming Dynasty.

钓鱼城的旅游价值不只局限于古代战争故事和相关的军事遗址，城堡里还有其他的人文景观，如：护国寺、悬空卧佛、千佛石窟。在众多的人文景观中，悬空卧佛堪称"钓鱼城一绝"。该卧佛雕凿在钓鱼台西面的悬空崖壁上。卧佛像身长11米，肩宽2.2米，两耳间距1.8米，双脚间宽1.2米，背倚石岩，面临绝壁。一块巨石从岩上伸出，在卧佛上方形成了天然的遮盖物。在遮盖的岩石下，佛像微眯着眼睛，庄严地侧卧着。卧佛雕刻精美大气，饱满的面形好像流露出端庄和宁静的笑容。这座雕刻初建于晚唐，尽管历经了近千年历史变迁，至今依然保存完好。在卧佛头部上端的崖壁上，有宋代文学家王休题书"一卧千古"，字体宏大，笔触飘逸。卧佛脚上端的崖壁上，也有若干题刻，其中有明代合州知州刘士逵书题的"鱼山古迹"。

Well, so much for my introduction to Hechuan Diaoyu Town. Please get off the bus now and go sightseeing with me. We start from the South Pier of the Water Forces and end our tour at the Monument to Wang Jian's Merits and Virtues. On the way, we will take a view of Shiguan Gate, Feilai Temple, Huguo Gate, the Ruins of the Ancient Military Training

Field, Huguo Temple, Diaoyu Platform, as well as the Statue of the Suspension Reclining Buddha, the Thousand-Buddha Stone Cave and the Stone Sculpture of the Three Sages. The whole trip takes two hours. By the way, please remember the parking place, the departure time and my phone number. Don't hesitate to contact me whenever you need assistance.

好了，合川钓鱼城的讲解到此为止。请下车随我参观游览。我们从南水军码头出发，在王坚纪功碑前结束游览。中途经过始关门、飞来寺、护国门、校场遗址、护国寺、钓鱼台、悬空卧佛、千佛崖、三圣岩。游览时间为两小时。顺便说一下，请记住停车地点、发车时间，以及我的手机号码。有需要请随时与我联系。

07

White Crane Ridge in Fuling County
涪陵白鹤梁

The White Crane Ridge (Baiheliang) is a natural rock ridge that stretches from west to east. As a tiny island, the ridge is about 2,200 meters long and 15 meters wide. It is located in the upper reaches of the Three Gorges Reservoir on the Yangtze River, north of Fuling City and 119 kilometers from the center of Chongqing.

白鹤梁是一道天然石梁,自西向东延伸,为袖珍小岛,长约2200米,宽15米。它位于长江三峡库区上游,涪陵城北,距离重庆市中心119公里。

In ancient times, the White Crane Ridge was called Baziliang. As for the origins of its name, there is a story that the ridge is named after a group of white cranes that gather on this ridge. Another saying is that Er Zhu, a Taoist priest of the Tang Dynasty, cultivated himself on the ridge. After he attained the Tao, he rode off the ridge on a red-crowned crane.

白鹤梁,古称巴子梁。关于白鹤梁名称的来历,一说是因为白鹤群聚集梁上而得此名,还有一说是唐时尔朱真人在梁上修炼,后得道,乘仙鹤离梁而去。

Before the impoundment of the Three Gorges Reservoir, the White Crane Ridge was parallel to the river flow and tilted toward the center of the river at an inclination of 14.5 degrees. For most of the year, the ridge was submerged under the river. Only at the turn of winter and spring every year when the water level was low, did part of the ridge rise above the river. After the water impoundment, the ridge remained underwater at a depth of several dozen meters and no longer surfaced ever since then.

三峡大坝蓄水前，白鹤梁与江流平行，呈14.5度的斜度向江心倾斜。在一年的大部分时间里，白鹤梁伏没于江中。只有每年冬春交替之时，水位较低，部分白鹤梁才会露出水面。蓄水之后，它便沉入几十米的水底，再也不能露出水面了。

Since the Tang Dynasty, 36 stone fishes have had carved onto the White Crane Ridge, thus creating the use of "stone fish" to mark the low water level at a certain time. However, the stone fish become blurred by age. However, the two carps were found to have been carved by stone-cutters at the order of Xiao Xing, governor of Fuzhou in the Qing Dynasty. They also chiselled an old saying, "Once the stone fish appear, it will be a sign of the coming harvest year." Thus, the stone fish are used as a sign of whether a year's crop is productive or not. In the 20th century, the stone fish on the ridge came out of water three times, respectively in 1953, 1963 and 1973. In those years, there were bumper harvests in local areas. After the first stone fish was carved on the ridge in the Tang Dynasty, the ancient people recorded the low water level of the Yangtze River by "carving stones to keep a records of events" on the same ridge. Meanwhile, they carved "stone fish" as a hydrological sign. Therefore, the ridge not only occupies an important position in the history of world hydrological observation, but also obtains the title of the "World's First Hydrometrical Station". So far, the ridge is known as the earliest and well-preserved ancient hydrometrical station with "stone fish" as a sign of low water.

自唐代以来，人们在白鹤梁上共凿刻了36尾石鱼，从而创立了用"石鱼"来标记某时的枯水水位。因年代久远，这些石鱼已经模糊不清。不过，人们发现，有两尾鲤鱼是由清代涪州知州萧星命石工所刻，并凿古人云"石鱼出，兆丰年"，石鱼由此被当作可以预知一年丰歉的信号。20世纪，白鹤梁上的石鱼三次露出了水面，分别是1953年、1963年和1973年，而那几年当地都大获丰收。自唐代第一尾石鱼刻在梁上后，古人便在白鹤梁上以"刻石记事"的方式记录长江的枯水水位，并刻石鱼作为水文标志。为此，白鹤梁在世界水文观察史上不仅占有重要的地位，还获得"世界第一水文站"之称。迄今为止，白鹤梁被誉为我国最早的、保存完好的，以"石鱼"作为枯水标志的古代水文站。

In ancient times, whenever the stone fish came out of the water, literati, officials or merchants would take boats to the ridge. There, they wrote poems or *fu* (descriptive prose interspersed with verses) and inscribed them on the rocks on the ridge. Gradually, the number of the rock inscriptions grew larger, thus it developed into a large collection of rock inscriptions, also known the "Underwater Forest of Steles". Up to now, 167 inscriptions have been found. These include one from the Tang Dynasty, 98 from the Song Dynasty, five from the Yuan Dynasty, 16 from the Ming Dynasty, 24 from the Qing Dynasty, 14 from the modern times, and seven others of the unknown ages. All these inscriptions are written in Chinese, except for one with six characters carved onto a piece of rock that is 55 centimeters high and 44 centimeters wide. No one in the local area understands the meaning of these characters. It is assumed that these characters might be the Mongolian Phags-pa script. This writing system was invented by Phags-pa, a state teacher during the reign of Kublai Khan, the first emperor of the Yuan Dynasty. But with the demise of the Mongol Empire, the Phags-pa script was gradually abandoned and became a "dead language". So far, it is impossible to verify who wrote it and when the Phags-pa script was carved on the rock.

In addition, the ridge inscriptions also involve more than 300 people whose names are well documented. Some were senior ministers in the central imperial government, some were local officials, and many others were literati. Their inscriptions became important historical records from the Tang Dynasty to modern times. Experts of cultural relics believe that the ancient inscriptions on the White Crane Ridge have the following high value. Firstly, it is important scientific and historical data of hydrology, water conservation, agriculture, meteorology, navigation and other aspects in the regions along the middle and upper reaches of the Yangtze River. Secondly, it is an important material object to study the evolution of various calligraphy styles from the Song Dynasty to modern times. Thirdly, it provides important information about the human geography and folk geography in the Sichuan section of the Yangtze River. Fourthly, it is an important part of the natural landscape and cultural sites in the Three Gorges area.

在古代，每当石鱼出水，文人雅士、官吏商贾，都会乘船到白鹤梁，在那里吟诗作赋并将诗文题刻于岩上。于是，岩石题刻渐渐增多，成为一处大型题刻收藏地，又有了"水中碑林"之称。迄今为止，已发现167处题刻，其中唐代1段、宋代98段、元代5段、明代16段、清代24段、近代14段、年代不详者7段。所有的题刻都是用汉字书写的，唯有一段题刻，共六个字，刻在高55厘米、宽44厘米岩石上。当地没有人认得这些字，推测是用蒙古族八思巴文写的。该文字系统为元世祖忽必烈的国师八思巴所制，但随着元帝国的消亡，八思巴文亦被逐渐废弃，成为一种"死文字"。迄今为止，人们无法考证何人所书，何时八思巴文题刻在了岩石上。此外，白鹤梁题刻者多达300余人，其姓名有据可考；有的为朝中重臣，有的是地方官吏，还有众多文人墨客，他们的题留成了由唐代至近代的重要记录。文物专家认为白鹤梁题刻具有以下很高的价值：第一，它是研究长江中上游地区水文、水利、农业、气象、航运等方面的重要的科学史料。第三，它是研究宋代至近现代各种书法风格演变的重要实物资料。

第三，它提供了关于川江地区人文地理、民俗地理的重要信息。第四，它是三峡地区自然景观、人文景观的重要组成部分。

However, due to the high water level in the Three Gorges Reservoir, a protective housing has been specially built on the site of the White Crane Ridge to protect these inscriptions. The construction project started in February 2003 and was completed at the end of 2007. At present, the housing is composed of four parts, namely, the Underwater Museum, the Passageway Connection, the Underwater Crash-Proof Piers and the Onshore Exhibition Hall.

不过，因三峡水库高位蓄水，为保护题刻，在白鹤梁原址上专门修建了一个保护壳体。该修建项目于2003年2月开工，2007年底竣工。目前，壳体由"水下博物馆"、"连接交通廊道"、"水中防撞墩"和"岸上陈列馆"四部分组成。

Well, so much for my brief introduction to the White Crane Ridge. Today, our tour route goes like this: we go through the security check and take an elevator down to the Underwater Museum. Next, we walk through a 150-meter-long passageway, pass through the door of the steel structure housing and enter into the circular sightseeing corridor. In the corridor, you can watch the White Crane Ridge up close through web-cameras or computer screens. I'd like to let you know that the museum offers free guide service. An audio guide service is also available in Chinese, English, Japanese, Korean, and French. Rent an audio guide if you think it's necessary.

好了，白鹤梁的简介到此为止。今天，我们的游览路线是，过安检，然后乘电梯到水下博物馆；经过150米长的走廊，再穿过钢制的壳体舱门，进入环形参观走廊。在走廊里，可以通过摄像头或电脑屏幕近距离观看白鹤梁。注意：本馆免费提供导游讲解服务，也有中、英、日、韩、法文语音导览。如果你认为有必要，可租用语音导览器。

Chongqing Municipality
重庆市

08

The Heaven Pit and Ground Seam in Fengjie County
奉节天坑地缝

The Heaven Pit and Ground Seam in Fengjie (Tiankeng Difeng) is located Xiaozhai Village, about 90 kilometers away from Fengjie County, Chongqing. Tiankeng Difeng is a national key scenic area, covering an area of more than 300 square kilometers, with ten main sections. They include Xiaozhai Tiankeng, Tianjing Gorge Difeng, the Mazy River, the Dragon Bridge Creek, the Nine-Bend River, Taoyuan River, the Dragon Gate Bridge, Maocao Grassland, and Qingyan Village. Today, we will go and visit Xiaozhai Tiankeng, Tianjing Gorge Difeng, the Mazy River and the Dragon Bridge Creek.

奉节天坑地缝位于小寨村，距离重庆奉节县城90多公里。天坑地缝为国家重点风景名胜区，占地300余平方公里，分为小寨天坑、天井峡地缝、迷宫河、龙桥河、九盘河、桃源河、龙门桥、茅草坝、青岩村等十大片区。今天我们将游览小寨天坑、天井峡地缝、迷宫河和龙桥河。

In science, sinkhole is usually called "the giant funnel of karst collapse" or "the world-class giant funnel". In terms of its appearance, it looks like a huge hollow in the ground, with its vertical cliffs surrounding the hollow like majestic walls. Seen from a distance, the sinkhole looks like the earth's huge mouth opening to the sky. As for earth cave, it is mainly a fault zone, another unique karst landform. It is a typical "thin-strip-of-sky" canyon landscape formed tens of millions of years ago due to the process of the mountain orogeny. Seen from a distance, the earth cave looks like a giant and narrow opening crack in the ground.

在科学界，天坑通常称作"岩溶塌陷大漏斗"或"世界级的巨型大漏斗"。从外观上看，天坑像是地面上的巨大坑洞，直立的峭壁围住坑洞，如雄伟森然的四壁。从远处看，天坑就像是大地对着天空张开的大嘴。地缝则多为断裂带，是另一种奇特的喀斯特地貌，是数千万年前因造山运动形成的典型的"一线天"峡谷景观。远远望去，地缝宛如地上裂开的一条大而狭窄的缝隙。

In Xiaozhai Village there are many sinkholes. There is a sinkhole almost every few hundred meters. Some are as small as teacups, and some are as big as stadiums. One sinkhole is particularly large, equivalent to five medium reservoirs. Its depth is 662.2 meters. Its maximum diameter is 626 meters at the mouth of the pit, while its maximum diameter is 522 meters at the bottom of the pit. So far, this sinkhole is the largest funnel ever found on earth, ranking the first in depth and volume, compared with similar karst funnels in the world. It is not only exceptionally huge, but also extremely rich in color. Its rock vein on the cliff take on a distinctive color, with red alternating with yellow or black, like a traditional Chinese painting. In addition, birds fly in and out of the cracks in the rock, chirping and foraging. Along the northeast cliffs there is a trail leading to the bottom of the pit. The cliffs have two terraces. One terrace is located at a depth of 300 meters and ranging in width from two to ten meters, with two houses on it. It is said that there once secluded two families who grew konjac on the terrace for their living. The narrow, winding trail on the cliff was the only passage to the outside world. The other terrace, located 400 meters below, is a slope overgrown with trees and grass. There are some springs on the cliff, pouring down like cascades. At the bottom of the pit is an underground river that rushes noisily out of a cave. The water flows uproariously for a few hundred meters and then disappears into another huge cave. Explorers from China and the West have explored the sinkhole many times and found the underground river flowing toward the Mazy River. They believe that the river may come from a mysterious earth cave in the earth.

小寨村一带有许多天坑,几乎每隔几百米就有一个,有些洞口小如茶杯,还有些大如球场。有个天坑特别大,相当于5个中型水库,坑深为666.2米,坑口面最大直径为626米,坑底的最大直径为522米。迄今为止,这座天坑是世界上所发现的最大的漏斗,其深度和容积均居世界同类喀斯特岩溶漏斗的首位。它不仅巨大,而且色彩也极其丰富。绝壁上的岩纹呈现出独特的颜色,红、黄、黑相间,犹如一幅中国传统绘画。此外,飞禽在岩缝中飞进飞出,鸣叫,觅食。沿着东北方向的坑壁上,有一条小道可通到坑底。坑壁有两级台地;其中一级台地位于300米深处,宽2至10米,上面有两间房屋。据说有两户人家在这里隐居,曾在台地上种植魔芋得以生存。既窄又弯曲的坑壁小道是他们与外界的唯一通道。另一级台地在400米以下,呈斜坡状,上面草木丛生。坑壁上有几处泉水,像瀑布一样倾泻而下。在坑底有一条地下河,河水从一个洞穴中咆哮而出,一路咆哮数百米后便消失在另一巨大的洞穴里。来自国内和西方的探险者曾多次深入天坑探险,发现天坑中暗河流向迷宫河,认为暗河来自神秘的大地缝。

Tianjing Fissure Gorge belongs to the same karst system as Xiaozhai sinkholes. It has a length of about 37 kilometers, a width from one to 500 meters and a depth from four to 900 meters. It is divided into upper and lower parts. As for its upper part, it is the hidden crevice, which is about eight kilometers from Daxiang Hill to the Chigu Channel. Visitors can enter the bottom of the crevice from Tianjing Gorge of Daxiang Hill. The section of the crevice in Tianjing Gorge is 10-30 meters wide at the top, and 1-30 meters wide at the bottom. There, the crevice cliffs reach a depth of 300 meters. Rocks on both sides of the gorge hold different postures and shapes and plants grow thick on the rocks and darken the sky. Typically, it looks like a "thin-strip-of-sky" canyon landscape. As for its lower part, it is a hidden cave. It is about 6,000 meters long, stretching from sinkhole to the Mazy Valley. Along this section, there are the Jade-Shuttle Waterfalls, the Plough-Share-Bay Waterfalls, the Image-Changeable Peak, the Giant Elephant Exploring Springs, the Stone Statue of Guanyin Bodhisattva, the Gate of Hell, the *Yin* and *Yang* Fissure, the Double-Wind Tunnel and other scenic spots.

天井峡地缝与小寨天坑属同一岩溶系统，全长37公里，宽1至500米，深4至900米。地缝分上、下两段，上段从大象山至迟谷槽，为隐伏于地下的暗缝，长约8公里。游客可以从大象山的天井峡进入缝底。天井峡地缝一段，上部宽10~30米，谷底宽1~30米，地缝悬崖深处达300米，峡谷两侧岩石千姿百态，岩壁上丛林茂密，遮天蔽日，是一条典型的"一线天"峡谷景观。地缝下段是长约6000米的暗洞，从天坑延伸到迷宫峡，沿途有玉梭瀑布、犁头湾瀑布、变幻峰、巨象探泉、石观音、鬼门关、阴阳缝、双风洞等景点。

In 1996, the Heaven Pit and Ground Seam in Fengjie were designated as a "Provincial Scenic Attraction" by Chongqing Municipal People's Government. In early 2004, the State Council formally approved it as a "National Key Scenic Attraction". Nowadays, the Heaven Pit and Ground Seam in Fengjie has become a paradise for adventurers and a resort for domestic and overseas tourists.

1996年，奉节县天坑地缝被重庆市人民政府命名为"省级风景名胜区"，2004年初被国务院正式批准为"国家重点风景名胜区"。如今，天坑地缝已成为探险者的乐园和海内外游客的度假胜地。

Well, so much for the brief introduction to the Heaven Pit and Ground Seam. Now let's get ready for our trip to the scenic area. The temperature in the canyon is about 10℃ lower than that on the top of the hill, so be sure to bring warm jackets and waterproof coats. Also, I'd like to advise female tourists not to wear high-heeled shoes, as most trails are stone steps.

好了,天坑地缝的简介到此为止。现在大家去准备景区的旅游吧。山谷里的温度比山顶低10℃左右,记住随身带上保暖衣和防水外套。此外,景区内多是石阶路,女性游客最好不要穿高跟鞋。